ANTON CHEKHOV
AND HIS TIMES

ANTON CHEKHOV AND HIS TIMES

TRANSLATED FROM THE RUSSIAN BY
Cynthia Carlile (Reminiscences)
and Sharon McKee (Letters)

COMPILED BY ANDREI TURKOV

UNIVERSITY OF ARKANSAS PRESS
FAYETTEVILLE 1995

Originally published by Progress Publishers, Moscow

American edition copyright 1995 by the Board of Trustees of the University of Arkansas

99　98　97　96　95　　5　4　3　2　1

Designed by Ellen Beeler

Library of Congress Cataloging-in-Publication Data

Anton Chekhov and his times / translated from the Russian by Cynthia Carlile (Reminiscences) and Sharon McKee (Letters) ; compiled and with an introduction by Andrei Turkov.

     p.　cm.

  Originally published: Moscow : Progress Publishers, 1990.

  ISBN 1-55728-391-5 (c : alk. paper). —ISBN 1-55728-390-7 (p)

   1. Chekhov, Anton Pavlovich, 1860–1904—Biography. 2. Chekhov, Anton Pavlovich, 1860–1904—Friends and associates. 3. Chekhov, Anton, 1860–1904—Correspondence. 4. Authors, Russian—19th century—Biography. I. Carlile, Cynthia. II. McKee, Sharon. III. Turkov, Andreï Mikhaïlovich.

PG3458.A657　1995

891.72'3—dc20

[B]　　　　　　　　　　　　　　　　　　　　　　　　　　95-5839
　　　　　　　　　　　　　　　　　　　　　　　　　　　　　CIP

CONTENTS

INTRODUCTION

"I saw the noblest, finest, most inspired face I had ever come across in my life," declared the Russian writer Alexander Kuprin, recalling his introduction to Anton Pavlovich. Nor is this by any means the only reference to Chekhov's captivating mind, talent, kindness, and lively spirit. Such was his charm that it not only captivated those who had the good fortune to meet Chekhov in person, but still captivates those who read his letters and reminiscences about him.

Chekhov himself did not like recounting events of the past, and even jokingly expressed his regret that he suffered from "autobiographobia." In his correspondence he also said little or nothing about his purely personal circumstances and feelings. However, his lively response to all that was going on around him, his keen powers of observation, unfailing sense of humor, tact, and sensitivity are so manifest in his letters that, whether their author wished it or no, they have become a unique self-portrait.

Alexander Blok declared that the works of every writer are merely the "external results" of the subterranean growth of his spirit. These words often come to mind when one thinks of Chekhov's life and works.

This anthology includes selected correspondence and reminiscences by a number of contemporaries who were close to Anton Pavlovich. We hope that they will help the reader to trace the continual development of Chekhov's personality and talent.

In a letter to his friend Nemirovich-Danchenko about his prose works, Chekhov remarked, "You are getting better and better, and each year it is as if another layer had been added to your talent." Using a similar metaphor we might remark that the "first layer" of Chekhov's character and talent remain for us, as for his contemporaries, shrouded in mystery.

One of the decisive periods in Chekhov's life—his last years at high school—was spent alone in Taganrog, far from his family, who were gradually moving to Moscow. When he appeared in the university, and later in literary circles, his new acquaintances, and even his own family, discovered someone who had already matured in many respects and was possessed of enormous self-restraint, extraordinary will-power, and modest reticence, "elusiveness."

Even many years later, in a laconic outline of his biography, Anton Chekhov passed over in silence his reasons for deciding to become a doctor: "For reasons I cannot recall, I chose the medical faculty. . . ." This inevitably recalls the conversation in *The Three Sisters:*

> MASHA: Did you love my mother?
> CHEBUTYKIN: Very much.
> MASHA: And did she love you?
> CHEBUTYKIN (after a pause): That I don't remember now.

It is obvious that the old doctor is defending the privacy of his secret, perhaps the dearest possession of his life. Just as it is impossible to take the doctor's words seriously, so it is impossible to believe that Chekhov had "forgotten" the reasons for such an important step!

Whereas Chekhov remained totally silent about the circumstances of this "lawful marriage" (everyone knows Chekhov's famous words to the effect that medicine was his lawful wife, and literature—his mistress), his "affair" with the second was often mentioned both in his correspondence and in conversation, though with deliberate light-heartedness. "In his own words," wrote Korolenko, "he began his literary work almost as a trifle, seeing it in part as enjoyment and entertainment, in part as a means of completing his university course and supporting his family." In his obituary on Chekhov, the publisher Suvorin movingly related that Anton Pavlovich had allegedly written his first story only in order to earn some money to buy a birthday cake for his mother.

It is perfectly possible that this legend was artfully invented by Chekhov himself, not only to remove any trace of a halo surrounding his entry into literature by making it seem purely fortuitous, but also so as to veil in shadow all his previous "literary efforts."

Many authors of reminiscences succeed in conveying the atmosphere which surrounded Chekhov, his infectious charm, endless inventiveness, and amusing improvisation. It is a pure pleasure to read such pages, which bring to life the captivating figure of a young writer, his generous disposition, his genuine love of life, which had begun at last to smile on him a little—after the difficult years in Taganrog and, to begin with, in Moscow—bestowing on him the joy of literary success, the ties of friendship, and sincere admiration both of his talent and his personal qualities. Memoirs refer to the "captivation" and "intoxication" by Chekhov which their authors experienced.

The references to "dear Chekhia," as Pleshcheyev, a kindly and simple-hearted poet, termed the family of his young friend, are full of affection. All speak of "the atmosphere of a united, loving family . . . a happy idyll" (Korolenko), of "the wonderful old folks"—"dear" Pavel Yegorovich, and the "timid" Yevgenia Yakovlevna (Shchepkina-Kupernik).

This "layer" in Chekhov's life, when the young student and debutante writer took from his father onto his own still immature shoulders the full burden of supporting a large family, is carefully concealed from the outside world; and if it is mentioned in memoirs, then in purely "Dickensian" style: "With tender emotion she told me," writes Shchepkina-Kupernik about Chekhov's mother, "of a moment she would never forget, when Antosha—still only a young student—came to her and said, 'Well, Mother, from now on I shall pay for Masha to go to school!'"

One must assume, however, that the "transfer of authority" in the family did not always proceed smoothly, and that difficulties and problems continued. Ten years later, in a letter to Shcheglov (18 April 1888), Chekhov spoke of the "family miter" to which he had become "accustomed . . . like a bump on the head" (a definition far from idyllic!). He wrote almost at the same time to his brother Alexander, speaking even more bluntly of "adults gathered together under one roof only because, by force of certain inexplicable circumstances, they cannot go their several ways," and of the fact that their "conversations . . . had become wearisome."

All such evidence from Chekhov himself and from certain authors of reminiscences must be taken into account. Not, of course, in order to "blacken" any of Chekhov's family, but in order to fully appreciate the assertion by one of Chekhov's contemporaries that his most outstanding virtue was his patience, and to recognize his enormous self-sacrifice. ("Your whole life is spent for others, as if you desire no life of your own!" Lidia Mizinova once wrote to him, and surely it was not only personal, subjective motives which compelled her to write those words.)

The "optical illusion" affecting a number of those who wrote reminiscences about Chekhov is not limited to just this aspect of his life.

The enchantment of unpretentious dinners, lighthearted improvisations, and friendly games is seen by some as the main, even the sole content of Chekhov's life during this period (perhaps, without any offense being intended, by analogy with their own lives). One author of such reminiscences describes with total conviction an entire period in Chekhov's life—from 1886 to 1896—as "the happiest half of his personal life," years which "passed . . . absurdly, ineluctably, like a sweet, springtime dream, passed in unthinking, extravagant bustle, leaving behind bright, festive patches of light in the memory. . . ."

This is a strange way of describing the period when Chekhov was writing "Nervous Breakdown," "A Dreary Tale," "Ward No. 6," and "The Black Friar"; when he undertook the arduous journey to Sakhalin—an expedition into the dreadful world of Russian penal labor, so unexpected on the part of the carefree, merry fellow so many thought him to be—to study it in depth (suffice it to say that Chekhov carried out single-handedly a census of the local population). This was also the period when Chekhov clearly revealed the dramatic singularity of his literary position, which rejected many of the outworn canons of late-populist ideology and liberal criticism. Konstantin Korovin, on the other hand, who recorded a day spent with Chekhov both on canvas and in his memoirs with the vividness characteristic of his own exuberant personality, did not omit from this picture the bitter argument between Chekhov and some student acquaintances who heatedly criticized the supposed ideological poverty of his writings.

The motif running through Korovin's memoirs of Chekhov's resolute, at times even demonstrative ("I have absolutely no ideas. . . ."), opposition to inflexible and intrusive demands on the arts is also to be found in other memoirs.

How, indeed, was it possible for the writer not to wax indignant in the face of the pretensions of the "daily" criticism of the 1880s and even later? With bitter irony he wrote to A. M. Gorky: "The critics are like the gadflies which prevent a horse from plowing. . . . The horse is working, all his muscles are stretched as taut as the strings of a double bass, and then a gadfly settles on his crupper, stinging and buzzing, so he has to twitch his hide and flick his tail."

Published reminiscences contain a record of the many and most diverse instances of "painful incomprehension" suffered by the writer. Of these, the most famous, of course, is the story of the failure of the play *The Seagull* at the Alexandrinsky Theater in St. Petersburg. The play proved incomprehensible not only to the particular audience which came to the benefit performance given by the comedy actress Levkeyeva, but even to the performers and most of the reviewers. Many of those who wrote reminiscences have left us a vivid picture of this event, which the writer Potapenko, a friend of Chekhov, described as "one of the most absurd . . . in the history of the state theaters of St. Petersburg."

This "absurdity" had, however, its own logic. "What was lacking—the general tone of the play, the unity of its mood—was fundamental and made itself felt not only here, but in other productions," remarked the same Potapenko. Chekhov's *The Seagull* was, as it were, the herald of the theatrical future being ushered in by the experimentation of Stanislavsky and Nemirovich-Danchenko.

The "sentences" passed on Chekhov's prose by many influential critics were less resounding but sufficiently definitive. The characteristic absence of any overt moralizing, of the "pointing finger" and clear "hints" to the reader—who was left the right to judge for himself what the writer had depicted—was taken by the critics not as a particular and original literary style, but as a major conceptual and literary defect. Even Chekhov's preference for the short story, sometimes exceptionally laconic, was taken as yet further evidence of his "limitations" or, at best, the "immaturity" of his talent. "They required that I write a novel, otherwise I could not be called a writer," recalled Chekhov.

This inability to recognize the creative originality of Chekhov's talent naturally influenced the interpretation of his general position as a writer. Since, in the words of Kuprin, he "did not expend himself in empty words," he was accused of indifference. As he loved people without loud phrases, he was accused of social insensibility.

At the turn of the century, during the years of democratic upsurge which preceded the first Russian revolution (1905), the years when *The Seagull* returned to the stage in triumph and Chekhov collaborated successfully with the young Arts Theater, new "layers" were added to his talent. However, the qualities revealed in his previous writing also matured.

Chekhov's principled position and open manifestation of his civic and aesthetic sentiment reached their peak with his refusal, together with Korolenko, to accept the title of honorary academician in protest over the shameful annulment of Gorky's election to the Academy of Sciences after the tsar had voiced his displeasure. This event rightly impressed itself on the memory of many of those who later wrote their reminiscences. For some, this incident served to "open their eyes" for the first time to the real Chekhov, since the clear stance he had taken, for example, over the notorious Dreyfus Affair at the end of the century, and which had brought him into sharp conflict with Suvorin, had not been so widely publicized.

However, the numerous allusions to Chekhov's warm sympathy for the mounting social protest and to his hopes for the future of his country were not merely the result of sudden "illumination" on the part of those writing their reminiscences, but were also marked changes in the outlook of Chekhov himself.

As Chekhov's house in Yalta rose floor by floor, so the writer himself also increased in stature—in his later works, in his understanding of events—although he saw his illness and his enforced stay in Yalta as a major obstacle to learning about the new, changing Russia.

The reminiscences of all those who visited Chekhov in the Crimea speak of the writer's eagerness to "absorb" all the information reaching him about what was happening at the "epicenter" of escalating events.

Alas, the power of his spirit, his thought, his growing stature as a writer were in tragic contrast with his relentlessly progressing illness. Many of the recollections of meetings with him during these years contain, wittingly or unwittingly, details, still painful to read today, of his physical decline: increasingly noticeable weakness and thinness, his hands resting on angular knees, his racking bouts of coughing in which he also coughed up blood and after which, in his own words, he became "rattling bones."

Even then Chekhov did not lose his enormous capacity for restraint, and it was only in a few conversations remembered by those who wrote about him later that we can hear, in what Stanislavsky describes as "sudden explosions of depression," a muffled echo of that bitter reflection which, it seems, he expressed only once directly and seriously to M. M. Kovalevsky in a brief nighttime conversation while they were traveling together: "As a doctor I know that my life will be short."

Perhaps the "vaudeville" theme which he related to Shchepkina-Kupernik in Melikhovo ("a couple are waiting in a threshing barn for the rain to stop, they joke, laugh, dry their umbrellas, profess their love for each other—and then the rain passes, the sun comes out—and suddenly he dies of a heart attack!") was born of sad pondering on the little time allotted to him.

The beginning of a new century, with the hopes it aroused in all, including Chekhov, could not but aggravate such sentiments: "the rain passes, the sun comes out—and suddenly he dies!"

In the memory of his contemporaries, the writer who died before "the sun came out" remained its herald, a man of "unusually upright heart" who brought into the world notes of elevated humanity and resolute rejection of all injustice.

No doubt Chekhov, given his extraordinary modesty, felt extremely embarrassed when Lev Tolstoy, with tears in his eyes, expressed his enthusiastic admiration for "The Darling" with the words:

> It resembles a piece of lace woven by a maid; there were such young lace-makers in the country, "old maids" who put their whole life, all their dreams of happiness, into their lace.

It would be difficult, however, to convey more accurately the impression created by Chekhov's work, and by the man himself.

"It's a fine thing to be able to remember such a man," wrote Gorky. "A feeling of cheerfulness immediately returns to your life, a clear sense of purpose invests it once again."

A. Turkov

REMINISCENCES

He went out into the dusk. The last
Ray of the sun glowed in the clouds,
Like a funeral torch lighting his path.

YAKOV POLONSKY

K. A. KOROVIN

FROM MY MEETINGS
WITH ANTON CHEKHOV

I

It was, if I remember rightly, in 1883.

At the corner of Dyakovskaya Street and Sadovaya Street in Moscow there stood a hotel called Oriental Rooms—why "Oriental" no one knew. They were extremely shabby. At the "main" entrance, three bricks hung on a rope attached to the door, so that it would close properly.

Anton Pavlovich Chekhov had a room on the ground floor,[1] and up above, on the first floor, lived I. I. Levitan, then still a student at the College of Painting, Sculpture, and Architecture.

It was spring. Levitan and I were returning from the college on Myasnitskaya Street after the third and final examination in art, for which we had been awarded silver medals: I for drawing, and Levitan for painting.[2]

When we entered the hotel, Levitan said to me, "Let's call on Antosha" (that is, Chekhov).

Anton Pavlovich's room was full of tobacco smoke, and a samovar was standing on the table. There were also small loaves of bread, sausage, and beer. The divan was covered with sheets of paper and college notebooks—Anton was preparing for his medical finals at the university.[3]

He was sitting on the edge of the divan and wearing a gray jacket of the kind many students wore in those days. There were some other young people in the room, students.

The students were talking and arguing heatedly, drinking tea and beer and eating sausage. Anton Pavlovich sat in silence, only occasionally replying to questions addressed to him.

He was handsome with a large, open face and kindly, laughing eyes. When conversing with someone, he would sometimes gaze into their face, but then immediately drop his head and give a curious, gentle smile. The whole of his figure, his open face and broad chest inspired particular trust in him, as if he radiated sincerity and protectiveness. Despite his youth, almost adolescence, he already had something of the kindly uncle whom one wanted to approach to ask about the truth, about grief, and confide in him that something particularly important which each of us has buried somewhere in our heart. Anton Pavlovich was simple and natural. He struck no pose, was without any shadow of self-display or self-satisfaction. Innate modesty, even shyness were integral to him.

It was a sunny spring day. Levitan and I invited Anton Pavlovich to go with us to Sokolniki.* We told him about our medals. One of the students asked, "What, are you going to wear it round your neck, like doormen?"

Levitan replied, "No, they aren't worn. They're simply awarded. A mark of excellence on graduation."

"Like the ones they give champion dogs at dog shows," another student remarked.

The students were not like Anton Pavlovich. They were great arguers, and always in some strange opposition to everything.

"If you don't have convictions," one student said, turning to Chekhov, "then you can't be a writer."

"No one could say I don't have convictions," another said. "I don't even understand how it's possible not to have them."

"I have no convictions," replied Anton Pavlovich.

"You're saying you're someone with no convictions? How can you write without ideas? Don't you have any ideas?"

"I haven't any ideas or convictions," replied Chekhov.

They argued strangely, these students. They were clearly dissatisfied with Anton Pavlovich. It was obvious that he did not correspond to some didactic trend in their thinking, to their ideological and instructive interpretation of things. They wanted to guide, instruct, lead, influence. They knew everything—understood everything. Anton Pavlovich apparently found it all very boring.

* The name of the park—Sokolniki—is derived from "sokol," the Russian for "falcon."—Tr.

4

"Who needs your stories? What's their purpose? They don't contain any opposition, any ideas. The *Russkiye Vedomosh* (Russian Herald)[4] doesn't need you, for example. Just entertainment, that's all."

"That's all," replied Anton Pavlovich.

"And why, if I may ask, do you sign yourself Chekhonte? Why a Chinese nom de plume?"

Chekhov laughed.

"And is it," the student went on, "because, when you become a doctor of medicine, you'll feel guilty that you wrote without ideas, without protest."

"You're quite right," replied Chekhov, continuing to laugh. Then he added, "Let's go to Sokolniki. It's a wonderful day. The violets are already in bloom. Fresh air, spring."

And we set off for Sokolniki.

At Krasnye Vorota we got on a horse-drawn tram and passed the railway stations, Krasny Prud, and wooden houses with green and red iron roofs. We were traveling through the outskirts of Moscow.

Dear Levitan was continuing our interrupted conversation.

"What do you think?" he said. "I don't have any ideas either. Can I become an artist or can't I?"

"Impossible," a student replied, "no one can be without any ideas."

"You're just like a crocodile!" Levitan retorted to the student. "What am I to do now? Give it all up?"

"Give it up."

Anton Pavlovich joined in the conversation, laughing, "How can he drop painting? No! Isaac the wily won't drop it. He's been given a medal to wear round his neck. Now he's waiting for the Order of Stanislav. And Stanislav isn't as easy as that. That's what they call it: Stanislav, don't slap my face."

We laughed, the students became angry.

"What ideas, when what I want to draw is pine trees in the sunshine, spring."

"Just a minute, a pine tree is a product. You understand? A product of construction. You understand? Timber belongs to the nation. Nature produces it for the people. You understand?" The student was growing heated, "For the people."

"But I don't like it when a tree is cut down. They're living things, just like us, and birds sing in their branches. They—the birds—are better than we are. I'm drawing, and I don't think: this is timber. I can't think that. You really are a crocodile!" Levitan protested.

"And why are singing birds better than us? Just a minute," the student replied indignantly.

"I'm offended, too," said Anton Pavlovich. "Isaac, you'll have to prove that."

"Try to prove it," the student insisted, perfectly serious and looking sharply at Levitan with an expression of extraordinary importance.

Anton Pavlovich laughed.

"Stupid," Levitan snapped back.

"We'll arrive soon, we're already approaching Sokolniki."

A woman from the trading class who was sitting next to Levitan held out a red Easter egg and said, "Take it, you're a fine-looking fellow. (Levitan was very good-looking.) My father died . . . it's forty days now. Say a prayer for him."

Levitan and Chekhov laughed. Levitan took the egg and asked the father's name, so he would know who it was he was to pray for.

"What, are you a priest, my fine boy?" the woman was a little tipsy.

"Students, students—a book under the arm, and nothing else."

We arrived at the Sokolniki tram terminus.

As we got out of the tram, the woman who had been traveling with us turned to Levitan and said, "Remember my father. His name was Nikita Nikitich. And when you finish at the seminary, you'll have a fine head of hair. Come to Pechatniki. Everyone knows Anfisa Nikitishna. I'll give you something to eat. You probably don't get enough to eat, even if you are scholars."

Anton Pavlovich laughed, but the students were serious. They were subdued, as if old mother care was treading on their heels. They were full of some persistent ideas. Something heavy and artificial weighed down upon them, like a duty hobbling their youth. They lacked simplicity and the ability simply to enjoy the present moment. Yet it was such a wonderful spring! However, when Levitan indicated the beauty of the forest saying, "Look how lovely it is," one of the students replied, "There's nothing so special about it—monotonous, that's all. A forest, and nothing more! What's so wonderful about that?"

"You don't understand anything, you misery," retorted Levitan.

We strolled down the avenue.

The forest was mysteriously beautiful. In the rays of the spring sunshine the tops of the pine trees sparkled like reddish flames against the deep, rich, dark-blue sky. Blackbirds sang incessantly, and in the distance cuckoos counted out how many years of life were left for whom upon our mysterious earth.

The students, traveling rugs thrown over their shoulders, also livened up and began to sing:

> To he who wrote "What's To Be Done?"
> Our glasses we shall raise,
> And drink a toast to that ideal
> We'll follow all our days.

Anton Pavlovich and Levitan walked side by side, with the students walking ahead. From a distance one could see their hair, worn long in the fashion of the day, lying on the traveling rugs round their shoulders.

"What's that flying over there?" one of them asked, turning to Levitan.

"It's probably a falcon," Anton Pavlovich replied jokingly.

It was a crow!

"I doubt if there are any falcons left in Sokolniki," Chekhov added. "I never saw which falcon, bright falcon . . . what are you thinking of, my little falcons? Falcons and hunting with falcons must have once been widespread in Russia."

We had arrived at the edge of the forest. There was a clearing in front of us, across which there ran a railway line. There were tables with tablecloths. A great many people were drinking tea. Samovars were boiling. We also sat down at one of the tables—it was the custom to drink tea in Sokolniki. Waiters immediately came to serve us. Their trays were piled with buns, rusks, cured sturgeon, smoked sausage.

"Yes, gentlemen?"

At another table nearby there were traders of the kind you find on Okhotny Ryad, clearly drunk and giving us unfriendly looks.

"You students," one of them, clearly the worse for drink, suddenly turned towards us and said, "who if. . . ." and he raised his fist.

Another tried to persuade him to leave us alone.

"Let them be. What are you bothering them for? Perhaps they aren't students at all. Don't bother them."

"Let the servant serve, the jester jest," the drunk with bleary eyes said, looking at us.

It was obvious that we were not popular with this group of people—their barely comprehensible hostility to us "students" was breaking through the surface.

Anton Pavlovich took out a small notebook and quickly jotted something down. As we were walking back, I remember he said to me, "And yet in spring there's a kind of melancholy, a deep melancholy and restlessness. Everything is full of life, but although nature is alive, there is some strange sadness within her."

When we had said good-bye to our student companions, he smiled at Levitan and me and said, "Those students will become excellent doctors. A fine group of people. I envy them for having their heads full of ideas."

II

A long time had passed since our walk in Sokolniki, and on arriving in the Crimea, in Yalta—in the spring of 1904—I visited Anton Pavlovich Chekhov at his home in Verkhnaya Autka. When I went through the gate, there was a crane in the yard, standing on one leg, his neck stretched forward. On seeing me, he spread his wings and began to hop and dance about, as if showing me the figures he was capable of.

I found Anton Pavlovich in his room. He was sitting at the window, reading the newspaper *Novoye Vremya* (New Times).

"What a friendly crane you have," I said to Anton Pavlovich, "he dances so amusingly."

"Yes, a wonderful, affectionate creature. He loves all of us," said Anton Pavlovich. "He returned a second time to us this spring, you know. He flew off for the winter to travel to other, different lands, to visit the hippopotami, and now he's come back to us. We're all very fond of him, Masha (Anton's sister) and I. It's strange and mysterious, isn't it—to fly away, and then fly back? I don't think it's only because of the frogs that he devours here, in the garden. No, he's also proud of the fact that we ask him to dance. He's a performer, and he loves it when we laugh at his entertaining dances. Performers love to perform in various places, and then fly away. My wife has just flown away to Moscow, to the Arts Theater."

Anton Pavlovich picked up from the table a piece of paper rolled up into a small tube, coughed and spat into it, and then threw it into a jar containing some solution.

Anton Pavlovich's room was neat and tidy, bright and simple—rather like the room of a sick man. There was the smell of creosote. On the table there was a calendar and a number of photographs spread out like a fan in a special stand—pictures of actors and acquaintances. There were also photographs on the walls—once again portraits, including Tolstoy, Mikhailovsky, Suvorin, Potapenko, Levitan, and others.

Maria Pavlovna came into the room and said that the cook had fallen ill and was lying down with a severe headache. At first Anton Pavlovich did not pay this any attention, but then he suddenly got up and said, "Oh, I forgot. I'm a doctor. Isn't that so, a doctor. I'll go and see what's the matter with her."

He went out into the kitchen to see the sick woman. I followed and, I remember, noticed how his illness had affected him; he was thin, and his angular shoulders revealed how his cruel illness had sapped his strength.

The kitchen was to one side of the house. I remained in the yard with the crane, who again began to dance, finally spreading his wings out of sheer exuberance and taking off. He circled the yard and then again landed in front of me.

"Crane, crane!" I called to him, and he came up to me, glancing at me sideways with his sharp little eye, no doubt expecting some reward for his artistry. I offered him an empty hand. He looked, and then squawked something. What? Probably "swindler!" or something worse still, as I had paid him nothing for his performance.

Later I showed Anton Pavlovich some paintings I had done in the Crimea and brought with me, thinking to divert him a little—large ships sleeping in the night. He asked me to leave them with him.

"Leave them here. I would like to take another look at them, alone," he said.

Anton Pavlovich was planning to go to Moscow. I advised him not to go—he looked very ill and was coughing hoarsely. At dinner he said to me, "Why aren't you drinking any wine? If I were well, I would drink some. I so enjoy a glass of wine."

The stamp of illness and sadness lay on everything.

I told him that I wanted to buy a small piece of land in the Crimea for a studio, not in Yalta itself, but somewhere close by.

"Masha," he said to his sister, "you know what—let's give him our piece of land. Would you like that? It's in Gurzuf, by the cliffs. I lived there for two years, right by the sea. Listen Masha, I'll give that land to Konstantin Alexeyevich. Would you like it? Only you can hear the sea breaking there, 'eternally.' Would you like it? And there's a little house there as well. I'll be glad if you'll take it."

I thanked Anton Pavlovich, but I also could not have lived right beside the sea—I can't sleep when it's so close, my heart begins to palpitate.

That was my last meeting with Anton Chekhov.

Afterwards I lived in Gurzuf, where I had a studio built. From the window I could see the little house by the cliffs where Anton Pavlovich had once lived. This house often appeared in my paintings. Roses . . . and the little house of Anton Pavlovich was intimately visible against the sea. It evoked the mood of a distant land, and the waves crashed not far from the forlorn little house where a great writer had lived, little understood in his own day.

"Women do not like me. They all think I'm a scoffer, a joker, but that's not true," Anton Pavlovich would say to me.

V. G. KOROLENKO

ANTON PAVLOVICH CHEKHOV

I

I first met Chekhov in 1886 or the beginning of 1887 (I don't remember exactly). By that time he had already published two anthologies of his stories. The first, which I saw on Chekhov's table during one of my visits, was called *Tales of Melpomene*[5] and had been published, as I recall, by some satirical journal. Its very exterior bore the stamp typical of our satirical press. On the cover I saw "A. Chekhonte," a picture of an easel, and standing in front of it the caricature of a long-haired artist. If my memory does not deceive me, this vignette was by Anton Pavlovich's brother, an artist. He died at the end of the eighties or beginning of the nineties. He had been very talented, so it was said, but unlucky. This first book by Chekhov went virtually unnoticed by the public, and now, very probably, there are few who remember it. However, some (though not all, as far as I know) of the stories were included in later publications.

Then, as I remember, at the beginning of 1887, there appeared a larger book, *Motley Stories,* published by *Budilnik, Strekoza,* and *Oskolki,* this time under the name A. P. Chekhov. It immediately attracted the attention of a wide reading public. People wrote about it, talked about it—variously, but a great deal—and it proved to be a great success. In newspaper obituaries and commentaries there were remarks to the effect that A. S. Suvorin[6] had been the first to recognize among the amorphous mass of our dull Russian "humor" the genuine pearls of Chekhov's talent. That would not seem to be accurate. The first to recognize them was D. V. Grigorovich,[7] who apparently noticed the sparkle of these original works when they were still scattered about the pages of various satirical journals or, perhaps, in the first anthology of "A. Chekhonte." It seems it was Grigorovich who arranged for the publication of *Motley Stories,* and it was most probably thanks to this publication that Suvorin discovered Chekhov and invited him to work for *Novoye Vtemya*. During my first meetings with Chekhov, Anton Pavlovich showed me letters he had received from Grigorovich. One of them had been sent from abroad. Grigorovich wrote of the homesickness he felt at the spa where he was staying, of his illness and presentiment of approaching death. Chekhov, showing me this letter as well, added, "Well, so much for fame, career, handsome royalties."

At the time I took this as merely a passing note of pessimism from a humorous author of humorous tales before whom life had just opened up a promising future. Later, however, I often remembered those words, and they no longer seemed merely fortuitous.

After the publication of *Motley Stories,* the name of Anton Pavlovich Chekhov immediately became famous, although the evaluation of this new talent provoked disagreement and controversy. The whole book, while still marked with carefree youthfulness, and even a slightly frivolous attitude to life and literature, nonetheless sparkled with humor and frequent flashes of genuine wit, combined with unusual brevity and powerful images. The notes of pensiveness, lyricism, and that melancholy unique to Chekhov which could already be heard amidst the lively humor, only served to set off the youthful light-heartedness of these truly *Motley Stories.*

II

At the time there was a journal published in St Petersburg called *Severny vestnik*. The publisher was A. M. Yevreinova, and the editorial board was composed (initially) of members who had previously worked with *Otechestvenniye zapiski* and headed by Nikolai Mikhailovsky.[8] Gleb Uspensky[9] and S. N. Yuzhakov[10] were close collaborators, and A. N. Pleshcheyev[11] was an editor with the department of belles-lettres and poetry. I was also invited to take a more active part in the work of the journal, and I went to St Petersburg for this reason also. By this time I had already read the stories of Chekhov, and I wanted to make the acquaintance of their author while passing through Moscow.

Chekhov's family was then living on Sadovaya, in Kudrin, in a small, red, pleasant house of the kind, it seems, one can now only find in Moscow. It was a stone building adjoining a large house, but itself constituting a separate, two-story dwelling. I was met down-stairs by Chekhov's sister and younger brother, Mikhail Pavlovich, then still a student. A few moments later Anton Pavlovich came down the stairs.

In front of me I saw a young man, even more youthful looking than his years, a little above average height, with a long face, regular features and a fresh complexion which had still not lost the contours typical of youth. The face had something unusual about it which I could not identify immediately, and which my wife later defined very aptly in my opinion, having also made Chekhov's acquaintance. In her view, Chekhov's face, despite its undoubted air of intelligence and culture, had something sweet about it, reminiscent of a simple-hearted country lad, and this had a particular attractiveness. Even Chekhov's eyes, blue, with a sparkle in their depths, radiated not only thought, but also an almost childlike directness. The simplicity of all his movements, gestures, and speech was the dominant feature of his whole person, as of all his writings. This first meeting with Chekhov left me with the impression of a man with a profound love of life. His eyes seemed to sparkle with the inexhaustible wit and direct merriment which filled his stories. Yet there was also a hint of something more profound, something which still had to develop, and develop for the good. The total impression was one of wholeness and charm, despite the fact that I myself was far from being in sympathy with everything he wrote. However, even his "freedom from any party" seemed to me then to have its good side. Russian life had managed to conclude one of its short cycles without, as usual, having resolved any concrete issue, and there was a feeling in the air that a "review" was needed before launching into the next battle and further search. Therefore Chekhov's very freedom from any party of the day, given his great talent and enormous sincerity, seemed to me then to give him a certain advantage. All the same, I thought to myself, it's not for long. Among his stories there was one (entitled, if I remember correctly, "En Route") in which, at some relay station, a dissatisfied young woman meets a young man, also dissatisfied, badly injured by life, a Russian "seeker" after a better world. The character was only briefly sketched, but bore a striking resemblance to one of the notable people I had come across in my life. I was amazed that this carefree young writer had been able, *en passant,* without experience, by the sheer intuition of his immediate talent, to pluck so accurately and so perceptively the most intimate chords of this long-lived character, still to be found in our midst. Chekhov seemed to me to be like a young oak sending out shoots in various directions, still rough and, at times, somehow shapeless, but already revealing the strength and integral beauty of his future powerful growth.

When, in St. Petersburg, I described to the staff of the *Severny vestnik* my meeting with Chekhov and the impression he had produced on me, my words provoked a great deal of discussion. Chekhov's talent was unanimously recognized, but that to which he directed the still immature power of that talent was viewed with a certain degree of doubt. Mikhailovsky's attitude to Chekhov is already known to the reader: he often and with great interest returned to Chekhov's works, recognized the vast range of his talent, but was therefore all the more severe in noting certain features in which he perceived a mistaken view of literature and its purpose. However, Mikhailovsky wrote more about Chekhov than about any other of his contemporaries, and in his later years, as everyone also knows, he felt very sympathetic towards him. Whatever the case may be, at the time I am speaking of, Mikhailovsky's *Severny vestnik* would have liked to see Chekhov among its contributors, and I had to listen to the reproach that during my visit I (still a debutante in journalism) had not thought to invite Chekhov to work for the journal.

During my next visit to Chekhov, I spoke of this "matter," but A. N. Pleshcheyev had already brought it up when he had called to see Chekhov while passing through Moscow on his way to the Caucasus. Chekhov himself told me about this meeting and confirmed the promise he had made to Pleshcheyev, but also expressed certain hesitations. In his own words, he had started to write almost as a joke, viewed it in part as a pleasure and entertainment, in part as a means of finishing his university course and supporting his family.★

"Do you know how I write my little stories? Here. . . ."

He glanced at the table, picked up the first thing that met his eye— it was an ashtray—placed it in front of me and said, "If you like, you can have a story tomorrow entitled 'The Ashtray.'"

His eyes sparkled with merriment. It was as if some vague images,

★ By this time Chekhov was already a doctor, although without a practice, and his brother, Mikhail, was also beginning to publish his works in satirical journals (under a nom de plume). Note by V. G. Korolenko.

ideas and adventures, still without form but already invested with humor, were beginning to gather over the ashtray.

Now, on recalling this conversation, the small lounge where his elderly mother sat behind the samovar, the sympathetic smiles of his sister and brother, in short, the whole atmosphere of this united, loving family, in the center of which stood this young man, charming and talented and with such an apparently cheerful view of life—it seems to me that this was the happiest, and the last happy period in the life of the whole family, a joyous idyll just before the approaching drama. I recall in the expression on Chekhov's face at the time, and in his gestures, a certain ambivalence: in one sense this was still the carefree Antosha Chekhonte, cheerful, successful, ready to laugh at the clever *dvornik*★ who advises people to read in the kitchen, and at the barber who learns, while cutting someone's hair, that his fiancee is going to marry someone else, and then leaves his customer's head untended.[12] The images came to him in a merry, lighthearted throng, amusing him, but rarely disturbing him. They filled the comfortable little flat, coming, it seemed, all at once to visit the entire family. Anton Pavlovich's sister told me that her brother, whose room was separated from her bedroom only by a thin partition, often knocked on the partition at night in order to tell her about an idea he had had, or even a complete story that had suddenly occurred to him. And both were happily surprised at the unexpected combinations. Now, however, there was a marked alteration in that carefree approach: Anton Pavlovich and his family could not help but notice that Anton possessed something which was not just an entertaining, and at times useful, plaything, but a rare gift which might bring with it great responsibility. The sketch "On Holy Night" had, it seems, already been published by then (in *Novoye Vremya),* a wonderful picture full of penetrating, captivating sadness, still conciliatory and robust, yet already as far removed from the thoughtlessly humorous tone of the majority of his *Motley Stories* as the sky from the earth. And the face of Chekhov himself, only recently a lighthearted contributor to the journal *Oskolki,* had now acquired a certain expression which in former times would have been termed "the first glow of fame." I remember how, when his mother spoke of him, apparently happy and proud of her son's success, one could already hear a note of sadness. Anton Pavlovich and I

★ A man whose job is to ensure that the courtyard and adjoining part of the pavement are kept swept and tidy.—Tr.

were talking about a trip to St. Petersburg, and about where we would meet there, and his mother said with a sigh:

"Yes, it seems that Antosha is no longer mine."

As is often the case, the mother's presentiment proved true.

We agreed to meet in St. Petersburg in the editorial offices of *Oskolki,* where I indeed found Chekhov on the appointed day, in the office of Leikin, one of the editors. It was here, by the way, that a small incident occurred: the day before, Leikin had been enthusing to Chekhov about a wonderful story sent in to *Oskolki* by a still unknown debutante writer from Tsarskoye Selo. The editor was full of praise for it, and had invited the author to come to discuss the possibility of working for the journal. Chekhov had expressed the wish to read the manuscript. It turned out that it was nothing other than one of his own sketches carefully copied out from print and signed with a name no one had heard of. The best proof of fame: the plagiarist had obviously recognized the new talent and had been drawn to it like some parasitic plant.

III

Some time later, Chekhov wrote his first story for a journal. It was called "The Steppe." During my stay in St. Petersburg, Pleshcheyev received a letter from Moscow in which Chekhov wrote that his work was progressing rapidly. "I don't know what it will finally be, but I can smell the flowers and grasses of the steppe all around me"—that was roughly (I'm quoting from memory) how Chekhov described the atmosphere of his work, and it is this, without any doubt, which can be felt as one reads it. This first "major" work also, it is true, bears the stamp of Chekhov's customary form. Some of the critics noted that "The Steppe" seems to be made up of several small pictures set within one frame. That the pictures within this one large frame, however, breathe one and the same atmosphere is beyond dispute. It is as if the reader can himself feel the wind blowing freely across the steppe, filled with the perfume of flowers, can himself follow the sparkle of a steppe butterfly winging through the air, and the dreamily heavy flight of a solitary and predatory bird. All the figures sketched against this background are also imbued with this unique aura of the steppe. Shortly after the story had appeared in *Severny vestnik,* Chekhov junior (Mikhail

Pavlovich) told me that it contained many autobiographical, personal recollections.

The story also contains one detail which seemed to me typical of Chekhov at that time. One of the characters in the story is a young peasant lad called Deniska, a coachman. The coach with the travelers stops for a rest in the steppe in the stifling heat of midday. The burning rays of the sun beat down on their heads, and from somewhere comes the sound of a song, "soft, slow and doleful like a lament and almost undetectable to the ear . . . as if an invisible spirit was flying over the steppe and singing" or as if the steppe itself "burnt, half-dead, already doomed, without words, but piteously and sincerely it was trying to convince someone that it was in no way to blame, that it had not deserved to be burnt up by the sun . . . it was not at fault, but it was still asking someone's forgiveness, avowing that it was suffering from unbearable pain and was feeling sad and sorry for itself." Meanwhile, Deniska is the first of the travelers to wake up, and he goes to a nearby stream and washes himself, drinking, splashing, and snorting. Despite the oppressive heat, the melancholic view in every direction, the even more melancholic song coming from no one knows where and speaking of no one knows what guilt, Deniska is brimming with good spirits and energy.

"Well, and who'll reach the sedge first!" he says to Yegorushka, the central character in the story, and he not only wins the victory over Yegorushka, wearied by the heat, but, still not satisfied with this, immediately suggests that they race back.

I once said to Chekhov, jokingly, that he himself was like his Deniska. Indeed, at the peak of the mood of the eighties, when society resembled that steppe with its wordless, weary and melancholic song, he was carefree, cheerful, full of high spirits and energy. From somewhere or other various projects would come to him, moreover, suddenly and ready-planned down to the finest details. Once he began to spread before me the plan for a journal to be published by men of letters, twenty-five of them, "and all debutantes, all of them young." Another time he looked at me, his fine eyes expressive of an idea which had suddenly matured, and said, "Listen, Korolenko, I'll come to stay with you in Nizhny [Novgorod]."

"I'll be only too happy. Just see that you do."

"Of course I'll come. We'll work together. We'll write a play. In four acts. In two weeks."

I laughed. Deniska again.

"No, Anton Pavlovich. I couldn't keep up with you. You'll write the play yourself, but come to Nizhny just the same."

IV

He kept his word, came to Nizhny and charmed everyone who met him there on that occasion. On my next trip to Moscow, I found him already working on a play. He came out of his study, but took hold of my arm when I was about to leave, not wishing to disturb him.

"I really am writing a play, and I'll finish it," he said. "'Ivan Ivanovich Ivanov.' Understand? There are thousands of Ivanovs—the most ordinary man in the world, nothing of the hero about him at all. And that's precisely why it's so difficult. Do you sometimes find, when you're working, between two episodes that you can see quite clearly in your imagination—suddenly a blank?"

"Across which," I replied, "you have to build a bridge not with your imagination, but with logic?"

"Yes, that's it exactly."

"Yes, it happens sometimes, but then I stop working and wait."

"Yes, but you can't write a play without bridges like that."

He seemed a little absent-minded, dissatisfied, and tired. Chekhov had considerable difficulty writing that first play, and experienced his first serious, purely literary worries and setbacks, not to mention the problems over the stage production, the agonizing over the distance between the word and the image, between the theatrical presentation and the word. This was the play that first revealed a radical change in Chekhov's approach. I remember how much was written and spoken about a few of Ivanov's careless phrases, such as "My friend, heed my advice: don't marry a Jewess, or a psychopath, or a student." True, this was said by Ivanov, but Russian society was so painfully sensitive to certain issues of the day that the public was not prepared to separate the author from the hero; indeed, to be frank, *Ivanov* did not have that note of spontaneity and carefree impartiality which could be heard in Chekhov's previous works. The drama of Russian life had sucked into its vortex a writer who had stepped out onto the literary arena. One could not but feel in his play some underlying tendency, that the author was attacking something, defending something, and the argument was over what exactly he was defending and what exactly he was attacking. This first play, which Chekhov reworked several times, could provide invaluable material for a thoughtful biographer who wishes to trace the history of the spiritual turning point which took Chekhov from *Novoye Vremya*—to which he happily contributed at the beginning, and to which he sent not a line in his later years—to *Russkiye Vedomosti, Zhizn* and *Russkaya mysl*. Lighthearted spontaneity had come fatefully to an end, and now, equally fatefully, began the period of reflection and a heavy sense of responsibility for his talent.★

After "The Steppe" came the story "Name Day"★★ which was also published in *Severny vestnik*. Then came the third story ("The Lights"). The prevailing mood in this story was far more complex, and was even darkened by a sad and skeptical, if slightly cynical, undertone. Chekhov himself, in his correspondence, several times expressed his dissatisfaction with this story.[13] The rest is undoubtedly known and remembered by the whole of reading Russia. *Motley Stories* was followed by an anthology suggestively entitled *In the Twilight*. Then came *Gloomy Folk*, after which *Russkaya mysl* published "Ward No. 6"—a work of amazing power and depth, and expressing that new mood of Chekhov which I would term his second period. That mood was now clearly defined, and everyone realized that there had been an unexpected change: a man who had only recently approached life with merry laughter and humor, who had been cheerfully lighthearted and witty had suddenly, on looking more closely into the depths of life, discovered himself to be a pessimist. I would classify as his third period the stories, and even the plays, of his later years, in which one can detect a desire to see a better world, belief in that world, hope. Through the mist of sadness, sometimes very beautiful, sometimes corrosive and sharp, but always poetic, this hope shines like the domes of a distant church, barely visible through the hot dust and stifling haze of a difficult journey. . . . And above everything there hovers the melancholic awareness:

> A pity that neither of us,
> little Vanya,
> Will live to behold that
> most wonderful day.[14]

★ The drama Ivanov was published in *Severny vestnik* (March, 1889). Note by V. G. Korolenko.

★★ Traditionally the Russians celebrated the feast day of the saint after whom they were named, usually the saint on whose feast day they were born.—Tr.

V

Following these early meetings, which were fairly frequent at the beginning of our acquaintance, I saw less and less of Chekhov. In the late eighties and early nineties our literary connections and preferences (I am speaking of our personal connections and preferences in the literary world) differed, and it also turned out that they rarely crossed thereafter, even when he joined the literary circles I frequented. It was then (at the end of the eighties) that I tried to introduce Chekhov to Mikhailovsky and Uspensky. We set off together as agreed for the Palais-Royal, where Mikhailovsky was staying at the time, and where we also met Gleb Ivanovich Uspensky and Alexandra Arkadyevna Davydova (who later published the journal *Mir Bozhi*). However, nothing came of this meeting. Gleb Ivanovich remained reticently silent (the first signs of mental exhaustion were already manifesting themselves, heralding his approaching illness). Mikhailovsky kept the conversation going, and even Alexandra Arkadyevna—an unusually cultured and tactful person—offended Chekhov with some sharp comment about one of his literary friends. When Chekhov had left, I could tell that the attempt had failed. Gleb Ivanovich, with whom I left Mikhailovsky's, noted with his customary sensitivity that I was down-hearted over something, and said, "You're fond of Chekhov?"

I tried to define what it was I felt for Chekhov, and the impression which he made on me. He listened with his usual pensive attention and said, "Fine," but remained reticent.

Now I realize that Uspensky found the lightheartedness of the author of *Motley Stories* alien and unpleasant. He himself had once been possessed of a profound and original sense of humor, the sharpness of which, however, had soon turned to bitterness. In his article on Uspensky, Mikhailovsky gave an extraordinarily accurate and perceptive description of that reticence with which Uspensky deliberately restrained his inclination to amusing sentences and humorous images, fearing to profane the tragic motifs of Russian reality. Whether that was right or wrong I shall not discuss here, though I believe, of course, that it would be wonderful if people with such a natural fund of humor could find in themselves and the world around them sufficient strength to conquer the massive melancholy of Russian life with the even more powerful force of their laughter. Perhaps we would then produce world classics of satirical literature. One can dream, however, about whatever one likes, but the fact remains that modern

Russian melancholy conquers Russian humor, and this, with the ineluctability of a fatal law, was reflected—unfortunately, only too soon—in Chekhov himself.

At the time, however, the matter still stood differently, and I remember with what sad incomprehension the deep eyes of Uspensky probed the open, cheerful face of this talented arrival from another world where it was still possible to laugh so lightheartedly. Chekhov also instinctively held aloof from the mood which had ripened in Uspensky and which was lying in wait for him, and they parted rather coolly, with an instinctive dislike for each other.

Both of them are now gone. Uspensky died first, and Chekhov's grave is still open even as I write these words. However, each departed with hope for the future and bitter regret for the present.

I recall yet another conversation with Chekhov, about Garshin.[15] I don't recall whether it was after Garshin's death or just before the end of his clouded life. I had not long returned from Siberia, and the profound impression made upon me by its majestically severe landscape and its people was still vivid and fresh. I believed that if Garshin could be distracted from the painful impressions created by the reality of life around us, removed for a time from the world of literature and politics and, most important of all, if his weary soul could be relieved of that awareness of shared responsibility which so weighs down on every Russian with a sensitive conscience, and instead find himself face to face with primordial nature and man, then, so it seemed to me, his sick spirit might yet recover. However, Chekhov objected with the categorical refusal of a doctor:

"No, it's incurable: some molecules in the brain have moved apart, and there's no way to bring them back together."

Later I often recalled these words. A year or two later, "molecules moved apart" in Uspensky, and though he sought a cure in the "healing expanses" of his native land, though he traveled the steppes and ravines of the Southern Urals, the mountain peaks of the Caucasus, the Volga and the "remote rivers" of Central Russia, he was unable to throw off the depression eating ever deeper into his soul, nor the awareness of "shared responsibility" before the truth for all the untruths. And then the "molecules moved apart" in Chekhov. Molecules in the lungs, it is true, and not in the brain, which retained its lucidity to the end. Yet who can say what role was played in this physical illness by the profound and corroding sadness which constituted the background for all Chekhov's mental, and therefore also physical, processes.

In the second half of the nineties, my meetings with Chekhov were infrequent and fortuitous. In the period when his illness was already clearly diagnosed, we met only three or four times. One of these was in 1897, in the editorial offices of *Russkaya mysl*. At the time I was also ill. Chekhov asked after my health with the interest of a friend and a doctor, and when we were outside in the street, he warmly shook my hand and said:

"Never mind, you'll recover, I can promise you, you'll recover."

"And so will you, Anton Pavlovich!" I said with a confidence born of my strong desire to believe it.

"Yes, yes, I hope so. I feel better already," he said, and we parted.

I saw Chekhov for the last time in 1902, in Yalta, where I had gone to discuss a joint statement.[16] Chekhov wrote to me to say that he wanted to stop in Poltava, but I went to see him instead, knowing how difficult that would be for him to come to me. He was living in his country house, which he had built (with artistic impracticability) some distance out of Yalta; his sister and his wife were living with him. As on our first meeting, Chekhov's sister met me downstairs, and as then, Chekhov came down from the first floor. I felt my heart contract painfully at the memory. It was the same Chekhov, but what had happened to his confident, calm joy of life? His features had sharpened, had become as if harsher, and it was only his eyes that still occasionally shone affectionately. More often, however, one could see in them the frozen expression of sadness. His sister said that sometimes he would sit for hours looking at one spot. During our conversation he picked up a book lying on the table, recently recommended to the reader by Lev Tolstoy.

"Polenz, *Der Büttnerbauer*.[17] Have you read it? A good book," he said. "Now if I could still write a book like that, I would think that was enough. Then I could die."

He died before he could.

VI

Yet again a comparison comes inevitably to mind: Gogol, Uspensky, Shchedrin—and now, Chekhov. These names constitute virtually an exhaustive list of great Russian writers with a marked inclination to humor. Two of them died quite simply from acute depression, the other two—from a sense of hopeless gloom. Pushkin called Gogol "the cheerful melancholic," and that apt definition applies equally well to the others, Gogol, Uspensky, Shchedrin, Chekhov.

Could it be that Russian humor indeed contains something fatal? Does the reaction of innate humor to Russian reality—to use the terminology of the chemist—inevitably yield a poisonous residue which destroys more effectively than anything else the vessel in which the reaction takes place—that is, the writer's soul?

T. L. Shchepkina-Kupernik

On Chekhov

It is a universally acknowledged truth that in our younger years we live usually only for the present. The past does not interest us, and we do not think about the future, unable to imagine that it might change anything in our life; the specter of loss, of separation, of death does not trouble us, we squander the wealth without thinking, and we later regret. It was during just such a thoughtless youth that I first met Chekhov. There is no difficulty in tracing back the sources of this meeting. My aunt, A. P. Shchepkina, an actress with the Maly Theater, was on friendly terms with the artist S. P. Kuvshinnikova, known as a close friend of Isaac Levitan. Her acquaintances included Lidia Stakhievna Mizinova (the "Lika" of Chekhov's letters). Lika was an unusually beautiful girl, a genuine "Queen of the Swans" from Russian fairy tales. Her ash-colored, wavy hair, wonderful gray eyes beneath dark, glossy eyebrows, her extraordinary femininity, gentleness, and elusive charm, combined with a total absence of affectation and an almost severe simplicity, made her captivating; but it was as if she did not realize how beautiful she was, and was embarrassed or offended if someone from Kuvshinnikova's group of friends remarked on it in her presence with the familiarity typical of artists' temperament. However, she could not prevent people turning to look at her in the street or in the theater. Lika was a close friend of Anton Pavlovich's sister, Maria Pavlovna, and she introduced us. Maria Pavlovna painted and taught at the Rzhevskaya High School. She was serious and seemingly aloof, and I, used to the extrovert theatrical world, was rather afraid of her at first, but I soon came to appreciate her fine character, her Chekhovian humor and quiet gaiety, and became very fond of her. We became friends with the ease of youth, and it was through her that I met her brother. I met him as "Masha's brother" and "Lika's friend," and approached him simply and confidently. We often met in Moscow, and shortly thereafter Maria Pavlovna invited me to visit them in Melikhovo, and I began to go there. However interesting it was in Moscow at that time, these trips were always like a holiday for me. Anton Pavlovich, who probably realized that I was coming to visit not him but Maria, did not find my visits wearisome, and was always happy to see me.

In Moscow I met Chekhov in the editorial offices of the journals and newspapers which published his works and for which I was also working: *Russkaya mysl, Artist, Russkiye Vedomosti*. It is a pity that I did not keep a diary during that period: it was not only the period of my youth, it was also an interesting time for Moscow. Literary and artistic life was in a ferment. In the theater, under the allusions of poetry, and on canvas, the muffled forces of protest and struggle were being prepared and summoned to life. The Arts Theater appeared and flourished in Moscow. The young Chaliapine, of simple peasant stock, sang at Mamontov's, the Jewish artist Levitan captivated people with his exhibitions: admiration for these two was already a form of protest and a slogan. Reviews and lectures, some authorized and some prohibited, alternated with concerts, exhibitions, benefits by popular performers. Everything revolved around the arts. In the midst of all of this they sometimes gathered together and amused themselves like children—suddenly everyone was playing forfeits; and Ivanyukov, a venerable professor of political economy, crawled beneath a table and began barking like a dog, while the writer Mikheyev, who was as round as a barrel, danced a pas de deux. Chekhov also found himself in our group. When he came to Moscow, he always stayed in Bolshaya Moskovskaya Hotel opposite Iverskaya, where he had his favorite room. The news "Chekhov is in town!" spread through Moscow with the speed of the telegraph. He was feted so often that he even nicknamed himself "Aveland"—a naval minister who, because of good Franco-Russian relations, was always being feted, either in Russia or else in France. So, when "Aveland" arrived, our "joint cruises," as he termed them, began; he was inexhaustible when it came to comic nicknames and titles. I have in front of me a little note on pale blue note paper, written in his fine, humorous handwriting:

. . . At last the waves have tossed the madman ashore . . . [several lines of dots] . . . And stretched out his hands to two white seagulls. . . .

Not an extract from some mystery novel, but simply a note to say that Anton Pavlovich has arrived and wants to see us—my friend, the young actress L. B. Yavorskaya, and myself. This was followed by breakfast in the editorial offices of *Artist* with Kumanin, then tea in the editorial offices of *Russkye Vedomosti* with our common friend, "uncle Sablin," then a photography session with Trunov. This is the period when the three of us were photographed together: Yavorskaya, Chekhov, and myself. Kumanin took us to Trunov, who photographed us for *Artist*. We were photographed together and separately, and then we decided to be photographed together as a souvenir. We took a long time seating ourselves, laughed a great deal, and when the photographer said, "Look at the camera," Anton Pavlovich turned away and set his face like stone, and we could not stop laughing, and kept pestering him over something or other—with the result that Chekhov called the photograph "The Temptations of St. Anthony."

He was taken out to dinners, to the theater, to literary gatherings and the like. As he himself wrote of that time, he lived "in constant intoxication," and finally it was not without relief that he left for Melikhovo.

In Moscow he shared our amusements, our interests, talked about everything Moscow was talking about, went to see the same plays we saw, visited the same circles we visited, sat up all night listening to music; yet I could not free myself from the impression that he was "not with us," that he was a spectator, and not one of the dramatis personae, a distant and definitely senior spectator, although many members of our group, such as Sablin, Professor Goltsev, the old Tikhomirov, editor of *Detskoye chteniye,* and others, were much older. Yet nonetheless he was the older one playing with children, giving the impression that he found it interesting—but in fact he was not interested at all. Somewhere behind the glass of his pince-nez, behind his humorous smile, behind his jokes, one could feel sadness and loneliness. Whether this was because of his illness, which was already making itself felt and was manifest to him as a doctor, or whether it was dissatisfaction with his personal life, Anton Pavlovich lacked gaiety, and his fine, intelligent eyes always looked at everything "from a distance." It was no coincidence that he once showed me a talisman which he always had with him, and which had the inscription: "For the lonely man, the whole world is a desert." Melikhovo, however, was an oasis in this desert, and there he was completely different than in Moscow.

For me also Melikhovo was like an oasis.

I was a true city child, moreover without any family, living in the incessant kaleidoscope of new faces and impressions, work, different things to be done, excitement and amusement. This sometimes proved to be an intolerable burden, and then a trip to Melikhovo was both calming and cleansing. After the stifling air of Moscow, the clatter of the carters and the press of the crowd, I would emerge from the stifling train compartment at the little station at Lopasnya, and suddenly breathe in the fresh air, especially pure, fragrant with the perfume of the earth, grass and pine trees—fragrant even in winter, as if something aromatic lay concealed beneath the snow. Then I would get into a *tarantass* or a sled and drive across the fields, breathing in that blessed quietness, that broad expanse, sad, pensive, and mellow, which is to be found only in Russia. This one feeling alone was joyous and soothing for nerves wearied by the bustle of Moscow. It was as if one had suddenly stopped in the middle of a sprint to take one's breath. The gray sky, the white birches, the reddening rowanberries breathed tranquillity and delight along the way. (Chekhov would slate that phrase as "banal"—but it fully expresses the mood which used to seize hold of me then.) And this feeling continued and increased as I approached the low little house, when I found myself in the comfortable rooms of Melikhovo, in the atmosphere of the Chekhov family.

I first visited Melikhovo about a year after this small, abandoned country house had been purchased. Chekhov bought it unmindfully, not even looking around it. It then comprised a long-untended garden, a great deal of wasteland and bleak little house. A year after the purchase, it had altered beyond all recognition. The whole family had joined in the work: one had taken charge of the garden, another of the vegetable plot, another of the sowing, and with the help of two assistants they had tidied, planted, and sown without a break. All the Chekhovs have one trait in common; they all have "green fingers." "Just push a stick in the ground, and it will grow," said Anton Pavlovich. He himself was an enthusiastic gardener and used to say, like Tchaikovsky, that the dream of his life, "when he could no longer write," was to work in his garden. The house was repaired, freshly painted, wallpapered, reconstructed in some places, and a separate kitchen was built. Melikhovo became truly "Chekhov's country house": not a romantic corner in the style of Turgenev, with summer houses named "Pleasant View" and "Aeolian Harp," not a Shchedrin village with its dreadful memories, but also not a "summer cottage," although everything was new. A new, low-roofed house without any style, but with its own particular comfort. The pleasantest room in the house was made into a study for Chekhov. It was large, with enormous Venetian windows, a tambour to prevent drafts, a fireplace and a large Turkish divan. In winter the snow came halfway up the windows. Sometimes hares would look in through them from the snowdrifts, standing on their hind legs. Chekhov used to tell Lika that they were admiring her. In spring the windows looked out onto blossoming apple trees which Chekhov himself tended. He particularly liked blossoming apple and cherry trees, and in his play *The Cherry Orchard* what he liked most of all was the title. The blossoming of fruit trees evoked in him joyful associations—perhaps the gardens he had known as a child in a small southern town, but when he looked at pinkish-white apple blossoms, his eyes became tender and happy.

The house had nine or ten rooms, and when Anton Pavlovich first took me round, he showed me every room about three times, and each time gave them a different name: first, for example, "the communicating room," and then "Pushkinskaya"—because of the large portrait of Pushkin which hung there—and then "the guest room," or "the corner room," and then "the divan room," and the "study." He explained that it was like this in provincial theaters when there were not enough actors for "the crowd" or "the troops" and the same part-time players crossed the stage several times, sometimes walking, sometimes running, sometimes singly, and sometimes in groups, in order to create the impression of large numbers. This stratagem was later used brilliantly by Stanislavsky in his production of *Julius Caesar*, and I remembered Chekhov's little joke.

Although the house had only belonged to the Chekhovs for one year, when I went I had the impression that they had lived there from time immemorial, and that Pavel Yegorovich, Chekhov's father, had grown old in his "little cell," and the children had been born in this now so comfortable house. The setting was modest in the extreme, without any trimmings; the main ornament was irreproachable cleanliness, abundant fresh air and flowers. The rooms somehow matched those who lived in them: Pavel Yegorovich's little room with its icon stands and icon lamp, the smell of medicinal herbs, and the large books in which he wrote down each event of the day in one line, thus:

14. The girls brought lilies of the valley from the wood.
15. Maryushka made wonderful country cheese pancakes.
16. A shepherd has been killed by lightning.
17. Misha has married.
18. Guests came, there were not enough mattresses.
Anton is annoyed.
The peonies are in flower, et cetera.

With epic calm—joys, griefs, news—all in one line. From such notes one could understand whence Anton Pavlovich had the ability to convey an entire picture so briefly and concisely; in one single phrase— just "the neck of the bottle, shining on the weir"—he has evoked a moonlit night.

The room of Yevgenia Yakovlevna, the so very mild and kind-hearted mother of Anton Pavlovich, had curtains of dazzling whiteness at the windows, a vast wardrobe and chest in which were kept all the things that might possibly be needed by the household, and a comfortable armchair in which, however, she rarely sat, as she was forever bustling about.

The girl's room of Maria Pavlovna, white, with flowers and a narrow, white bed and a huge portrait of her brother, who reigned here as he did in her heart. A living room with a piano, and a terrace overlooking the garden.

Finally, Anton Pavlovich's study, with its windows looking brightly, like his own eyes, out onto the world, with its books and writing desk on which, together with pages of his latest story in his ornate but legible handwriting, there lay plans, sketches, and estimates for hospitals, schools, and other construction projects in the Serpukhov district, and with sketches by Levitan and the late N. P. Chekhov—a talented artist—on the walls.

I was always amazed that this family, which had started out in the provinces, in the lower middle classes, in poverty, could reveal such taste, culture, and elegance. There was no single thing which offended the eye, nothing ostentatious; one could feel in the Chekhov's house and its furnishings some inner dignity—as one could feel in the Chekhovs themselves. I have seen many apartments in Moscow and St. Petersburg belonging to "men of letters." They usually came in two kinds: either a tendency to the ostentatious, with pictures, furniture upholstered in silk, and specially purchased "antiques"; or else, scantily furnished, with the remains of herring on the table, furniture upholstered in oilcloth from which the bast was escaping. But here all was cleanliness, neatness, with nothing superfluous.

I am talking about the house in Melikhovo because now no one can see it as it was then. The house in Yalta—which has miraculously survived—has been preserved, and one can still visit it; but the house in Melikhovo is no more,[18] and those who once visited it are also, for the most part, no longer with us.

Chekhov himself grew very attached to Melikhovo. At Melikhovo he was a completely different man, and there I never saw him with that absent-minded look he had in Moscow. At Melikhovo he was not a spectator, but actively involved. Probably his happiest years are linked with Melikhovo. After a difficult childhood, deprivation and poverty, after having to chase after fees of three rubles and live in a succession of cheap rooms, he suddenly had the feeling of possessing his own home, somewhere he did not have to leave, from which he did not have to hasten elsewhere. He wrote of Melikhovo:

> Here everything is in miniature: a small avenue of lime trees, a pond the size of an aquarium, a small garden and tiny park, small trees—but you walk through it once or twice, look at it, and the impression of smallness disappears: there is plenty of space. . . .

I cannot help but see a parallel with his short stories: one or two pages, then you read it once or twice, think about it—and the impression of something small disappears, and what an expanse of thought, of mood, what a broad picture of Russian life!

I usually arrived at Melikhovo when there were no "guests." In summer I was almost always traveling around Europe. However, it was precisely in summer that so many guests, invited and uninvited, arrived at the Chekhovs' house that sometimes there was not enough room to provide everyone with a bed, Chekhov's mother and Maria Pavlovna were overwhelmed, and Anton Pavlovich fled to his own little wing of the house to work without disturbance. It was in this little wing of the house, where the writing desk barely fit into one room, and in the little bedroom, which Anton Pavlovich called his "oven"—the bed— that he wrote *The Seagull*.

I was not afraid of the muddy autumn roads and usually arrived when only the family were there. I remember one occasion when I was planning to go there in November, and Chekhov wrote to warn me:

I will be overjoyed if you come to see us—but I'm afraid you may dislocate your delicious gristle and bone. The road is in a dreadful state, the *tarantass* jumps up and down in pain, and loses its wheels at every step. When I came the last time from the station, the jolts dislodged my heart, and now I'm incapable of love.

However, when I did not take fright and arrived, he was very glad, as he felt that I loved both him and his family, and their whole way of life.

On another occasion, in early spring, Ivan Pavlovich and I took about five hours to travel the ten versts★ from Melikhovo to the station. Sometimes it was the sled which sunk into the snow and froze to it so that we had to dig it out, sometimes the horses sank into the snow and froze to it so that we had to pull them out.

My "fearlessness" was appreciated and I was joyfully and cordially welcomed. If Anton Pavlovich was away when I came, he would write to his sister, "Tanya must stay and wait for me. Otherwise it will be the worse for her." Before I went to visit them, he usually sent me lists of things to bring with me, such as:

> Dear Tanya, bring two bottles of red wine, Udelny, 1 lb of Swiss cheese, one cooked and one smoked sausage, and 1 lb of olive oil. Do please bring them, or else you yourself will have nothing to eat. Your affectionate celibate priest Anthony. If you can manage it, bring 2 lbs of cheese.

Or:

> Dear godmother, get 2 lbs of starch from Keller's on Nikolskaya, the very best, to make chemises and panties soft and white. Also from there get half a pound of olive oil, the cheaper kind—for guests. And also go to the Arbat, to the tailor Sobakin, and ask if he sews well. I remain your affectionate godfather-miller, or Satan in a barrel.

The old folk never left Melikhovo, and Maria Pavlovna also spent the greater part of her time at home, but Anton Pavlovich's brothers, Ivan Pavlovich and Mikhail Pavlovich, were always visiting them.

The old folk were wonderful. The father, Pavel Yegorovich, tall, well built and of noble aspect, had once been stern and had brought up

---

★ *Verst*—a former Russian unit of linear measure, equal to 3,500 feet.

his children the old-fashioned way, almost along the lines of *domostroi*—strict and exacting. In his day "spare the rod, spoil the child" was a common belief, and he was strict with his sons not because he was himself a harsh man but, as he was deeply convinced, because it was for their benefit. At the time I met him, however, he fully acknowledged that Anton Pavlovich was the head of the household. He felt, with all an old man's powerful sense of justice, that he had not managed his household successfully, had not been able to provide for his family; but "Antosha" had taken all of that into his own hands, and now he was supporting them in their old age, providing them with a roof over their heads—and both of them, his aging parents, considered "Antosha" the head of the household. Pavel Yegorovich always stressed that he was not the master, not the head, despite the touchingly respectful and playful gentleness which the young Chekhovs showed them; this very playfulness, however, already revealed total freedom from parental authority, previously rather severe. Yet the old man displayed not the slightest bitterness or irritation over it.

He lived in his attic, which resembled a monastic cell, worked a great deal in the garden during the day, and then read his favorite "divine books"—enormous folios of the lives of the saints, *Rules of Faith,* and others. He was very devout: he loved to go to church, burnt incense in the house on the eve of holy days, kept all the rituals, and held his own evensong in his cell, reading in a low voice and singing the psalms. I remember that often, when I was passing his room on my way to mine on a winter's evening, I would hear the soft singing of church chants from the other side of his door, and it gave a particular sense of calm to the approaching night.

He was very well disposed towards me. I had always loved old folk, and often, when I was young, had made them the heroes of my stories, feeling all the unspoken pathos of age and approaching departure. I never found it boring to listen to their stories and lectures; and therefore, Pavel Yegorovich gladly welcomed me into his cell, let me read his diary, took me to church, and occasionally expressed his regret that Antosha had sung so well in the church choir in Taganrog, his voice, when still a boy, had been angelic, but now he had stopped, did not sing—why not call in at the church and do a little singing?

Dear Pavel Yegorovich! When he fell ill and died—while his son was away—I shall never forget how the mild Yevgenia Yakovlevna grieved and wept, and kept repeating helplessly, with the typically southern accent, "My dear friend, and I have pickled some plums—he was so fond of them, and now he won't be able to try them, my dear friend!"

There was so much love and regret in that simple, "Chekhovian" phrase, so much of the cares of a life lived together which it would be impossible to express in a long, splendid speech.

I never saw Yevgenia Yakovlevna sitting down idle; she was forever sewing something, or cutting something out, cooking, baking. She was an expert on salting, pickling, and preserves, and loved to invite others to sample the results of her efforts. It was as if here, too, she was compensating for the scarcity that had marked her former life. Before, when they themselves had barely anything, if she had managed to cook enough potatoes she had eagerly invited others to dine with them. Now, when it was no longer necessary to economize and count every piece, she was in her element. She received and served her guests like an old-fashioned lady of the manor, with this one difference—she did everything with her own skilled hands, retiring after everyone else, and rising before everyone else.

I remember her motherly figure in her gown and cap when she would come to see me at night, as I was about to fall asleep, and put on the table beside my bed a piece of meat and mushroom pie or something else, saying with her agreeable aspiration, "Perhaps my little one will feel hungry?"

I also loved to sit in her room and listen to her recollections. For the most part they centered on "Antosha."

With tender emotion she told me about that moment she would never forget, when Antosha—still a very young student—had come to her and said, "Well, Mother, from now on I will pay for Masha to go to school!" (Up till then some well-wishers had provided the fees.)

"From then on everything began to look up," said the old lady. "And the very first thing he did was to pay for everything himself, and earn enough for us all. And his eyes would shine—'I'll pay,' he said, 'myself.'" As she was telling me, her own eyes shone, and as she smiled there appeared at the corners of her eyes the laughter lines that made the Chekhov smile so captivating. She transmitted this smile to Anton and Maria.

Maria Pavlovna helped with everything, but particularly the vegetable garden. This slender, fragile girl pulled on heavy men's boots, tied a white scarf round her head, which set off her shining eyes, and disappeared from morning to evening in the fields or the barn, trying wherever possible to spare her brother extra work.

I have never seen anything to compare with the bond between Anton Pavlovich and his sister, Ma-Pa as he called her. She never married and denied herself her own personal life so as not to upset that of her brother. She had every right to personal happiness but refused everyone, certain that Anton would never marry. Indeed, he did not wish to marry, declaring more than once that he never would, and he married quite late, when it was difficult to imagine that he would because of his health. Maria remained unmarried, and after her brother's death she devoted the rest of her life to looking after the Chekhov museum in their old house in Yalta.

The elder of the four brothers, Ivan Pavlovich, was a quiet, serious man with a head resembling paintings of Christ. We were close friends, and I worked with him in the public reading room in Moscow, snatching days from my overloaded Moscow timetable. The younger brother, Mikhail, was lighthearted and witty, talented at everything, a master of all trades. He also wrote (stories and short plays) but never envied his brother's fame and bore his own literary "anonymity" quite calmly. We enjoyed ourselves together in Moscow, celebrated my name day, and so on. Later he published the journal *Zolotoye detstvo,* which he wrote entirely by himself, his own children inventing riddles and charades while his wife composed the "supplement" in the form of patterns for dolls, et cetera. Our friendship continued to his death.

Life in Melikhovo flowed peacefully and quietly. Anton Pavlovich spent all his leisure time in the garden. He planted, sowed, smeared the apple trees with something white, pruned the roses, and was proud of his garden. He wrote:

> . . . Yes, it's pleasant now, in the countryside. Not just pleasant, but wonderful. A splendid spring, the trees are coming into leaf, it's very warm. The nightingales sing, and frogs are croaking in various voices. I haven't a penny, but I reason thus: not he is rich who has a great deal of money, but he who has the means to live now in the luxury of an early spring.

Each rosebush, each flower which he himself had sown, stirred him to action, was remarked upon and seen as a treasure. Each avenue, each tree was shown in a particular light: "These pine trees are exceptionally fine in the sunset, when the trunks turn quite red. . . . And the

Mamvriisky oak [the name he gave to an old, spreading oak which had remained from the previous garden] should be seen at dusk—then it has such an aura of the mysterious." With what pride he would show me each new rosebush, each tulip which bloomed in the spring, and would declare that for him there was no greater pleasure than to watch "how it comes up through the soil, how it tries"—and then blooms magnificently. I have rarely met a man, except perhaps gardeners, who so loved and knew flowers. There was nothing extraordinary about giving him flowers, although one did not normally present a man with a bouquet. I remember, however, how, when he was leaving to go abroad, I wanted to take him some flowers as a farewell present; and I gave him a bouquet of lilac-colored hyacinths and lemon-yellow tulips, a combination which pleased him very much. One of the books which he gave me (a slim volume of plays) has the following humorous inscription: "To the tulip of my soul, and the hyacinth of my heart, dear T. L." When he was writing that dedication he no doubt remembered Moscow, the first thaw, the March wind with its promise of spring, and our merry group which had come to Kursky Station to see him off and drink a toast to wish him a good journey. When Chekhov wrote about flowers he found his own words. The phrase he puts in the mouth of Sarah in *Ivanov* begs to be set in verse:

The flowers return with every spring
But joys—never. . . .

And the words of Nina in *The Seagull,* about "feelings which resemble fragile, delicate flowers. . . ."

When away from his flowers, Anton Pavlovich concerned himself about them as he might about his own children. As early as March he wrote to his sister, "Put some sticks around the lilies and tulips, or else they will be trampled on. We have two lilies: one opposite the windows of your room, the other near the white rose, on the path to the daffodils." What a charming address! Or: "Don't prune the roses until I come back. Just cut off those stems which have frozen during the winter, or else which are in a very poor condition—but carefully remember that the sick sometimes recover." His letters are full of such instructions and requests.

In general he had an increasing need to be close to nature. In the countryside he became himself. I cannot say that Melikhovo and its environs were particularly beautiful. However, the expanse of the fields, the dark, blue-green band of the forest on the horizon, the scarlet sunsets over the strips of harvested wheat had their own specifically Russian charm. When we sat in his favorite spot just in front of the gates, overlooking the fields, Anton Pavlovich's eyes lost their usual sadness and became clear and calm.

"The depths of the countryside, peacefulness, elks," he wrote about this part of the world and valued it. The proximity of the village did not bother him. He was soon on the best of terms with the peasants.

Chekhov never pronounced the pompous phrases about "serving the people" or "loving our minor brethren" so abundant in the liberal circles of the day, where these topics were discussed over a glass of red wine or champagne. However, to use the elevated style which he himself disliked and which he always warned against, his entire life was spent in precisely such service to the people.

Without any high-flown phrases Chekhov wrote of patriotism:

> The world is a wonderful place—there is only one thing that is not wonderful: we ourselves. How little of justice there is in us! How badly we understand patriotism! A drunken, dissipated, profligate husband loves his wife and children—but of what benefit is it? We, so the newspapers say, love our native land—but in what does that love express itself? Instead of knowledge— insolence and self-importance beyond all bound; instead of work—idleness and swinishness, no justice. . . .
>
> . . . We need to work—and to the devil with all the rest! What matters is to be just, and everything else will fall into place.

Indeed, he did work, and he was just. His sense of justice did not make exceptions in personal relations. He did not hold forth on his political convictions, but when, for example, the whole of Europe was arguing over the Dreyfus Affair, Chekhov—who was, naturally, on the side of Dreyfus—broke off his long-standing friendship with the old Suvorin, unable to forgive the position he and his newspaper took over this issue.

As for how he worked, that is a subject in itself.

Let us begin with medicine, which he used to say, jokingly, was "his lawful wife, while literature was his mistress."

While still a student at the medical faculty he used to treat people. The late V. Ya. Zelenin, son-in-law of the actress Yermolova, and himself later a doctor, told me how Anton Pavlovich had cured him of a severe case of typhus when he was still a high-school student and was sharing furnished rooms with Chekhov. Every summer, wherever he happened to be, he would either treat peasants or work in local hospitals, taking no payment and losing no opportunity to increase his medical knowledge. When he arrived in Melikhovo, his fame as a doctor was known throughout the whole district. He never refused anyone advice. Here is one curious coincidence. When, having graduated from high school in Kiev, I returned to my native Moscow, about one year before I met the Chekhovs, I went to see my old nanny, who lived in a village not far from the Lopasnya railway station. She had what was then called consumption. I was very worried and began to inquire if there was a doctor nearby and whether he had medicines; and she replied, "Don't worry, my dear, we have a doctor here better than any you'd find in Moscow. He lives about six versts away. Anton Pavlovich, he's such a godsend, such a godsend—he even gives me my medicines himself."

It was only later, after I had met the Chekhovs and visited Melikhovo, that I realized who this "godsend" Anton Pavlovich actually was. In Melikhovo he devoted a great deal of his time to his gratis patients. We accepted as normal the fact that we would only just be sitting down to our morning tea in the dining room and Anton Pavlovich would already be returning from somewhere or other— sometimes from a patient who had sent for him during the night— and he would hurriedly drink a cup of tea and then go to his work. Or else he would put on his coat and leave in dreadful weather, despite all the cries of protest on the part of Yevgenia Yakovlevna, "Antosha, where are you going? Wait until the storm dies down!" And he would reply as he left, "Dysentery won't wait, Mother!"

He not only treated, but also provided his patients with medicines, spending what was for him at the time quite a considerable amount of money.

His fame as a doctor spread quickly, and soon he was elected as a member of the Serpukhov sanitary council. At that time a cholera epidemic was threatening Russia. It was proposed that he, as a doctor and member of the council, should take responsibility for the sanitary arrangements. He immediately agreed and, of course, offered his services gratis. The local government had few resources, and Anton Pavlovich began to collect. He traveled around to the local manufacturers and landowners and persuaded them to donate money to combat cholera.

He saw not a few types of humanity during that period—from the local rich to a most elegant country countess with diamonds worth thousands in her ears, the very sight of which, as he admitted, made him want to "say something rude to her, like a high-school student." Much of this was later reflected in his stories. He achieved a great deal: barracks were built at the factories, the necessary equipment was prepared.

"I would no doubt make a very good beggar," he used to say. "I've managed to collect so much money!"

He was proud of the fact that all the preparations had cost the local council not so much as a kopeck—all the resources had been "begged from the residents."

As a result he had in his sanitary district twenty-five villages, four factories and one monastery; and he supervised them alone, with the help of a medical assistant who, as he complained, was unable to take a step without him, and "saw him as his superior."

He traveled around the villages, saw the sick, read lectures on how to combat cholera, lost his temper, persuaded, was fired with enthusiasm for his work—and wrote to his friends, "While I'm serving with the local government, don't consider me a writer." However, he was, of course, unable not to write. He would return home exhausted, with a headache, but behaved as if he was engaged in trifles, joking with everyone. Then he was unable to sleep at night or woke up from nightmares.

When I was ill he also treated me. I still have one of his prescriptions. All his medical advice was extraordinarily simple and reasonable. He kept up with all the latest achievements of medical science, and they interested him. He thought highly of Dr. Khavkin, who was fighting the plague, and was indignant over the fact that no one in Russia had heard of him, though all of Europe admired him.

More than once he said to me, "Study medicine, my friend, if you want to be a real writer. Particularly psychiatry. That helped me a great deal and prevented me from making mistakes."

During that time I would often hear in Moscow: "Chekhov is not actively involved in the life of society." That, however, was, to say the least, shortsighted. His increasing literary fame somehow concealed from the public his social work, while he himself never spoke about it. However, such statements were profoundly mistaken.

In such a brief sketch I cannot go in detail into all Anton Pavlovich's activities, but I would like to recall certain periods in his life.

In 1890 he set off for Sakhalin on his own initiative and his own more than modest means. The question of penal servitude preyed on

his mind. "One needs to see it, to see it for oneself, study it personally," he said. "Sakhalin cannot be unnecessary for a society which sends
thousands of people there and spends millions on it."

He spent two months on Sakhalin, and had the patience to carry
out a census of the entire Sakhalin population single-handedly. He
traveled round all the settlements, went into every hut, spoke to everyone. Using the card system, he registered over ten thousand inhabitants. My honored friend A. F. Kony[19] told me that this book made a
powerful impression upon him both by its factual material, and also
by the passionate indignation over the horrors of Sakhalin which
could be felt in every page. As a result of this work, Sakhalin became
an object of attention; work began on the constructions of orphan-
ages, nurseries, schools, et cetera, and, most importantly, flogging was
abolished. This had so shocked Chekhov that thereafter he often saw
those dreadful scenes in nightmares and woke up in a cold sweat.

Later, in 1892, a famine struck Russia. Many *gubernias* were declared
to be "suffering from crop failure"—the official term for famine. The
gubernias of Nizhny Novgorod and Voronezh were particularly badly
affected. Chekhov had a friend on the Nizhny Novgorod local council. Anton Pavlovich organized a wide network of contributors and
set off in the harsh winter weather. There he set up canteens, fed the
peasants, did everything he could. Moreover, the starving population
either sold their livestock for next to nothing because they had no fodder, or else killed it, thereby condemning themselves to another hungry year. Chekhov organized the purchase of horses in the provinces
and the provision of fodder for them at public expense so that they
could be given in the spring to peasants who had no horse.

While living in Melikhovo, he was always looking for some way to
help the peasants. He was elected a member of the Serpukhov local
council, and he took his duties very seriously. He plunged himself into
questions of popular education and medical services. Talezh,
Novoselky, and Melikhovo owe their schools to him. He himself
supervised their construction, purchased building materials, drew up
the plans and estimates. He was actively involved in the construction
of the local hospital, managed to have a road built from Lopasnya to
Melikhovo, built fire stations in the villages, et cetera.

Chekhov did not limit his activity to his own district. He was, so
to speak, the founder of the library in his own native town of
Taganrog. He began by handing over his own splendid collection of
books brought together over many years, leaving himself only those

he needed for personal use. Not content with this, he got in touch with the mayor of Taganrog, Iordanov, and took upon himself the task of constantly adding to the library's stocks. Soon it became one of the best libraries in the province; he sent whole wagonloads of books, both bought at his own expense and "requested" from writers, publishers, and editors of his acquaintance. On his suggestion, something akin to a reference bureau was set up, attached to the library, where anyone could call for information, ranging from government instructions to the latest news in the arts, and which assisted the reader in all branches of knowledge—history, medicine, et cetera. However, he immediately wrote to Iordanov, "Only tell no one of my involvement in the library's affairs, I don't like it when people talk about me."

Anton Pavlovich also took an interest in the Taganrog museum, gave advice on its "organization and expansion"; and while he was in Paris he made the acquaintance of the famous sculptor Antokolsky especially so as to commission a statue of Peter the Great to be erected as a memorial in Taganrog, himself selecting the site for the memorial.

Despite the pressure of such activities, he wrote many of his most significant works in Melikhovo at that time. It was here, for example, that he wrote "Neighbors," "Ward No. 6," "Peasants," "A Story Told by an Anonymous Man," "Women's Kingdom," "The Black Friar," "Volodya the Elder and Volodya the Younger," "Three Years," "Ariadna," "The House with the Mansard," *The Seagull,* and others.

Anton Pavlovich would lock himself in his room to work and would afterwards emerge in a good mood, with his usual joke for everyone. He said little about what he was writing, perhaps just mentioning the title of the story and summing up the content in a couple of words: "I'm writing about a doctor who has hallucinations." Or else he would take out his notebook and read the name of some railway station or individual that had struck him, such as "Rosalia Aromat," or some note (as for Trigorin: "Heliotrope, heavy perfume, color of widow's weeds—remember when describing a summer's evening"), or a phrase heard on a steamboat (which later appeared in "Ariadna"): "Jean, your little bird is feeling seasick." He would then add quite seriously, "Well, godmother, when I give you in marriage to Yezhov,[20] that is how you must talk to your husband."

Anton Pavlovich began to call me "godmother" after he and I had been godparents to the daughter of a neighbor of his, Shakhovskoy. Moreover, he assured me that he had deliberately chosen to be a godparent with me, or else I would have obliged him to marry me. (In those days it was forbidden for godparents to marry.) He explained that we could not possibly marry because he was a writer, and I was a writer, and we "would inevitably begin backbiting."

He was always teasing me, but he did it in such a good spirit that it was impossible to be offended, and I was the first to laugh, particularly since I knew that Anton Pavlovich only teased those he liked. It seems there was only Lika he teased more than me.

Over his fireplace he hung a portrait of me, wearing a ball dress and holding a fan, and on it he wrote "Lisez Schepkin-Coupernic!" (Read Shchepkina-Kupernik!)—imitating A. I. Urusov, a famous lawyer and literary critic who had so admired Flaubert that when he was asked for his autograph for a charity collection, he wrote on his portrait in French "Lisez Flaubert!" (Read Flaubert!).

Anton Pavlovich called me "a great woman writer of the Russian land," "an eminent belletrist," and so on. He also nicknamed me "Tatiana Ye[zho]va"—the surname of a journalist he knew, apparently not very prepossessing in appearance (I never revealed his name)—and threatened to marry me to him.

One of his favorite stories went as follows: He, Anton Pavlovich, would be "a director of imperial theaters" and would sprawl out in his chair "no worse than your excellency." And then the courier informs him, "Your Excellency, some women have come with plays!" (Just as here, women with mushrooms come to Masha.)

"'Well, let them in!' And suddenly, in you come, godmother, and immediately give a deep bow. 'Who's this? Tatiana Ye-va! Ah! Tatiana Ye-va! An old acquaintance! Well, that settles the matter; I'll take your play for old-times' sake.'"

On one occasion Anton Pavlovich decided that he and I should write a one-act play together, and he sent me the first, long monologue for it. The play was to be called *A Day in the Life of a Woman Writer*. The monologue contained a great many jokes aimed at me, and began as follows: "I am a writer! You don't believe it? Look at these hands: they are the hands of an honest working woman. Look—even an ink stain!" (I always had an ink stain on my third finger—I was not yet using a typewriter.)

For some reason I remembered this opening, remembered how the woman writer, exhausted by the bustle of life, by admirers and work, dreamed of going to the countryside: "There should be snow, quiet, dogs barking in the distance, and someone playing a harmonica, a la some Chekhov or other."

I had not had time to finish my part when I lost the notebook somewhere, and with it the monologue written in Chekhov's hand. At the time I was not very sorry about it—somehow it never occurred to me that the day would come when every line he had written would be collected and carefully preserved; he was simply dear Anton Pavlovich, who joked so lightheartedly with me.

I recall how we once returned to his house after a long walk. We had been caught in the rain and had waited for it to pass in an empty barn. Chekhov, holding his wet umbrella, said, "I should write some kind of vaudeville: two people waiting for the rain to pass in an empty barn, joking, laughing, drying their umbrellas, professing their love for each other; and then the rain stops, the sun comes out—and he suddenly dies of a heart attack!"

"Good heavens!" I exclaimed. "What kind of vaudeville is that?"

"But very true to life. Don't things like that happen? Here we are, joking, laughing, and suddenly—bang! The end!"

Of course, he never wrote that vaudeville.

And here is his harshest joke. In Melikhovo, white-flecked, coffee-colored pigeons of the kind called Egyptian wandered around in "the naive yard," as Chekhov had nicknamed it, and with them a cat of exactly the same coloring. Anton Pavlovich persuaded me that these pigeons were the result of crossing the cat with ordinary, gray pigeons. In those days, natural science was not taught at high school, and I was an absolute ignoramus on the subject. Although the story seemed very strange, I could not bring myself not to believe such an authority as Anton Pavlovich; and when I returned to Moscow, I told someone about his wonderful pigeons. You can easily imagine the enthusiasm this provoked in literary circles, and how long I was obliged to blush for my ignorance.

The merriest hours at Melikhovo were meal times, at which Anton Pavlovich was always in a good mood, friendly and affectionate. He did not bring with him his sleepless nights, nor the concentration of his work. He joked, laughed, and was a cordial host. He summoned those at table "to the murky spring"—an expression that had become a household phrase, and which had its own history. Pavel Yegorovich had once gone with me to church; a village curate had preached to the peasants a sermon which Pavel Yegorovich had liked very much; on returning home he said, "Well, Anton, you never go to church, and what a good sermon the curate gave—a joy to listen to!"

Anton Pavlovich asked me in serious voice, but with laughing eyes, to tell him the content of the sermon, "What was it in the sermon that father had so liked?"

The sermon went roughly as follows: "What would you say," the curate had asked the parishioners, "if you saw a traveler parched with thirst, and next to him, two springs—one crystal clear, the other murky and polluted—and suddenly the traveler, to quench his thirst, ignores the pure spring and drinks from the murky one? You would call him irrational! But do you not do the same thing when, on your day of rest, instead of coming to the clear waters of the service, to the reading of the message of salvation, you go to a tavern and get drunk there?" And so on. (This was before the introduction of the state monopoly on vodka, and such sermons were encouraged, whereas later they were forbidden.)

Anton Pavlovich listened, and then praised the sermon and said, "Well, and now let's go to the murky spring, because wonderful salted mushrooms grow along its banks!"

Thereafter this expression had become part of the family.

After dinner we usually began to play with the dogs. There were two dachshunds, Anton Pavlovich's favorites: the brown Khina Markovna, nicknamed "the sufferer" (because she put on so much weight), and whom he was always persuading to "go to hospital"—"You'd feel much better there!"—and Brom Isaich, whose eyes, according to Anton Pavlovich, were just like Levitan's. Brom did indeed have very dark, sad eyes.

The favorite game was to tease the dogs with the sable wrap I wore around my shoulders. The dogs went mad, barking and jumping around it. I grew weary of the noise, and I was also afraid of what might happen to my sable, so I hid it. After this I was amazed to discover that the dogs barked just as furiously when Anton Pavlovich pointed to a cigar box on the mantelpiece. They barked and jumped, straining to get at the box! It turned out that Anton Pavlovich had surreptitiously removed my sable from the commode and hidden it in the box.

Such pranks were sometimes accompanied by serious conversations. Anton Pavlovich gave me some advice, but very tactfully; he had the ability to feel interest in and deep inner sympathy for the literary efforts of others, be they ever so modest. I remember that he once said to me, speaking of one of my stories, "It's well written, good literary style. However, for example, you have 'and she was ready to thank fate, poor girl, for the suffering sent to her.' But it's the reader who, when he reads that she thanked fate for her suffering, should say 'poor girl.'

Or again, 'it was moving to see this picture' (how the seamstress looked after the sick girl). But it is the reader himself who should say 'what a moving picture.' In general, 'Love your heroes, but never say so aloud!'"

In particular, Anton Pavlovich advised me to abandon "ready-made phrases" and clichés of the kind: "the gathering dusk wrapped the earth in darkness," "the strangely-wrought outline of the mountains," "the icy embrace of melancholy." He jokingly threatened me that if he came across "little stars" or "little flowers" in my verse, he would marry me off to Ye-va.

Even when Anton Pavlovich praised me, he did it mainly with a touch of the humorous. He would say, for example, that some of my verses were so good that I must have taken them from some old journals. Or he wrote: "Today, at nine o'clock in the morning, sitting in a cold classroom on Basmannaya Street, I read your 'Loneliness' and forgave you all your faults. The story is definitely good, and there's no doubt that you are intelligent and inexhaustibly ingenious. Most of all I was moved by the artistry of the story. However, you don't understand anything."

True, he did sometimes write to me in a serious vein: "They say your story is going to be published in *Nedelya* (my story 'Happiness'). I'm very glad for you, and congratulate you from my heart: *Nedelya* is a reputable and pleasant journal. Good-bye, dear friend."

I highly valued his kind comments. Moreover, I never saw a writer who viewed his younger brethren with such warmth and kindness as Chekhov. He was always visiting editorial offices on someone else's behalf, trying to get someone's work accepted for publication, and was genuinely happy when he found a writer who appeared talented. I need only mention his relations with the young Gorky, the letters he wrote to him, to show how alien to Chekhov was any sentiment of professional jealousy. In the mouth of his Trigorin *(The Seagull)* he says, "Why push? There's room for everyone!" And not only did he not push, but was always willing to hold out a helping hand to a junior. Somewhere he wrote, "One should be clear in one's thoughts, morally clean, and neat physically." Such was his principle, and he, like his whole family, never swerved from it.

In Melikhovo Chekhov wrote *The Seagull,* and that same year[21] read it at Yavorskaya's, in the unforgettable blue living room. Chekhov's relations with Yavorskaya were rather ambivalent, sometimes he liked her, sometimes he did not, and he certainly found her attractive as a woman. It was he who first recommended her to Suvorin, and she later left Korsh to join Suvorin's theater—he had seen plays which she performed. Their relations did not have the simplicity which existed between Chekhov and myself. They involved something akin to a flirtation. I recall that she was then appearing in the Indian drama *Vasantasena,* where the heroine, with blue lotus flowers behind her ears, goes on her knees in front of the one she loves and says, "My only one, impenetrable, wonderful. . . ." When Anton Pavlovich arrived and went into the blue living room, Yavorskaya took the pose of the Indian heroine, went down on her knees on the carpet and stretched out her slender arms, exclaiming, "My only one, great, wonderful," and so on. I found an echo of this later in *The Seagull,* where Arkadina goes on her knees in front of Trigorin and calls him her only one, great one, et cetera. There is also an echo in *The Seagull* of Yavorskaya's roles in *La Dame aux Camélias* and *The Fumes of Life.*[22] However, the resemblance is no more than superficial.

A large number of people, our usual professorial-literary company, gathered for the reading. Korsh was also there. He considered Chekhov "his author" as he had staged Chekhov's first play, *Ivanov.* Both he and Yavorskaya had long been awaiting a new play by Chekhov, and were counting on receiving "a tasty morsel." I remember the impression created by the play. It could be compared to Arkadina's reaction to Treplev's play, "Decadence." "New forms?" The play surprised with its originality those who, like Korsh and Yavorskaya, recognized only striking dramas such as those by Sardou, Dumas, and the like. It was impossible that they should like it, just as the wealthy public who attended the Levkeyeva benefit in St. Petersburg did not like it. I remember the arguments, the controversy, Lidia's insincere exclamations, Korsh's surprise: "My dear fellow, it's not scenic—you oblige a man to shoot himself offstage and don't even give him the opportunity to say a few words before he dies!" I recall the expression, whether of confusion or indignation, on Chekhov's face. This play was only understood and conveyed to us, of course, by the Arts Theater several years later.

My own impression was also rather vague. I remember that the first phrases in Nina's monologue made a strong impression on me: "In short, all living things have completed their sad circle and expired." My throat contracted, and it was as if a breeze from far off had blown into the blue living room.

The monologue moved me, but many only saw in it "a satirical comment on the new literature." I thought that perhaps I liked the play because of my partiality for Anton Pavlovich. In any case, I could not view it objectively because of the lines taken from life which were scattered through it: that phrase by Yavorskaya, Masha's [the heroine's— *Ed.*] habit of taking snuff and "having a glass," taken from a young girl we both knew and who had this habit. Most of all, I constantly had the impression that the fate of Nina coincided with that of a girl close to me and to Anton Pavlovich and who, at the time, was living through a painful and sad affair with a writer; and I was disturbed by the idea that her life might end as tragically as that of the poor Seagull.

I should say that I have often noticed that writers, including Chekhov, their attention drawn by some "typical" character, then portray it in a totally fictional context and circumstances and oblige you to live through events imagined by the author. Moreover, it often happens—such is the power of intuition—that these typical characters later find themselves in a situation analogous to that of the fictional heroes and heroines. Such was the case with this girl. The writer left her, her child died. However, this all happened about three years after *The Seagull* had been written.[23]

It was precisely such intuition which lay behind the unpleasant affair between Chekhov and Levitan, one which cost Chekhov a great deal of unhappiness. Levitan was a great friend of Chekhov, and then suddenly a serious dispute arose between them, and it erupted because of S. P. Kuvshinnikova. It happened as follows: Chekhov had written one of his best stories, "The Butterfly," undoubtedly inspired by some incident in Kuvshinnikova's life. Only a writer can understand how the impressions produced by something he has heard and seen in real life are then refracted and combined in the world of art.

With the naiveté of an artist selecting the colors he needs wherever he can, Chekhov had taken just some elements from the externals of Kuvshinnikova's surroundings—her "Russian" dining-room, with sickles and towels, her taciturn husband, who ran the household and invited people to supper, her artist friends. He made his heroine a charming blonde, and her husband a talented young scholar. However, Kuvshinnikova recognized herself and took offense. Referring to this incident in one of his letters, Anton Pavlovich wrote:

> Just imagine, an acquaintance of mine, a forty-two-year-old lady, recognized herself in the twenty-year-old heroine of my "The Butterfly," and now the whole of Moscow is accusing me of writing a lampoon.

The main piece of evidence is the external resemblance: the

lady paints in colors, her husband is a doctor, and she lives with an artist.

Levitan, who also "recognized himself" in the artist, was equally offended, although in effect there was nothing offensive in it for him; and the author should have been "absolved from all his sins" just for the incomparable genius of the story. However, friends and acquaintances became involved, indignation and anger rose, the whole incident developed into a serious business; the two friends did not see each other or talk to each other for more than a year, both suffering deeply from their estrangement.

Chekhov had undoubtedly touched some sore point in Kuvshinnikova's life. No one knew that her relations with Levitan were already under a strain which was to lead to total rupture—again about two or three years after this story was written.

Just when poor Kuvshinnikova was living through the last pages of her affair with Levitan, as her unusual husband expressed it, I was preparing to go to Melikhovo. It was winter, and I called to see Levitan, who had promised to show me some sketches which he had drawn that summer in Udomlya, where we had stayed together. Levitan had a fine studio in shades of brown provided for him by Savva Morozov in a house on one of the boulevards. He met me wearing a velvet blouse and looking like a portrait by Velasquez; I was loaded with various purchases, as I always was when I went to Melikhovo. On learning where I was going, Levitan began as usual to sigh and say how he regretted the silly estrangement between them and how he would like to go there again.

"So what's stopping you?" I said with the energy and resolution of youth. "If that's what you want to do—then you should go. Come with me, now!"

"What? Now? Just like that?"

"Just like that, only wash your hands!" (They were covered in paint.)

"What if it suddenly proves inconvenient? What if he takes it wrongly?"

"I promise you that it won't be inconvenient!" I replied definitively.

Levitan became agitated, seized hold of the idea, and suddenly made up his mind. He threw down his brush, washed his hands, and a few hours later we were already approaching the house in Melikhovo.

During the whole of the journey Levitan was ill at ease, sighing and saying anxiously, "Tanechka, what if we're doing the wrong thing?" (He spoke with a pleasant burr in his voice.)

I tried to reassure him, but his nervousness also infected me, and my heart began to thump. What if I was indeed about to create a painful situation? Although, on the other hand, I knew Anton Pavlovich and was certain that there would be nothing of the kind.

We drew up to the house, the dogs began to bark, Masha ran out onto the porch; Anton Pavlovich appeared, wrapped up and peering to see who was with me. There was a short pause, then an enthusiastic handshake, and then they began to talk about the most ordinary things, about the trip, about the weather—just as if nothing had happened.

That marked the beginning of their renewed friendship, which continued till Levitan died. Anton Pavlovich visited him and treated him.

The Kuvshinnikova affair, however, was something Chekhov did not like to talk about. He constantly teased Lika over it, as she had remained on friendly terms with her; and once, in connection with one of my stories, he wrote to me, "But even so you haven't been able to restrain yourself, and on p. 180 you've nonetheless described S. P." He teased me over it to no purpose; in that story I did not describe her. Many years later, when neither she, nor Levitan, nor Dr. Kuvshinnikova were with us any longer, I did indeed describe this incident in the story "The Seniors," published in *Vestnik Yevropy*.

When Chekhov sold Melikhovo[24] and finally moved to Yalta, it was as if I had lost a piece of my own heart. My old nanny also died around this time, so I no longer had any reason to go to Lopasnya.

Chekhov sold his beloved Melikhovo because of his illness, which forced him to move to a warmer climate, and because his father had died. Chekhov senior died suddenly in 1898. After his death, Anton Pavlovich wrote to his sister, "I have the feeling that after father's death, life in Melikhovo will no longer be the same, as if the flow of life in Melikhovo ended with his diary." So it was—and the brightest days in Chekhov's life came to an end.

Chekhov was not in Moscow for the first performance of *The Seagull*. Perhaps that was deliberate—the failure of the play in St. Petersburg had been a great blow to him. He was in Yalta when the whole of the Arts Theater and all those close to him were anxiously awaiting the premiere. I was also very anxious. However, from the very start, from the very first words spoken by the incomparable Masha (Lilina and Medvedenko) Tikhomirov, I simply forgot that I was in a theater, that it was a play, but felt something I had never felt in a theater before: it was as if this were not a stage, and these were not actors, but we all found ourselves watching real life. All the spectators had the same feeling. Following the famous "deathly silence" which—after the curtain came down for the last time—lasted for several seconds (and who does not know how pitilessly the seconds tick away onstage), and which drove those taking part in the play almost to despair, as they took this silence on the part of the shaken public as proof of failure, there was suddenly a storm of applause. Even Efros—a critic and journalist, extraordinarily quiet, restrained and pensive—"went overboard": he jumped up onto his chair, shouted, raved, wept, demanded that a telegram be sent to Chekhov. From that moment the Arts Theater had conquered him, and also the whole of Moscow, with just a few exceptions.

On leaving the theater, I immediately sent Anton Pavlovich a telegram. He wrote in reply:

> My dear godmother, I wish you a happy New Year, and many more to come, and good health and happiness. I received your telegram and was moved to the depths of my heart. Your letter was also the first to arrive and the first swallow, so to speak, to bring me news about *The Seagull* was you, my dear, unforgettable godmother. How are you? When are you going to send me your book of verse? By the way, your poem *The Monastery* is simply wonderful, pure joy. Very, very good. Here in Yalta the warm weather continues. I wish there was some snow. I press your hand and wish you good health. Don't forget your godfather-cab-driver Anton.

The idea for the poem to which Anton Pavlovich refers, by the way, was inspired by his father's funeral at the Novodevichy Convent. During the whole of the winter following the premiere of *The Seagull*, I rejoiced over its success. It was played to a packed theater, and very often, as I went home in the late evening past the Hermitage Garden to Karetny Ryad, where the Arts Theater then stood, I would see the whole square in front of the theater filled with people—mainly young people, students—who were preparing to spend the night there, some comfortably, with a small folding chair, some standing under a street lamp with a book, others in groups and dancing in order to keep warm. The square was buzzing with life as they waited to buy a ticket early the next morning and then run to their lectures, not at all troubled by a sleepless night. Their youth warmed and supported them.

The Arts Theater rehabilitated and recreated *The Seagull,* but *The Seagull* also made the Arts Theater. Certainly, Chekhov's plays are the best thing the theater ever did. Chekhov even exaggerated the role played by the Arts Theater in the success of his plays, and I remember saying to him once (we were talking about *The Three Sisters*) that what is amazing about his plays is that, although you are sitting in a theater, you feel you are actually watching someone's life. He smiled, all the Chekhov laughter lines gathering round his eyes, and said, "It's their acting: they're very clever."

Chekhov asked me to come to Yalta, but my travels took me sometimes abroad, sometimes to St. Petersburg, so that I never went there. From time to time we would write to each other. He wrote in his usual humorous tone. He would suddenly send me the bill from a hotel abroad, demanding in the name of the proprietor that I pay immediately or else face legal action. Or from Yalta, for example, he asked me to send him a play:

> My dearest godmother, please be so good as to send me your play *Eternity in a Moment,* and as soon as possible: we want to stage it and pay you royalties of one ruble. I will send you a theater bill, and also a review in good time. (There are theater critics here. They write very well!) If for some reason you cannot send your play, let me know as quickly as possible. My address is Yalta, Bushev House. And also let me know how things are with you. I am as bored as a sturgeon. Don't forget to write sometimes. And in general, say less about yourself and honor the elderly. Your benefactor and godfather Povsekaky. Don't forget to write! I will stay here the whole month. Where can one buy *The Romantics?* You see how concerned I am about your fame. As soon as talk began about amateur dramatics, I immediately let you know.

In his next letter, Anton Pavlovich replied to my request for permission to stage his play *The Bear,* which A. P. Shchepkina so wanted to produce, at the Maly Theater.

> My dear godmother, I hasten to reply concerning *The Bear.* I repeat—I am very happy. I write "repeat" because two years ago, on your demand, I wrote to say I agreed and almost, I seem to recall, signed the terms. That *The Bear* will appear at the Maly Theater (or, more accurately, on the stage of the Maly Theater) is very flattering.

Tatiana Ye-va, a few days ago I sent you an open letter and asked you for *Eternity in a Moment*. Please send it. I want to give a lecture entitled "On the Decline of the Dramatic Art in Connection with Degeneration," and I shall have to read extracts from your play and show the public photographs of you and the actor G. [That was the actor Gorev, whom Chekhov admired, rightly believing him to be one of the best actors at the Maly Theater.]

Yes, you are right: women with plays are multiplying not by the day but by the hour, and I think there is only one way of fighting this plague—summon all the women to the Miur and Mereliz shop and set fire to it.

I have a group of acquaintances here—murky springs flow in every direction—there are women with plays and women without plays, but it is still boring. I feel heavy, as if I had eaten a huge bowl of cabbage soup. Come to Yalta, and we'll tour the environs. The food here is good. Your godfather, A. Chekhov.

In all his letters dating from that period, despite the humorous tone, there is a note of that boredom, even melancholy, which he often felt in Yalta. He did not like southern scenery in general, found it sham, and pined for the gray days of Moscow, for landscapes a la Levitan. Once, after a trip to Abbatcia, he said to me, "The greenery there is shiny, as if made of metal. No comparison with our birches and lindens!" Travels abroad left no mark on his works, nor on Chekhov himself. I often wondered why, and I think I have found the answer. Chekhov was a writer who was passionately interested in life and people. In order to write, he had to observe life and people. Abroad this was not possible for the simple reason that he spoke not a single foreign language; and therefore, his life there became for him something like a film. He felt as if he were deaf and dumb; the scenery alone—and that, "sham," excessively, emphatically beautiful—could not satisfy him. He could not abide emphatic beauty, deliberate beautifulness, did not like anything akin to pathos, and carefully protected his own experiences and his heroes against fine words, pathos, and literary posing. In this he perhaps went to the extreme. It rendered him unable to identify with tragedy; he never sympathized with Maria Nikolayevna Yermolova, just as she never sympathized with him as a writer. They were polar opposites: true-to-life realism and romantic realism. Those "heights" on which the great actress felt so free, moving away from reality only in order to show what reality *could be,* were alien to Chekhov; and he revealed life as it *was,* leaving the reader or the spectator to exclaim of his own accord, "We cannot go on living like this!"

I am still not sure whether Chekhov realized the role he was to play not only in Russian but also in foreign literature; how great was his talent. Of self-importance or ambition—which it is impossible to conceal—I felt nothing at all. Yet he was a wholly original writer who stood apart among the leading lights of literature. In my opinion, the most significant element in Chekhov's writing is the liberation of the story from the domination of the plot, from traditional "tangles and denouements." In order to move the heart of his reader, Chekhov only had to take a slice of everyday life and describe it in his own words. He needed neither dramatic exclamations, nor murders, nor exultation—but it was as if he revealed the meaning of the words by the old, forgotten poet K. Sluchevsky:

> A drop of water is full of grief
> And inescapability. . . .

Shchepkin said, "There are no minor roles—only minor actors." Chekhov could truly say, "There are no minor events—only minor writers." For him, no event in life was a minor one; everything was worthy of observation. As Goethe says in *Faust,* "Reach into life, it is a teeming ocean! . . . And where you seize it, it exerts a space!" Through these minor events he showed breadth and depth of vision. As one can see a vast panorama through a small piece of glass, so through each small event in Chekhov's stories we see a vast area of life. Chekhov was embarrassed by the small dimensions of his stories and was always planning to write "a long novel," declaring, smiling with his eyes alone, that he "envied Potapenko" (a very average writer, but extraordinarily prolific). His short stories, however, are worth many volumes of other works. Take, for example, "The Lady with the Dog." Turgenev would have written a whole novel on such a theme. Chekhov fitted it into a few dozen pages, but in these few pages we can see and feel not only the personal drama of two or three people, but also the entire lifestyle of the "cultured" society of the day, suffocating under the weight of its prejudices, misconceptions about propriety, et cetera, which often destroyed its members' lives and souls.

And other stories are only a few pages long. What a passionate sympathy and love they express towards their characters—*that love* about which he did not "talk out loud," and which shortsighted critics mistook for "objectivity to the point of indifference." One need only recall at random: the story "In Exile," the story "The Chorus Girl," the story "Vanka," the story "The Bishop." In the story "In Exile," the Tatar alone is worth an entire novel. The tragedy of "The Chorus Girl" is an accusation directed against society for its attitude towards "fallen women," while the tragedy of "Vanka" castigates, no less than a Dickensian novel, the fate of apprenticed children. The tragedy of "The Bishop" reveals the crushing loneliness of a man who must deal with the crowds. I have named but a few, many more could be cited—they are all stories written from the heart.

During Chekhov's life I often heard reproaches from "philistines" that he wrote about "boring people" and about a boring life.

I recall the idea which Goncharov put in the mouth of Raisky in *The Precipice:* "to write about boredom." "Life is indeed multifaceted and diverse, and if this boredom, as broad and bare as the steppe, is found in life itself—as boundless fields and sandy expanses are found in nature—then boredom can and should be an object of thought, of analysis, of the painter's brush." Goncharov saw boredom embodied in "the broad and bare steppe." Chekhov, however, wrote "The Steppe," a story with almost no content, with no plot or denouement, but how much he saw in that steppe, what a wealth of color, observations, and impressions! On reading it, you feel as if you can smell the fragrant steppe grasses, can see "the ash-gray clouds" scudding across the boundless sky, can hear the flutter of the bustard's wings and the simple speech of simple people—and you are unable to put the story down until you have finished it, and then you will read it again with renewed pleasure, as you look again with renewed pleasure at a favorite landscape painting. Thus, in that "human boredom" of which Goncharov was thinking, Chekhov was able to find and leave for us as much a wealth of thoughts, feelings, characters, and possibilities as there are colors and pictures in his story about "the broad, bare steppe."

There is another quality in Chekhov which allows us to see him as a great writer. We always read him *anew,* and in his stories, as we read and reread them year after year, we always find something fresh for ourselves, something we had previously not noted, something which we had not yet "matured" enough to perceive. Not long ago, for example, I experienced such a moment while reading *The Seagull.* In the first production of the play, and in those that followed on the Russian stage, there emerged the tradition of playing Nina in the last act in such a state of hysteria as to be almost madness, so that the spectator should not doubt for a moment that her end is imminent and inevitable—be it in a pond or beneath a train, she must die. Only recently, however, I heard the monologue from *The Seagull* read by Alisa Koonen at the Kamerny Theater, on a "bare stage"—and I suddenly realized that Nina would not die, that she cannot die. I realized this from Chekhov's very text. She "believes in her art, she has learned patience"—and this painful path of suffering will surely bring her to the realization that, as she herself vows, she will become an actress. Somehow we forget that only two years have passed since Nina left her parental home, an inexperienced girl. But what a two years these have been for her. She has been abandoned by the man she loved; she has lost her child. Is it surprising if she has not yet had the time to become an actress? However, she "cried out with talent, she died with talent," and, of course, she will have a talented life on stage!

Chekhov acknowledged and savored pathos and romanticism only in music. Here there were no boundaries or prohibitions. He used to take me to neighbors who were relatives of the poet Fet simply in order to listen to Beethoven: the lady of the house was an excellent pianist. When he listened to *The Moonlight Sonata,* his face became serious and attractive. He loved Tchaikovsky, loved certain romances by Glinka, for example, *Do Not Tempt Me Without Cause,* and very much loved to write when there was music or singing on the other side of the wall. Brag's *Serenade* sung by Lika to the accompaniment of a piano and violin was reflected in "The Black Friar."

During the last years of his life, Chekhov and I met only rarely, when he was in Moscow and I also happened to be there. However, I spent less and less time in Moscow. Our last meeting has remained vividly imprinted on my memory.

Anton Pavlovich came to Moscow in the autumn, but was in no hurry to leave, despite the dreadful weather. He was staying in a small apartment which his wife was sharing with Maria Pavlovna. I was amazed at the change in him. Pale, gray faced, with sunken cheeks—he bore no resemblance to the old Anton Pavlovich. It was as if he had shrunk in size.

It was difficult to believe that he was living in Yalta: it was supposed to conserve his health; everyone said that at his age this illness was not so dangerous—"people over forty don't die from consumption" he was told by those around him. However, there was no sign of any improvement. He had a stoop, was wrapped up in a traveling rug, and kept raising a jar to his lips to cough up phlegm.

His wife, the wonderful actress Olga Leonardovna Knipper, could not imagine her life without the Arts Theater, and the theater could not imagine itself without her. At the same time, their enforced separation weighed upon her, and she suggested to Anton Pavlovich that she would give up the theater and live in Yalta, but he did not wish her to make such a sacrifice.

Once, joking, Anton Pavlovich wrote to a friend:

> . . . There, I shall get married—if that pleases you—but on my conditions: everything must remain as it was before, that is, she should live in Moscow, and I shall live in the country and visit her. I promise to be a marvelous husband, only give me a wife who, like the moon, does not appear in my sky every day.

What sounded so cheerful in a humorous letter was not quite so in reality. Anton Pavlovich thought highly of O. L.'s talent and would not allow even the suggestion that she should leave the stage for his sake, expressing his opinion on this subject quite categorically. However, he pined in Yalta without her, felt lonely, particularly on dark, autumn evenings when a storm was sweeping across the sea and a hurricane was breaking the branches of the magnolias in his garden, the cypresses bending and creaking as if crying, while his cough prevented him from going outside. Indeed, no one would venture out in such a storm, and he read letters from Moscow describing the busy, cheerful life there, the theater, which breathed *his* spirit, *his* plays, while he was cut off from it all—from his wife, from the theater, and from his friends.

Understandably, though unwisely, he was always coming to Moscow and staying longer than planned, and these changes in climate had a fatal effect on his health.

On the evening I visited Chekhov, O. L. was taking part in a concert. The very respectable Nemirovich-Danchenko called for her wearing tails and an immaculately white shirt. O. L. came down in her evening dress, delicately perfumed, said an affectionate and tender good-bye to Anton Pavlovich, adding some lighthearted phrase to the effect that he was not to be bored without her, but "be good"—and then she disappeared.

Anton Pavlovich watched her go, and then began to cough, unable to stop for some time. He raised the jar to his lips, and when the bout of coughing had passed, remarked without any obvious relation to our previous conversation, which had revolved happily around Melikhovo, the past, and common friends, "Yes, godmother, it's time for me to die."

I never saw Anton Pavlovich again.

I learned about his death while I was abroad and visited his grave at Novodevichy Convent only several years later, after a long absence from Moscow. I found some young people there who had come to honor the remains of the beloved writer. The minutes, ticked off by the clock on the tower, fell like pearls into eternity. I stood there and thought, "No—he is still alive for us. He is with us in every gray day, in every girl pondering life, in every petal falling in a cherry orchard— and in the bright hope that 'life will one day be wonderful.'"

Sometimes Chekhov would remark in conversation that he would soon be forgotten. "I shall be read for seven or seven and a half years," he would say, "and then they'll forget me."

However, on one occasion he added, "But then a little time will pass, and they'll begin to read me again, and for a long time."

He proved right. His presentiments often proved correct.

When I reread Chekhov, I often come across phrases and statements which amaze me. In the story "Three Years," for example, his hero says, "Moscow is a city which still has to face a great deal of suffering." I recalled those words during the severe bombing of Moscow in the autumn of 1941. Here also one can check the accuracy of his presentiments.

The storm that swept the country during the first few years of the revolution overshadowed his pensive image from us for a while. However, when those years had passed, Russia again discovered Chekhov; and our bold age has decided to free him from the nickname "whiner" and "pessimist"—the hackneyed opinions of hackneyed critics—and has found in his stories, as sad as the Russian reality of his day, those germs of living faith in the people and their future, those notes of confidence in the victory of the new man which now ring out so clearly for literary researchers.

I sometimes wonder what Chekhov would have done, how he would have reacted, if he had lived to the great revolution. I always have my answer ready: Chekhov was a true Russian writer and a true Russian. He would never have left his country, but would have plunged himself into that new life about which he and his heroes dreamed.

V. I. Nemirovich-Danchenko

Chekhov

I have in front of me three portraits of Chekhov, each of them reflecting a period in his life.

The first is of the "promising" Chekhov. He is writing an endless number of stories, brief sometimes minuscule, mainly in satirical journals, and the vast majority with the signature "A. Chekhonte." How many such stories did he write? Many years later, when Chekhov was selling all his stories[25] and deciding what to publish and what not to publish, I asked him and he said, "Around a thousand"

All these stories were anecdotes, marvelously inventive, witty, apt, and with their own individual character.

However, he is already moving to longer stories.

He loves company, prefers to listen rather than talk. Not in the least concerted. There is no question that he is considered "undoubtedly talented," but who then would have thought that his works would be numbered among the Russian classics!

In the second portrait, Chekhov is already recognized as "one of the most talented" writers. His collection of stories *In the Twilight* received the full academic award. He is writing less, his style more restrained; people talk about every new story he publishes; he is a welcome visitor in every editorial office. However, Mikhailovsky, the then recognized leader of the young people, never ceases to emphasize that Chekhov is a writer without a message; and that has its effect, delaying his unanimous acclamation.

Lev Tolstoy, however declared, "Here is a writer it is pleasant to talk about."

The doyen Grigorovich, one of the so-called "leading lights" of

Russian literature, goes still further. When, in his presence, a comparison was drawn between Chekhov and one rather poor but very "ideological" writer, Grigorovich replied, "He's not even worthy to kiss the trail left by a flea which has bitten Chekhov." About the story "Cold Blood" he said, although in a whisper, as if it were still rather daring to say, "Put that story on the same shelf with Gogol," and then added, "You see how far I'm going."

Another such leading light of Russian literature, Boborykin, says that he allows himself the pleasure of reading one story by Chekhov without fail every day.

During this period Chekhov is in the very thick of life in the capital, attending circles of writers and artists in Moscow and St. Petersburg; he loves a gathering, witty conversation, the backstage of the theater. He travels a great deal around Russia and abroad; he is full of love of life, modest as always, and still prefers to listen and observe rather than talk. His fame is constantly growing.

The third portrait shows Chekhov at the Arts Theater.

The second period in my reminiscences ends somehow abruptly with the failure of *The Seagull* in St. Petersburg, as if it was this which delivered the blow, caused the dramatic change in his life. Until then, as I recall, no reference had ever been made to his illness, but after this I cannot recall Chekhov without thinking of a man visibly affected by some hidden affliction.

He is writing less, two or three things a year; he is more demanding of himself. The most remarkable new feature in his stories is that, while remaining objective, he is perfecting his enormous artistic skill, permitting his characters more and more frequently to reflect on life, mainly among the Russian intelligentsia, lost in contradictions and indulging in dreams and inertia. The thoughts of the author himself, intelligent, apt, noble, expressed elegantly and with great taste, can be identified with extraordinary clarity among these reflections.

Each new story by Chekhov is already a literary event.

Most important of all, however, during this period, is Chekhov the dramatist, Chekhov—creator of a new theater. He almost eclipses himself as a belletrist. His popularity is increasing; his image is acquiring a new charm through the theater. He is becoming the public's favorite; the refrain that he has nothing to say is fading. His name gives way only to that of Tolstoy, still with us, and still working incessantly.

However, even as his fame grows, his end is approaching. The reader greets every new work not with the usual lightheartedness, but with a kind of tender gratitude, aware that precious strength is being expended. Three portraits over the course of eighteen years. Chekhov died in his forty-fourth year, in 1904.

Writers' circles were often organized in Moscow, but they were always short-lived and soon collapsed. One such circle was headed by Nikolai Kicheyev, editor of the journal *Budilnik*. He was always very decent, correct, friendly, slightly aloof, and suffering from ill health, always spoke softly, and almost never laughed—it even seemed rather strange that he should be the editor of a satirical journal. However, he loved laughter most of all, felt its power, and was among those who consider wit to be the greatest gift of man. I had known him for a long time; in the years when I was just beginning my literary career, he and I headed the theatrical section in *Budilnik* under the joint signature "Niks and Kiks."

The circle was rather a mixture. In the political sense, however, it pursued one direction: liberal, but with rather abrupt swings to the left and the right. While, for some, the most important goal of a literary work lay in its "social tasks," others valued above all in a literary work its form, its vivid imagery, its living word. The first involved politics in absolutely every theme. Around the dinner table there were conversations whose content was such that one had to look at the servants waiting on tables to see whether or not there might be spies among them. Others remained cool, did not protest out of feelings of camaraderie, but then, in their various corners, termed these speeches "cocking a snook in one's pocket."

The true "liberals" accepted this label with pride. I can see now in front of me Goltsev attending a banquet. Until the end of his life he remained the most honest of men, a journalist wholly dedicated to progress. But he had only to begin a dinner speech and coldness emanated from him, and the more serious he became, the more boring. Everyone knew in advance what he would say. However, the liberally minded young ladies found this agreeable; his fine words pleased them and also, clearly, the majority of the listeners, who nodded sympathetically with blankly serious faces at every pause in Goltsev's speech and warmly applauded when he produced a well-placed full stop. They particularly liked the fact that they were also well acquainted with what he was saying.

I once went with Chekhov for a ride in a one-horse carriage; the driver was unable to swerve in time, and the carriage collided with a tram and overturned—confusion, panic, shouts. We got up unharmed and I said, "There you are, just a matter of a moment and we might all have been killed."

"That's not so dreadful," said Chekhov, "but Goltsev would have delivered the funeral speech—and that's far worse."

This, however, did not prevent us from having great respect for Goltsev.

Shchedrin was idolized by the writers. However, here also, not because of his considerable satirical talent but for his marked liberalism. It even became commonplace to send Shchedrin a greetings telegram (he lived in St. Petersburg) from every gathering with wine and speeches.

Purely literary aims were viewed with suspicion.

"Aha, art for art's sake? 'Nightingales, a sigh, a whisper?'[26] Our congratulations."

However, the opposing group of writers also expanded. They were weary of the same haunts, clichéd phrases, hackneyed ideas, emasculated philosophy. It was repellent to discover mediocrity or cunning behind the labels "an enlightened personality," "a champion of freedom."

Mikhailovsky, having captivated the minds of the young, held the literature of the young on the end of a leash. In all seriousness it was declared that success required suffering, exile for at least a few years. There was a period when the huge success and entire literary talent of the writer consisted in his long beard, but he had written a short story and presented it immediately on returning from political exile. Poetry was despised. There remained only "Sow what is wise, what is good, what is true" or "Forward without fear or doubt,"[27] cited ad nauseam. Pushkin and Lermontov gathered dust on the shelves.

Chekhov appeared at one of our gatherings in a separate room in a restaurant. Introducing us, Kicheyev whispered, "Here's someone who will go far."

He could be called rather handsome: above average height, agreeably wavy chestnut hair tossed back off the forehead, a small beard and mustache. He was retiring, but not excessively timid, and was restrained in his gestures. His voice was a low bass with a deep metallic ring; his diction genuinely Russian, with a hint of purely Great Russian turns of phrase, the intonation flexible, even sometimes slightly musical, but without the slightest sentimentality and, of course, completely free from the artificial.

Only an hour later one could discern yet another two notable characteristics. He had an internal equilibrium, a calm independence—no trace of that smile which never leaves the faces of two companions who have come together on some mutually agreeable topic, that familiar smile of forced amicability which says, "Ah, how pleasant it is for me to talk with you," or "You and I, of course, share the same tastes."

Chekhov's smile—the second characteristic—had its own particular quality. It appeared all of a sudden, rapidly, and then disappeared just as rapidly. It was a broad, open, sincere smile that lit up his whole face, but which was always brief, as if it had suddenly occurred to him that it was perhaps not fitting to continue to smile on that subject.

This was a characteristic which remained with Chekhov all his life. It was a family trait. His mother, his sister, and in particular his brother Ivan had precisely that same smile.

I was, of course, familiar with his stories. Many of them he already signed with his full name, though the signature "Chekhonte" was still to be found on trifling compositions.

Not long before this he had staged his first play, *Ivanov*, at Korsh's private theater. He had written it in eight days, at one sitting, so to speak. He made no attempt to have it staged in one of the imperial theaters, but handed it over to Korsh's theater, which then had the wonderful actor Davydov.

The actors, it seems, gave a good performance. Certainly, Chekhov's family frequently praised them for a long time afterwards. However, the play was not uniformly successful, and for a private theater this was the equivalent of failure.

Theatrical circles in Moscow at the time were very much influenced by the opinions of two theater critics—Flerov-Vasilyev and, to some degree, the rather foppish Pyotr Kicheyev, who shared only his surname in common with Nikolai Kicheyev, editor of *Budilnik*. Pyotr Kicheyev wrote a crude criticism of the play, trying, for whatever reason, to argue that Chekhov could not be a poet because he was a doctor. Flerov, who, in general terms, deserves to be remembered with gratitude, also criticized the play, but ended roughly as follows: "Yet nonetheless I cannot rid myself of the impression that this young author possesses genuine talent."

That this talent also required a new, specific theatrical approach to staging his plays was something which did not occur to the critics, or even to the author himself. Such an idea had yet to be born.

I first read *Ivanov* when the play had already been published. It seemed to me then to be merely a rough draft for an excellent play.

We were all deeply impressed by the first act, one of the best of Chekhov's "nocturnes." Moreover, we were won by the enviable boldness and ease with which the author tore off masks and hypocritical labels. However, the comical figures appeared more like caricatures, certain scenes were unnecessarily provocative, and the construction of the play was rather clumsy. Clearly, at the time I underestimated Chekhov's poetic gift. Myself being occupied with the development of scenic form and still under the powerful influence of the "art of the Maly Theater," I made the same demands of Chekhov. This occupation with a familiar scenic form concealed from me the inspired combination of simple, living, everyday truth and profound lyricism.

Prior to *Ivanov* Chekhov had written two one-act comedies, *The Bear* and *The Proposal*.[28] They proved very successful, and were frequently performed in every theater. Chekhov would often say, "Write vaudevilles, they will bring you a considerable income."

The charm of these little comedies lay not only in the comical situations, but also in the fact that these were real people and not vaudeville characters, and they spoke a language full of humor and the unexpected.

These little comedies, however, were also staged in private theaters.

Ivanov was published in one of the "fat" journals. As a rule the monthly journals did not print plays, but already an exception was made for Chekhov. True, the royalties he received were very small, so small that, as I recall, Chekhov could scarcely believe me when I told him that for one of my plays published in a weekly journal I had received more than three times that amount.

During the early period of our acquaintance, Chekhov and I did not meet very frequently, and neither of us could have termed the other "a friend." Indeed, I could not say that Anton Pavlovich was ever on very close terms with anyone. Was it even possible?

Chekhov had a large family: father, mother, four brothers and a sister. I formed the impression that he related to them differently, some he loved more, some less. On one side were his mother, two brothers and his sister—on the other, his father and the other two brothers. His brother Nikolai, a young artist, died of consumption during the early years of my acquaintance with Chekhov. I frequently met another brother, Ivan, whom I have already mentioned, at Anton Pavlovich's country house and in Yalta. His voice, his intonation, his habit of accentuating his words with a gesture of his hand were extraordinarily reminiscent of Anton Pavlovich, as I realized with particular force after his death.

I do not know exactly the relationship between Anton Pavlovich and his father, but here is what he once said to me, much later, when we were already close friends. We were both spending the winter on the French Riviera, and were returning together from a dinner for a few close friends at the home of Professor Maxim Kovalevsky, at the time a well-known figure. He had his own villa in Beaulieu. It was a "spring-like winter," and we were wearing light coats as we made our way past tropical greenery and spoke of our youth and our childhood. Then he said, "You know, I have *never* been able to forgive my father for beating me when I was a child."

Towards his mother, however, he had the tenderest feelings. His concern for her was such that wherever he went, he wrote her at least a couple of lines every day. This, however, did not prevent him from making little jokes about her piety. He would suddenly ask, "Mama, do monks wear pants?"

"There you go again! Antosha is always coming out with something like that!" She had a gentle, pleasant, low voice, very quiet. She herself was quiet, gentle, and extraordinarily pleasant.

Chekhov's sister, Maria Pavlovna, was the only daughter, and this alone gave her a privileged position in the family. However, her total devotion to Anton Pavlovich struck one immediately on first meeting her, and the longer one knew her, the more striking it was. In the end she ran the entire household and devoted the whole of her life to him and their mother. Following the death of Anton Pavlovich, she was occupied solely by her concern to preserve his memory, maintaining the house and its furnishings exactly as they had been, publishing his correspondence, et cetera.

Anton Pavlovich was also deeply devoted to his sister. Later, judging by the published correspondence, this sometimes even provoked his wife, O. L. Knipper, to jealousy.

Anton Pavlovich had become the "breadwinner" and head of the family, so to speak, very early on. I do not remember when his father died. I met him very rarely. I recall only a rather small, dry figure with a gray beard who made superfluous comments.

During the early years of his literary career, Anton Pavlovich, like all but a few Russian writers, was in constant need of money. His letters, again like the letters of the majority of writers of the time, were full of requests for money to be sent to him. The question of royalties, of who was receiving how much and how well various publishers paid, occupied a large place in our conversations.

I might also mention that in monetary matters, Anton Pavlovich was scrupulously correct. He could not bear to be in debt to anyone, was very careful in his expenditures, neither miserly nor a spendthrift. He saw money as a major necessity, and his attitude to the wealthy was as follows: their wealth is their private business, of no concern to him, and not capable of affecting his relations with them in the slightest.

When in Monte Carlo he would gamble, but only a little, and with restraint, never once staying for any length of time; on most occasions he made a modest winning. He never gambled in Moscow clubs.

He was very concerned to ensure that his mother and sister would be provided for after his death. When he thought of purchasing a property in the country and I asked him why he wanted to concern himself with such matters, he replied, "I shan't need to think any more about paying the rent, or stocking up firewood."

Particularly fortunate is the man who is constantly engaged in his favorite occupation. Moscow—one need not even mention the provinces—was full of people who did not like their work and saw it solely as a means of earning a living. The doctor treated his patients, saw them at his surgery or went to visit them at home purely for the money; the court assessor or civil lawyer, the official in any state institution—be it a bank, the railways, or an office—sat out the working day without any interest, any pleasure; the high-school teacher taught the same material year after year, lost interest in his subject, and in many cases lacked the energy and initiative to keep abreast of it in his leisure time.

The university with its professors and students, the theater, the institutions of music and art, and the editorial offices were the exception to this rule, but they formed a very small section of this huge, inert, philistine society. In this respect actors are the happiest of people: they are bound by all their interests to that which they love with all their heart. It is this which compels them to work; the company of their fellows fires their energy, and inevitably they give of their best.

The writer, the artist, the composer, on the contrary, is always alone; he must generate all his energy within himself. His very love of his work is put to the test. Chekhov made the following very apt comment about Gnedich, a writer of our generation:

He is a true writer. He is unable not to write. Whatever conditions you were to put him in, he would write—a story, a tale, a comedy, an anthology of anecdotes. He has married a rich woman, he has no need to earn his living, but now he writes even more. When he has no theme on which to write, he translates.

Anton Pavlovich was not constantly occupied as a writer; he was not a member of any editorial board, nor did he work for any particular theater. He was a doctor and placed great value on it. I cannot remember how much of his time and attention he devoted to his medical profession when he was living in Moscow, but I remember the situation in Melikhovo, where he moved with his whole family. There he willingly treated the peasants. On the registration list of patients he had seen in his surgery, recorded on individual sheets of paper spiked on a nail, I saw the number eight hundred plus for one year. He dealt with a variety of illnesses, and he said that there was a high percentage of women's ailments.

Nonetheless, however much he may have valued his medical diploma, his work as a writer forced his work as a doctor into second place. No one even referred to it, and that sometimes offended him.

"Excuse me, but I am a doctor, after all."

However, neither did he devote all his time to his writing. He did not write as much, nor so incessantly as Tolstoy, nor yet as Gorky when he was living on Capri. He read a great deal, but not avidly, and almost exclusively belles lettres.

Completely by the way, he once said to me that he had not read *Crime and Punishment* by Dostoyevsky.

"I'm saving that pleasure till I'm in my forties."

I asked him when he had already turned forty.

"Yes, I've read it, but it did not make a great impression on me."

He thought very highly of Maupassant, possibly more than of any other French writer.

In any case he had a great deal of free time which he spent on nothing in particular, and he was bored.

He did not like long discussions and arguments. That was a particular trait of his. He would listen attentively, often out of politeness, but also often with interest, himself saying nothing until he had found a way to express his own thoughts briefly, aptly, succinctly. Then he would say what he wanted to, give his broad, brief smile, and fall silent again.

With others he was courteous without being at all suave, simple, and with what I would call an inner refinement. However, he was also rather aloof. When greeting someone and shaking hands, for example, he would say "How are you?" automatically, not waiting for a reply.

When he was young, he enjoyed a drink, but drank less as he grew older. He said that one should not drink a little vodka with the midday meal and with the evening meal systematically, but that it did no harm to drink from time to time, even a great deal. However, I never saw him "merry" at a banquet or dinner. I simply cannot imagine him drunk.

It seems he was very popular with women. I say "it seems" because neither he nor I liked gossip on the subject. I am judging by rumors I happened to hear.

Nothing attracted a Russian woman of the intelligentsia more than talent. I should imagine he could be very captivating.

Two years had passed since *Ivanov*, and Chekhov had written a new play, *The Forest Demon*. This time he did not give it to Korsh, but to the new Abramova theatrical group (which promised to become a major theater). One of the leading actors in this group was Solovtsov, to whom Chekhov had dedicated his one-act comedy *The Bear*.

I do not remember now the reception the play received among the public, but its success, if any, was very muted.[29] Nor did the author's dramatization seem to me to be very successful. I recall that the major scene between two women in the second act made a powerful impression—the greater part of it was later carried over into *Uncle Vanya*. I remember the monologue by the forester himself (*The Forest Demon*). However, what I recall best of all is my own sense of the discrepancy between the lyrical intent and its scenic interpretation. The roles were played by fine actors, but it was impossible for me to discern any characters known to me in real life behind their speeches, gestures, and temperaments. Great care had been taken over the settings, but the decor, the side scenes, the canvas walls, the flapping doors and the noise in the wings never for a moment reminded me of the countryside I knew. Everything was reminiscent of the *stage* I knew, but not of *life* I knew.

I knew a great many people, intelligent people who loved literature and music, but who did not like going to the theater because they found it artificial, and who often laughed at the most "sacrosanct" scenic devices. We, judging from the point of view of the intelligentsia, called them old-fashioned or primitive, but that was unjust: what help was there for it if the illusion of the theater left them *sober*. Not they but the theater was to blame.

Can artistic stimulation come not from the familiar world of the stage but from the familiar world of life? Where lies the obstacle or inadequacy? Is it in the decor, in the organization of the play, in the dramatic art of the actors? This is a question which had only just begun to emerge.

Six or seven years passed between *The Forest Demon* and *The Seagull*. In the meantime *Uncle Vanya* had appeared. Chekhov did not like it when people said that it was a reworking of *The Forest Demon*. At one point he declared categorically that *Uncle Vanya* was a completely independent play. However, both the basic line and also several scenes had been transferred almost whole and entire from *The Forest Demon* to *Uncle Vanya*.

I find it now impossible to remember when and how he removed the one from circulation and when and where he published the other. I remember *Uncle Vanya* already published in a small collection of plays. Perhaps this was its first publication. To begin with it was performed in the provinces; I saw it performed in Odessa by the troupe of that same Solovtsov with whom Chekhov maintained his connection. Solovtsov had himself already become an entrepreneur, and the most successful in the provinces; my sister, the actress Nemirovich, was a member of his theater, and she played the role of Yelena in *Uncle Vanya*.

It was just another play. It was a success, but the very nature of this success was, so to speak, quite ordinary in the theatrical world. The public applauded, the actors took curtain calls, but the life of the play ended with the performance; the spectators did not take home with them any profound emotions; the play did not arouse in them any new understanding of things.

I repeat: that new reflection of life which the new poet brought with his play was lacking.

As a result, Chekhov ceased writing for the theater. Nonetheless, we managed to interest him in the world of theater. We were waging a battle in the Society of Dramatic Writers and involved Chekhov. At first he was unwilling, cautious, but finally he became interested.

The Society of Dramatic Writers, which had been founded by Ostrovsky,[30] smacked of officialdom. The whole business was run by a secretary who held a prominent post in the office of the governor-general. This secretary and the treasurer, also a prominent official, constituted the entire leadership of the society. Power had to be taken from them, writers brought onto the management board, new statutes drafted, et cetera. It was both a difficult and a complex business. The chairman of the society, the playwright and doyen d'age Shpazhinsky, who had replaced Ostrovsky, played a purely fictional role, was under the influence of the secretary, and feared that the secretary would take his revenge through the apparatus of the governor-general.

For the most part, the "conspirators" gathered at my apartment; and Sumbatov-Yuzhin, another playwright and lawyer, myself, and also Chekhov were appointed to the management board. The militant general meeting was a heated confrontation. We won. However, we had no intention of seizing the profitable posts of secretary and treasurer. Our aim was simply to draw up and pass a new statute, and this we spent the next year engaged upon, continuing our battle. Finally, however, we were defeated and ousted, the usual story in a party battle. We were too liberal, whereas we should have torn out the leadership by the roots, even at the risk of rupturing relations with the office of the governor-general.

During all this time Chekhov and I met frequently. He displayed no organizational abilities, nor did he make any claims in that direction. He was attentive, said very little, and, it seemed, was mainly engaged in observing and registering the amusing aspects.

He wrote no more plays, and did not seek to see his works staged in the imperial theaters, but he had some friends there. He met with Yuzhin and Lensky more frequently than the rest when attending premieres at the Maly Theater. He and Yuzhin were on intimate terms.

Yuzhin was one of the most prominent people in the Russian theatrical world. After the October Revolution it became customary to say that the theatrical world was based on three leviathans: Yuzhin, Stanislavsky, and Nemirovich-Danchenko.

Yuzhin was a man well known in society. He was the leading actor in the best theatrical troupe in the world, and he performed a large and powerful repertoire. He had joined the theater against the wishes of his father, and his real name was Prince Sumbatov. He kept this name for his dramatic compositions and performed on stage under the name of Yuzhin. He had been a playwright since his student days, and his plays were considered very effective on stage, were performed everywhere and always with great success. He took part in every kind of theatrical, literary, and social meeting and committee; he was very cultured and widely read, following the latest publications with enormous interest. He maintained a broad acquaintance with the "whole of Moscow"; he was a member of every major club, the founder and lifelong chairman of the Literary Artistic Circle so popular in Moscow. In addition, he was a gambler, that is, he was constantly involved in some major card game. There was not a single social gathering in Moscow at which Sumbatov-Yuzhin did not occupy one of the first places. He was one of Moscow's most popular figures. In summer, instead of a holiday, he went on tour in the provinces, then to Monte Carlo to try out a new "system" he had elaborated during the winter months, and thence to his estate in the country, to his wife, to write a play.

This was a man who did not know the word laziness, and who could serve as a model of the "self-made man." He created his own position, not relying on easy means but investing energy and stubborn persistence into every step.

In society he was full of inexhaustible wit and was able to monopolize any conversation. He was a great success with women.

He was splendidly hospitable and was able to find something good in everything. This was his winning quality. Innumerable meetings, gatherings, dinners, and suppers took place in his apartment.

When we were still young, people used to say of Sumbatov and I, "The devil has tied them together." Our friendship began in our second year at high school. However, even there we moved not together but in parallel. Our high school was the only one in our town. The school roll was a large one, and therefore every form was divided in two; I was in one half, and Sumbatov in the other. In the sixth form we joined battle while remaining friends. Both halves of the class put out their own literary journal. I do not now remember what subjects we argued over; I remember only that my journal—I was the editor— was called *Tovarishch,* and that we fired "criticism" and "anti-criticism," et cetera, at each other.

We began to appear in amateur dramatics at the same time in our native city of Tiflis.

We were the co-authors of a play which enjoyed considerable success outside.

We met at the Maly Theater as playwrights.

We married cousins; his wife was also a Baroness Korf.

Sumbatov was my only true friend throughout my life. Our friendship continued despite differences in our artistic taste. This was to be expected, as our artistic differences had begun while we were still young. With the appearance of the Arts Theater, this difference of opinion became quite sharp, and we often found ourselves adopting hostile positions. Our main interest—the theater—continued along parallel lines as it had in high school.

He was a romantic. Hugo he preferred almost more than any other poet. He had even received an award from the French Academy for his performance as Charles in *Hemani* and for his Ruy Blas. His artistic taste always and everywhere inclined towards romantic exultation.

On one occasion there was a long and heated argument on this subject between myself and Chekhov, on the one hand, and Yuzhin, on the other. It took place in his large, well-lit office on the street which, after his death, was renamed Yuzhinskaya in his honor.

The argument was mainly between Chekhov and Yuzhin, because I myself was the subject of dispute. My story "The Governor's Inspection" had been published only a short time before, and Chekhov had sent me the following short letter from his house in the country:

> I read "The Governor's Inspection" straight through. In its penetration, its finesse, and every other respect it is the best of your works with which I am familiar. It produces a powerful impression, and only the end, beginning with the conversation with the clerk, is slightly hectic, whereas one would prefer it to be *piano*★ because it is very sad. You have tremendous knowledge of life, and I repeat (I have said this once before), you are becoming better and better, as if each year a new layer is added to your talent.

Prior to "The Governor's Inspection" I had published another tale, "Dead Tissue," which had pleased Sumbatov. Now they were arguing over which was the better work. The argument moved from the particular to the general, and two differing artistic approaches were clearly revealed. Yuzhin liked vivid and dramatic images; Chekhov preferred, even in a play, simple and realistic images. Yuzhin liked the exceptional, Chekhov—the ordinary. Yuzhin, a Georgian, a fine son of his people, of fiery temperament akin to the Spanish, loved the striking entrance, the glitter. Chekhov, a pure Great Russian, preferred deeply concealed feelings, restraint.

Most important of all in this argument, the art of Yuzhin resounds and glitters so much as to eclipse life, while in Chekhov life, as he depicts it, eclipses the art.

★ (It.) restrained.

On this occasion Chekhov argued for an unusually long time. Normally he expressed his opinion, and then, if others continued to try to convince him differently, he would simply shake his head silently as if to say, "No, I stand by my opinion." On this occasion, however, he continued to search for more and more arguments.

True, this was an argument between the Maly Theater and a new, future theater which had not yet appeared, but with the difference that the Arts Theater would immediately adopt a militant tone, whereas Chekhov argued gently, his characteristic smile passing every now and again across his face. He paced up and down the room, his hands buried in his pockets, not as a "fighter," without passion. A little later the writer Trigorin in *The Seagull* would say, "Why push? There's room for everyone."

Both Sumbatov and I repeatedly urged Chekhov to continue writing for the theater. He heeded our advice and wrote *The Seagull*.

Chekhov wrote *The Seagull* in Melikhovo, which is about two or three hours by train from Moscow followed by eleven versts along a country road through the forest. The house was a fairly large, one-story building which received frequent visitors. Chekhov liked conversation and company. Nonetheless he was quite capable of suddenly leaving everyone and going to his study to write down some new idea, some new image.

There was a fine garden with a straight, attractive path running through it, like the one in *The Seagull* where Treplev organized his theater.

In the evenings everyone played lotto. It was the same in *The Seagull*.

During those years the new writer Potapenko was very close to Chekhov. He published two stories, "The Secretary of His Excellency" and "On Active Service," and immediately became famous. He came from the provinces, was very sociable, exceptionally agreeable, perceptive and realistic in his thinking, and infected and cheered everyone with his optimism. He also sang very nicely. He wrote a great deal, and very quickly; he did not think very highly of his own work and himself made jokes about it. He had an open purse, was sincere, simple, and rather weak willed; he was very fond of Chekhov and fully appreciated his superior qualities. He was very popular with women, mainly because he himself liked them and, most importantly, knew how to love.

Many thought that Trigorin in *The Seagull* was autobiographical.

Tolstoy once said it.[31] I cannot get rid of the idea that it was Potapenko who most probably served as the model for Trigorin.

Nina Zarechnaya gives Trigorin a medallion on which is inscribed a phrase taken from one of Trigorin's stories:"If ever you should need my life, come and take it."

This phrase is taken from one of Chekhov's own stories, and it is full of that self-sacrifice and simplicity typical of the women in Chekhov's works. This provided a basis for identifying Trigorin with the author himself. However, that is merely a coincidence. Perhaps Chekhov came to love this powerful yet gentle expression of a woman's loyal devotion and wished to repeat it.

The character of Trigorin is determined far more by his relation-ship to women, and in this he does not resemble Anton Pavlovich, but is closer to Potapenko.

In general, however, it is not "either/or" but rather both the one and the other, and also a third, a tenth.

The Seagull is an exceptionally sincere piece of work, and many of its details could be taken directly from life in Melikhovo. Even the girl who served as the model for Nina Zarechnaya was identified as a friend of Anton Pavlovich's sister. However, here also the similarities are mere coincidence. In those days there were many girls of that kind, girls who wanted to break free of provincial life, of gray routine, find a cause to which they could "give themselves" whole and entire, and passionately, lovingly sacrifice themselves to "him," to the talent which had aroused their dreams. While women's rights continued to be harshly restricted, theatrical schools were full of such girls from the provinces.

Anton Pavlovich sent me a manuscript, and then came to hear my opinion.

I cannot explain why his image, as I analyzed his play in detail and at length, so imprinted itself on my memory. I was sitting at my desk, the manuscript in front of me, and he was standing by the window, his back to me, his hands, as always, in his pockets. He did not turn round once, at least for a whole half hour, and did not say a single word. There was not the slightest doubt that he was listening to me with particular attention, yet at the same time it was as if he were carefully following something happening in the little garden in front of the windows of my apartment; sometimes he even moved closer to the glass to look through, and turned his head slightly. Was this a desire to make it easier for me to speak freely, not embarrass me by catching my eye or, on the contrary, was it to preserve his own dignity?

At Chekhov's home they did not like to open their hearts, and all his positive characters are sensitive, taciturn, and restrained.

It is difficult for me to say now what I told Chekhov about my first impressions, and in any case I fear I might begin to "invent." One of the greatest faults in reminiscences is that the narrator may confuse *when* something occurred, and he begins to imagine that he wonderfully predicted everything.

My subsequent conduct as regards *The Seagull* is sufficiently well known, and at the time I was indeed as if in love with Chekhov's work. Very probably, however, I gave him a great deal of advice concerning the architectonics of the play, its scenic presentation. I was considered an expert on drama and the stage, and in all probability I sincerely offered him some of my tried and tested scenic methods. It is unlikely that he had need of them.

One detail, however, I recall very clearly.

In that edition, the first act of the play ended with a wholly unexpected discovery in the scene between Masha and Doctor Dorn; it suddenly turns out that she is his daughter. Thereafter not another word is said about this fact in the play. I said that either this motif should be developed, or else dropped entirely, and all the more so as this came at the end of the first act. The end of the first act, by the very nature of the theater, should lead sharply into a situation which is to be developed subsequently in the course of the play.

Chekhov said, "But the public loves a loaded gun to be placed before it at the end of the first act."

"Quite correct," I replied, "but then it has to be fired, and not simply removed during the interval."

It seems that Chekhov later quoted that phrase more than once.

Chekhov agreed with me, and the end of the first act was rewritten.

When we began to talk about staging the play, I said that it was time at last for him to give the play to the Maly Theater. I had already begun to discuss the question of who could perform the various parts when Chekhov suddenly handed me a letter, from Lensky to Chekhov.

Lensky was one of the leading actors at the Maly Theater. Yuzhin had only recently come to occupy a similar position. He was one of the most charming Russian actors of the day, who would later be compared in this respect only with Kachalov. He was an amazing master of the new style of make-up and the intriguing image; he was interested in painting and himself painted a little. By this time he had already grown a little cool as regards acting, liked to prepare a role, perform it two or three times, and then found it boring. However, he devoted himself wholeheartedly to school education, to producing school plays and training people to work in the theater.

He hated the administration board of his theater and did not conceal it. He dreamed of creating new conditions for theatrical work and trained up a whole new troupe of performers from among his pupils.

I have referred to Lensky more than once in the course of my reminiscences. He performed in almost all my plays, and we were also close friends outside the theater; later, interest in school education and dissatisfaction with the management of the Maly Theater drew us even closer together.

Lensky was eight to ten years our senior. Chekhov placed great value on their friendship.

The letter was about *The Seagull*. It seemed that Lensky had already read it, and here is what he wrote:

> You know how highly I think of your talent, and how fond I am of you. And precisely for that reason I must be perfectly frank with you. Here is my most sincere advice as a friend: stop writing for the theater. It is simply not your genre.

Such was the drift of the letter, and its tone was quite categorical. As I recall, he even refused to undertake a critique of the play, finding it so unsuitable for the stage.

I do not remember whether Chekhov gave *The Seagull* to anyone else from the Maly Theater to read. Its future fate shifted immediately to St. Petersburg.

M. M. Chitau

The Premiere of *The Seagull*
(From the reminiscences of an actress)

By the time Chekhov's *The Seagull* was performed on the stage of the Alexandrinsky Theater, many young playwrights had finally become aware of the need to find "new tones," but this need had still not been fully recognized by the theater-going public. As for theatrical managers, always, moreover, somewhat indifferent when it came to the Russian theater, they were not interested in innovation.

I recall that the play *Darkness,* written by P. P. Gnedich as early as 1880 or 1881 as a first attempt at such new tones, never even appeared on stage: it was considered not suitable for dramatization.

As everyone knows, the first major play by A. P. Chekhov staged at the Alexandrinsky Theater was *Ivanov.* The play was a benefit for Davydov, the actors performed wonderfully, and the play was a brilliant success. Clearly its transitional tones were accurately conveyed by the performers and accepted by the public. However, the second play by Chekhov, *The Seagull,* suffered a harsh failure in that same theater. This had its direct and indirect reasons.

The Seagull was chosen by Ye. I. Levkeyeva for her benefit performance. The public had always seen her in comedy roles, and came to the performance in the hope of an amusing evening. In this instance, Chekhov's reputation as the witty "Chekhonte" was also able to provide a basis for such hopes.

Backstage, however, it was already being said that *The Seagull* was written in "completely, totally new tones." This attracted the interest of those who were to perform in the play and also provoked their apprehension, though this was soothed by the fact that the author himself was to read his play, and it was hoped that he would help us to understand these innovations.

The roles in the play were distributed by A. S. Suvorin himself. M. G. Savina was to play Nina Zarechnaya, with Dyuzhikova as Arkadina, Abarinova as Polina Andreyevna, and myself as Masha. The main male roles went to Davydov, Varlamov, Apollonsky, and Sazonov.

We gathered in the actors' foyer for the reading of the play. Only Savina and the author were absent. Savina sent to say that she was ill. However, it was not her presence that had interested the gathering but the presence of the author himself, and his reading.

We waited for a long time. At first very little was said, but then we began glancing every minute at the clock; we all became rather weary, and theatrical gossip began. Finally the chief producer, Ye. P. Karpov, appeared and informed us that Anton Pavlovich had sent a telegram from Moscow saying that he could not come to the reading. Everyone was disappointed by this news. Karpov then asked Kornev, the prompter, to read the play.

Levkeyeva, never one to lose heart, did not perform in *The Seagull* but chose a lighthearted comedy more suited to her to conclude the benefit evening. She had come to the reading, however, and at the time consoled herself with the fact that Chekhov was to conduct rehearsals himself and would serve as our tuning fork, as there was no one to match him among the theatrical producers.

Kornev's reading of the play was of no benefit as regards our comprehension of the new tones or even the basic meaning. We then sought to take it home with us to read.

Later, when I admired the performance of *The Seagull* at the Moscow Arts Theater, it seemed to me that the original had been considerably changed and more successfully adapted to the stage. Perhaps I am mistaken, and it was not a question of the text and the producers, but our poor performance of the play.

Rehearsals began. The author still had not arrived from Moscow. Savina continued to ail, and the part of Zarechnaya was read out by Polyakov, the assistant producer.

By the second rehearsal the author still had not arrived, and we learned that Savina, who had also not come to the theater, was withdrawing from the role of Nina, although she was willing to play Arkadina in place of Dyuzhikova. The role of Zarechnaya was given to Komissarzhevskaya. Every change in the cast inevitably had a regrettable effect on our work when we had only seven rehearsals to prepare the new play, although in this particular instance the change was for the better. Komissarzhevskaya arrived for the rehearsal, and Dyuzhikova also arrived to take the place of Savina. In order to help the play on, this hardworking, honest, and fine actress was even ready to play a dummy which was to be carried up to the attic as soon as the real character appeared. In fact, however, she was not able to be of much use, as it was impossible, of course, to anticipate or convey to the other actors how Savina would perform her role. Davydov gave some of us certain instructions in addition to those given by the producers, who were still counting on instructions to be given by the author. However, despite his enormous talent, even Davydov was unable to identify these new tones.

Only Komissarzhevskaya had succeeded in sketching the character of Nina Zarechnaya so artistically that the ever optimistic Levkeyeva, waving her hands with their widespread fingers, her prominent eyes shining, told me of her hopes that "Vera Fyodorovna would chip and hew something out of Nina, Savushka would be marvelous in the role of a provincial prima donna—that perhaps the play was being rehearsed on a wing and a prayer, but Anton Pavlovich would provide the final polish."

Many were curious and concerned about how the Alexandrinsky Theater audience would react to the monologue by Nina Zarechnaya on the improvised "stage on a stage." It was written not merely in new tones but apparently seeking some ultra-modernist trends in dramatic art.

Our backstage humorists had already supplemented it in their own style and spirit.

Komissarzhevskaya, however, emerged from this trial victorious. She began the monologue on the deepest note of her fine voice, gradually raising it and concentrating the listener's ear on its captivating modulations. Then she gradually lowered it again, as if dropping to a whisper, and as she ended with the phrase "All living things have completed their sad cycle and expired," her voice finally died away. Everything rested on the nuances, on the modulations of her wonderful voice. Many are familiar with such old methods of declamation, many have studied them, but few would be able to use them with such virtuosity.

The scene with the blanket, however, was one Komissarzhevskaya was unable to carry off successfully, "convincingly," and this was evident during the performance. The audience reacted with an explosion of laughter.

When I arrived in my dressing room for the third rehearsal, I found our chief costumer there. I had selected my dress from the theatrical wardrobe for the role of Masha with her, and I had asked her to make a few alterations. She seemed ill at ease, and when I began to hurry her on with the fitting, to my great surprise she declared that "Maria Gavrilovna [Savina] had found this dress perfectly suitable and was going to perform in it; and later, when it was possible to alter it, we could have a fitting."

My incomprehension was resolved by Levkeyeva herself, who then appeared and, unusually for her, seemed embarrassed. She explained that although Savina did not really understand *The Seagull* and had refused the roles both of Arkadina and Nina Zarechnaya, nonetheless, for the sake of her old friendship with Levkeyeva, she had offered to play the role of Masha in her benefit performance, would then play it a second time, and then give the role to me—Chitau. I would be rehearsing today, but Maria Gavrilovna would take the remaining rehearsals.

"What kind of rehearsal is that at all?!" I retorted furiously. "Four more have been taken from me. To speak the truth, the benefit performance won't be postponed just because the play will not be ready, but because we still don't even know how to go about it!"

This pointless statement, however, so upset Levkeyeva that I hastened to smooth over my mistake and then left for my last rehearsal.

The author still had not appeared. Some of the performers were irritated or dispirited by all this lack of organization, while others dismissed the whole thing and began to amuse themselves. As a result, not only were no new tones developed, but even rehearsing was impossible in such a situation, and everything began to fall apart. Only Komissarzhevskaya, who had already thought through, learned, and most importantly, identified with her role, carried on alone and improved with each rehearsal.

The following day I did not have to attend the rehearsal and did not go. However, that same evening Karpov came to see me and told me that Savina had withdrawn from the role of Masha as well, that Polyakov had read my role during the rehearsal, and that it was now being returned to me.

There has never been such a muddle and confusion!

A. P. Chekhov arrived at last and attended our rehearsals to the end.

However, either because he thought it too late or impossible to change anything, or for other reasons, he gave no suggestions whatsoever. The rehearsals continued to go nowhere, everyone began to lose heart, and only Komissarzhevskaya continued to improve in the role of Nina. Nor did Abarinova become discouraged but, believing she had found the key to the new tones, resolutely advised many of us, "The main thing is to speak despondently."

Then, rehearsing enthusiastically, she would say to Treplev with tears in her voice, "Well, now you have become a famous writer."

Levkeyeva, brought up on the "old tones," was completely at a loss to understand.

"But it's wonderful that he's become a famous writer," she whispered to me, "so why is Tosha [Abarinova] talking as if she were informing him that his favorite aunt had fallen ill?!"

It remains for me only to say a few words about the benefit performance itself.

Just before the curtain went up, rumors began to circulate that the "youngsters" would hiss the play. Where this rumor came from we did not know, but everyone decided that Anton Pavlovich was unpopular among the young people because he was apolitical, and because of his friendship with Suvorin. This rumor, absurd as it may have been, also had its effect on the mood of the majority of the performers: what could one do when the play was doomed to failure in advance?

Such was the atmosphere in which *The Seagull* began.

Much has already been written on how the play was received on the other side of the footlights by those who witnessed this spectacle. For my part I shall add that, as far as I know, there had never been such a painfully bad performance on the stage of the Alexandrinsky Theater, and never before had we heard not only hissing, but even bursts of hissing at attempts to applaud and shout "curtain call" or "give us the author." The performers sank into the blackness of failure. Everyone recognized, however, that above that darkness Komissarzhevskaya shone brightly, and when she came out alone to take her bow the audience applauded her enthusiastically. If the spectators who had come to the benefit performance of a comedy actress in order to laugh their fill had instead laughed at the amusing antics of Komissarzhevskaya with the "calico blanket" (as one author of reminiscences put it), it was no fault of Komissarzhevskaya, for the overall performance of *The Seagull* could in no way serve to radically change the mood of the festive audience.

I do not recall which act it was during which I called into the dress-
. ing room and found Levkeyeva there with Chekhov. She was looking
at him with an expression either of guilt or of sympathy in her prominent eyes and was not even gesturing with her hands. Anton Pavlovich
was sitting with his head slightly bowed, a lock of hair had fallen down
over his forehead, and his pince-nez were resting lopsidedly on the
bridge of his nose. Neither of them said a word. I also said nothing
as I stood beside them. A few seconds passed. Suddenly Chekhov stood
up and left quickly.

He left not only the theater but also St. Petersburg.

At the second performance a magic change occurred: the play was
given a wonderful reception, and there were numerous calls for the
author and performers. As for the enthusiastic reception given to
Komissarzhevskaya, nothing need be said. However, we did not, of
course, perform *The Seagull* any better the second time either.

Paris
1926

M. M. KOVALEVSKY

ON A. P. CHEKHOV

I was first introduced to A. P. Chekhov by an old friend, V. M. Sobolevsky, editor of *Russkiye Vedomosti*. I was living at that time just outside Nice, in the village of Beaulieu. Chekhov had been advised to live in a warm climate. Having spent some time in Biarritz, he had come with Sobolevsky to the warmer clime of Nice, and was staying for the winter in the Russian pension where Saltykov-Shchedrin had lived before him. I found Chekhov taciturn and somber, and the ice between us did not melt straight away. After a few weeks, however, we had become friends. I dined with him on several occasions at the pension in the company of the famous zoologist Korotnev, a professor at Kiev University, who was also staying there while organizing a biological station in Villa-Franca. Quite often they also came to visit me, or we went together on trips into the countryside Chekhov went to Nice for several winters in succession. When his health had improved, he was also not against a trip to Monte Carlo, Marseilles, or the Italian Riviera, and both Korotnev and myself accompanied him on more than one occasion. Before becoming a zoologist, Korotnev had completed a course at the medical faculty in Moscow. Chekhov had also received a medical education, and while living in the country outside Moscow had given the peasants medical treatment, without charge of course.

Love for medicine and the natural sciences inevitably drew the Kiev professor and Russian writer together. However, there was yet another interest they shared in common, love for art—the Russian countryside, and in particular the landscapes of Levitan. Over a number of years Korotnev had gathered a modest collection of pictures, mainly by Russians, but also by some foreign painters.

Our company usually included men of letters and artists who had arrived from Russia: Prince Sumbatov, Potapenko, Yakobi, and Yurasov, who was vice-consul in Menton but chose to live in Nice.

Chekhov liked to remain within this circle. There was little point in inviting him to attend a high-society salon. Even with his friends he was not always very sociable, particularly when he had begun to cough blood. Such attacks, however, were seldom. In the middle of winter he usually felt better after spending two or three months on the Riviera. Then he began to manifest a desire to leave Nice, and we went on trips with him which rarely lasted longer than a week. When he began writing, he would disappear for a number of days from our sight. He certainly did not write every day as is the habit of some belletrists whom I know. A story and a novella required assiduous work, often for a whole week. Then he did not even come down to attend the table at the pension. When he again appeared in our company, we could not but sadly note the change in his face. He had grown paler and seemed thinner than before. During our walks together he often fell silent as if troubled by his thoughts. At such times, no doubt, he was thinking about a story he planned to write.

Chekhov took his literary work very seriously. He once began to complain to me that his medical friends had urged him to leave his country house outside Moscow and move to the Crimea. "What do I need with Tatars?" he would say, half-joking, half-serious. "Before, I was surrounded by people whose whole life flowed before my eyes; I knew the peasants, knew the schoolteachers and provincial doctors. If I ever write a story about a village teacher, the most unhappy man in the whole of the empire, it will be based on knowing the lives of many dozens of them."

It was not easy to draw Chekhov into a conversation of any length which would have made it possible to gain some impression of his views on Russian reality. Sometimes, however, I nonetheless succeeded. From these conversations I became convinced that Chekhov saw it as inevitable and desirable that both the aristocratic landowner and the parvenu who bought up his estate at a low price should disappear from the countryside. The imminent felling of the "cherry orchard" did not trouble him. The Kolupayevs and Razuvayevs,[32] who had destroyed the woods and land of the former estates, also evoked no sympathy in him. He desired but one thing: the land should go to the peasants, and not to the commune but as private property, so that the peasants could live a free and untrammeled life in sobriety and sufficiency. And they should have an adequate number of schools and properly organized medical services.

Chekhov showed little interest in the question of republicanism versus monarchism, federalism, or parliamentarianism. He wished, however, to see Russia free, without any national enmities, and the peasantry given equal rights with other social estates, involved in local affairs, and represented on legislative bodies. Broad tolerance as regards religious beliefs, a press completely unfettered and free to evaluate current events, freedom of association and assembly, and the absolute equality of all before the law and the courts—such were the essential conditions of that better future towards which he consciously strove, and the approach of which he awaited.

How heated was Chekhov's reaction to any injustice on a national or religious basis can be judged by his attitude to the Dreyfus Affair. It began while he was staying in Nice.

Having studied it closely, Chekhov wrote a long letter to Suvorin, who was then living in Paris. This letter, as can be seen by the reply from the recipient, had the expected effect: Suvorin's conviction of Dreyfus' guilt was shaken, but this in no way altered the stance adopted by *Novoye Vremya* to this famous case.

When he came from Russia, Chekhov often presented me with some little volumes of his stories. I was always amazed at his ability to say so much in just a few pages. In this respect he had the same gift as Guy de Maupassant. Once, when talking with me about the author of *Une Vie* and so many inimitable tales and short stories, Turgenev said to me, "There is a man who has that quality which Homer would have described thus—taking the bull by the horns." This was precisely the quality which Chekhov possessed. Indeed, the French liked to compare the two. I was personally acquainted with several translators of Chekhov's work, including one physician from Paris. He told me that the resemblance between our writer and the author of *Une Vie* had to some extent an adverse effect on Chekhov's success with French readers, who preferred the vivid imagery of *The Lower Depths* by Maxim Gorky.

In Chekhov the thread of the story is not broken by digressions, fine descriptions of nature such as, for example, in Gogol's *Ukrainian Nights* or the well-known opening to *Bezhin Meadow* by Turgenev.

I once had occasion to discover for myself how Chekhov avoided any kind of unnecessary detail. It happened in Rome, during the first day of Lent. We left the Cathedral of St. Peter where we had seen a rather colorful procession, "smoking out the traces of carnival." "For a belletrist," I remarked, "what we have just seen is not without a certain attraction." "Not the slightest," he replied. "The modern novelist would be obliged to satisfy himself with the phrase: 'A silly procession dragged on.'"

When I think of Chekhov, I vividly recall one night which we spent on a train on our way to Rome. Neither of us was able to sleep. We began to talk about our plans and hopes. "I find it difficult," he said, "to think about any long-term work. As a doctor I know that my life will be short." Chekhov, who in his youth had been so full of life, who had infected with his laughter the readers of *Russky Kurier,* which had published his short stories,[33] was becoming more and more concentrated, though not gloomy, as a result of his illness. He faced the future without fear and did not complain about his fate, seeing it as ineluctable. Obliged to spend the winters far away from his native land, he nonetheless lived wholly absorbed by its concerns. I have never met anyone who was less a tourist. He liked the countryside, and not so much its impressive sights as its more modest, rural landscapes. Visiting museums, art galleries, and ruins exhausted rather than delighted him. In Rome I found myself obliged to assume the role of guide, showing him the forum, the ruins of the palace of the Caesars, the Capitol.

To all of this he remained more or less indifferent, but was willing to visit Tivoli, Frascati, and Albano. We were to continue our journey as far as Naples, but letters which he received with news that his new play was shortly to be staged, and the desire to see his family and friends drew him irresistibly to Russia. I persuaded him to wear my raccoon coat and accompanied him to the station. There we parted, never to meet again. As time passed I heard the news of his marriage, of the success of *Uncle Vanya* at the Arts Theater, and that his health was deteriorating. Then I heard the sad news of how he had died alone in Badenweiler, where he had gone on a cure.

Having known Chekhov for many years, I gained the impression that if fate had not endowed him with literary talent, he would have become famous as a scholar and physician. His was an extraordinarily positive mind, wholly devoid not only of mysticism, but also of any inclination to the metaphysical. He favored the exact sciences, and even in his writings he revealed a rare ability for precise analysis, implacable rejection of any sentimentality or exaggeration. He loved the work of a writer and treated it with utmost seriousness, making a detailed study of the topics he raised, and learning about life not from books but from direct contact with people. He captivated with his simplicity and an almost excessive fear of finding himself on stage.

In Chekhov, superficial coldness combined with warm sympathy for the sufferings of others and the desire to help not only fellow-writers, but even people with whom he had no connection whatsoever. Over a number of years he devoted himself enthusiastically to treating the peasants in his district free of charge, assisting the local physician.

Towards himself Chekhov was able to be rigorously critical. I saw him after he had spent several hours editing *The Three Sisters*. He was out of spirits, had found endless defects in his play, and swore that he would never write for the theater again. Fortunately, such moods passed very quickly, and when any of his friends permitted themselves criticism of one or another aspect of his comedy, he would skillfully and successfully defend what he had written, adding, "It's impossible to judge a play without having seen it performed on stage."

For me, however, Chekhov remains not so much a playwright as an incomparable storyteller who had a profound knowledge of Russian life, who carefully followed the shifts in the social mood of the country, who foresaw the coming changes, and who was able to predict with perfect accuracy the imminent future of our country. He was a writer of superb style who carefully polished every word, avoiding long phrases and everything unnecessary and secondary, immediately drawing the reader into the topics that interested him. In just a few words he sketched the Russian peasant drawn back to his village from the town but unable to find there any means of earning a livelihood, the young intellectual dreaming of universal happiness but unable to manage his own personal life, and that innumerable category of people for whom Chekhov invented a definition which has become part of our language: "The man who lived in a shell." In his recent statement, A. I. Kuprin termed Chekhov the creator of the modern Russian short story, I believe that historians of Russian literature will also one day agree with this evaluation.

K. S. STANISLAVSKY

A. P. CHEKHOV AT THE ARTS THEATER

I do not remember when and where I first met Anton Pavlovich Chekhov, but very probably it was in 1888.[34]

In the early period of our acquaintance, that is prior to the creation of the Arts Theater, we met now and again at official dinners, anniversaries, and theater performances. These meetings have left no trace in my memory, except for three occasions.

I recall a meeting in the bookshop of A. S. Suvorin in Moscow. The proprietor himself, at the time a publisher of Chekhov's works, was standing in the middle of the room and heatedly criticizing someone. A gentleman I did not know, wearing a black top hat and a gray mackintosh, was standing next to him in a respectful pose, holding a parcel of books he had only just purchased, while Anton Pavlovich was leaning on the counter and glancing at the covers of the books lying beside him, occasionally interrupting Suvorin with short phrases which were received with a burst of laughter.

The gentleman in the mackintosh was extremely amusing. In an excess of laughter and admiration he threw the parcel of books onto the counter and then calmly picked it up again when he grew serious.

Anton Pavlovich turned and addressed some friendly witticism to me as well, but at the time I did not appreciate his sense of humor.

It is difficult for me to apologize for the fact that then I did not find him particularly agreeable. He seemed to me to be proud, supercilious, and not without slyness. Perhaps it was his habit of throwing back his head which made him appear so—but that was due to his shortsightedness: it made it easier for him to look through his pince-nez. This habit of raising his head and looking down at the one talking to him, or his fussy manner of constantly adjusting his pince-nez, made him appear to me arrogant and insincere; but in actual fact this was all due to his touching shyness, which at the time I was unable to identify.

Another not very significant meeting which has remained in my memory took place in Moscow, at the Korsh theater, at a literary-musical evening in aid of the writers' fund. It was the first time I had appeared in front of a live audience in a real theater, and I was very much occupied with myself. It was no mere chance that I left my coat not backstage, as is the usual practice with performers, but in the stalls corridor. I was hoping to put it on there, surrounded by the curious glances of that audience which I was preparing to amaze.

In the event, things turned out otherwise. I had to hurry in order to leave unnoticed. It was at this critical moment that I met Anton Pavlovich. He came directly up to me and said in friendly tones, "They say you give a wonderful performance of my play *The Bear*. Listen, stage a performance for me, and I'll write a review."

After a moment's silence he added, "And I'll receive royalties for it."

Then, after another moment's silence, he concluded, "One ruble, twenty-five kopecks."

I must admit that at the time I was offended that he did not congratulate me on the role I had just performed. Now I recall those words with gratitude. No doubt Anton Pavlovich wished to cheer me up with his little joke after the failure I had just experienced.

The third and last meeting which I still remember from the early period of our acquaintance took place in the small, cramped office of the editor of a well-known journal. It was full of people I did not know, and hazy with tobacco smoke. An architect who was well known at the time and a friend of Chekhov was showing his plans for a social center, teahouse and theater.[35] I timidly objected on the basis of my own profession. Everyone listened with profound attention, and Anton Pavlovich paced up and down, making everyone smile and, quite frankly, getting in everyone's way. That evening he seemed particularly full of energy: large, solidly built, rosy cheeked, and smiling.

At the time I did not understand why he was so happy. Now I know. He was happy to see this new and noble enterprise in Moscow, happy that a small ray of light was to enlighten the ignorant. Later, too, throughout the whole of his life, he was cheered by anything which embellished human life.

"Listen, that's marvelous!" he would say on such occasions, and his frank childlike smile made him seem years younger.

The second period of my acquaintance with Anton Pavlovich is rich in recollections of great significance for me.

In the spring of 1897 the popular Moscow Arts Theater was born. It had been very difficult to find shareholders to invest in this new undertaking, as no one predicted its success. Anton Pavlovich responded to the first appeal and joined the shareholders. He took an interest in every detail of our preparatory work and asked that we write to him more often and at greater length. He was eager to come to Moscow, but his illness obliged him to remain in Yalta, which he called his "devil's island," and he compared himself to Dreyfus.[36]

Above all he was interested, naturally, in the repertoire of the new theater. He refused to consent to the staging of *The Seagull*. After the failure in St. Petersburg, this play had become for him an ailing and, therefore, cherished child.

Nonetheless, in August 1898, *The Seagull* was included in our repertoire. I do not know how Vladimir Nemirovich-Danchenko succeeded in arranging this.

I left for the Kharkov Gubernia to write the *mise en scène*. It was a difficult task as, to my shame, I did not understand the play. It was only while I was working on it that I began, without realizing it, to penetrate the meaning and came to love it. Such is the nature of Chekhov's plays. You give way to their captivation and wish to savor their fragrance.

Shortly thereafter I learned from letters I received that Anton Pavlovich had been unable to refrain any longer from coming to Moscow. No doubt he came in order to follow the rehearsals of *The Seagull*, which had already begun. He was very nervous. When I returned, he was no longer in Moscow. Bad weather had forced him to return to Yalta, and rehearsals were temporarily suspended.

The anxious days of the opening of the Arts Theater and the first months of its existence were now upon us. Things were going badly. With the exception of *Fyodor Ioannovich,* which brought in large receipts, nothing drew the public. All hopes were placed on Hauptmann's *Hanneles Himmelfahrt,* but the Moscow Metropolitan Bishop, Vladimir, censored it, and it was taken out of the repertoire.

Our position had become critical and all the more so as we were not placing any financial hopes on *The Seagull*. However, we had no choice but to stage it. Everyone realized that the fate of the theater depended on how the play was received. As if that were not enough, an even greater responsibility was placed upon us. On the eve of the first performance, at the end of the rather unsuccessful dress rehearsal,

Anton Pavlovich's sister, Maria Pavlovna Chekhova, arrived at the theater. She was very upset by bad news from Yalta. Given Chekhov's ailing condition, she was horrified by the thought of *The Seagull* failing a second time, and she could not accept the risk we had taken upon ourselves. We also took fright and even spoke of abandoning the play, which in effect meant the closure of the theater.

It is not easy to pass sentence on one's own creation and put a troupe of performers out of work. And the shareholders? What would they have to say? Our duty toward them was only too clear.

The next day, at eight o'clock, the curtain rose. The theater was far from full. How the first act passed off I do not know. I only remember that all the performers smelled of tincture of Valerian. I recall the horror I felt, sitting in the darkness with my back to the audience during the monologue of Zarechnaya, and that I surreptitiously held my leg steady to stop its trembling from nerves.

It seemed we had failed. The curtain dropped amidst total silence. The performers pressed close to each other apprehensively and strained their ears to hear the audience.

Deathly silence.

The backstage workers peeped out from the wings, also listening. Silence.

Someone began to cry. Knipper was trying to suppress hysterical sobs. We moved silently into the wings.

At that very moment the audience broke into shouts and applause. There was a rush to open the curtain.

We were standing, so they say, sideways to the audience, our faces distorted, and no one thought to bow to the audience. One of us was even seated. Obviously we did not realize what was happening.

The play was a great success with the public, and on stage the performers rejoiced, kissing everyone, including people who had dashed into the wings. Someone had an attack of hysteria. Many, including myself, danced wildly with joy and excitement. At the end of the evening the public demanded that a telegram be sent to the author.

From that evening on, the Arts Theater and Anton Pavlovich became as close as kith and kin.

The first season came to an end, it was spring and the trees were turning green. In the wake of the swallows, Anton Pavlovich also arrived in Moscow.

He stayed with his sister in her small apartment on Malaya Dmitrovka,

Degtyarny Lane, Sheshkov House. A very simple table stood in the middle of the living room, a simple inkwell, pen and pencil, a padded divan, a few chairs, a suitcase full of books and notes—in short, only what was essential and nothing superfluous. These were the typical furnishings of his improvised study when he was on a trip.

As time passed the furnishings of the living room were supplemented with several sketches by young artists, always talented, new in artistic approach, and simple. The theme of these pictures was, in most cases, also of the simplest—the Russian countryside a la Levitan: birch trees, a river, a field, a manor house, and the like.

Anton Pavlovich did not like frames, and therefore the pictures were usually just pinned to the wall.

Soon slim notebooks appeared on the writing desk. There were very many of them. At the time, Anton Pavlovich was busy correcting his small, long since forgotten stories from his early period. He was preparing a new edition of short stories for his publisher, Marks. As he reread them he would laugh benevolently, and then his rich baritone filled the whole of the small apartment.

In the next room one could often hear the hissing of the samovar, and visitors changed like a kaleidoscope around the dining table, some arriving, some departing.

Levitan had often been a visitor before his recent death. The poet Bunin, Vladimir Nemirovich-Danchenko, Vishnevsky, an actor with our theater, Sulerzhitsky,[37] and many others were frequent visitors who stayed for hours at a time.

This company of guests would usually include some taciturn man or woman whom almost no one knew, a woman admirer or a writer from Siberia, a neighbor from Melikhovo or an old friend from school or childhood whom the host himself did not remember. These visitors embarrassed everyone, and particularly Anton Pavlovich himself, but he did not hesitate to make use of a right he had established for himself—that of disappearing from his guests. Then one could hear him coughing now and again on the other side of the closed door and hear his measured tread as he paced the room. Everyone had grown accustomed to this disappearance and knew that if a company of guests gathered who were to his taste, he would appear more often and even sit with them, glancing through his pince-nez at the silent figure of his uninvited guest.

He himself was unable to refuse to receive a guest, and even less capable of hinting that he had outstayed his welcome. Moreover, he grew angry if someone did this for him, although he would smile with pleasure when someone dealt successfully with such a visitor. If the unknown guest stayed too long, Anton Pavlovich would sometimes open his door a little and call one of his family or friends.

"Listen," he would whisper resolutely, having firmly closed the door, "tell him that I don't know him, that I never studied in a high school. He has a story in his pocket, I'm sure. He'll stay for dinner, and then he'll read it. You shouldn't act that way. It's impossible. Listen . . ."

When there was a ring at the doorbell—something which Anton Pavlovich did not like—he would quickly take his seat on the divan and sit there quietly, trying not to cough. The apartment would fall silent, and the guests said nothing or concealed themselves in corners, so that when the door opened the new arrival would not guess there was any-one in the apartment. One could hear the rustle of Maria Pavlovna's skirts, then the rattle of the door chain and two voices talking.

"Busy?" exclaimed an unfamiliar voice.

A long pause.

"Aha," the voice clearly acquiesced.

Silence again. Then snatches of conversation reached us.

"Only just arrived in town . . . just a couple of minutes."

"Very well. I'll give it to him," Maria Pavlovna replied.

"Only a short story, a play . . .," the unknown voice persuaded.

"Good-bye," said Maria Pavlovna.

"Convey my deepest regards . . . the competent opinion of such a man . . ."

"Very well, I shall tell him," Maria Pavlovna repeated.

"Support for young talent . . . the need for enlightened patron-age . . ."

"Most certainly. Good-bye," Maria Pavlovna repeated even more politely.

"Oh, my apologies!" There was the sound of a parcel falling to the floor, the rustle of paper, then the sound of someone putting on over-shoes, and again, "Good-bye! Profound regards, deeply grateful . . . moments of aesthetic . . . profound . . . deeply grateful . . ."

At last the door closed, and Maria Pavlovna placed on the writing table a few pages of crumpled manuscript whose string had snapped.

"Tell them that I don't write anymore. There's no point in writing." Anton Pavlovich would say, looking at the manuscript.

Nonetheless Anton Pavlovich not only read all these manuscripts but even replied to those who sent them.

It would be a mistake to think that the success of *The Seagull* and the several years during which Chekhov was away meant that our next meeting was a moving affair. Anton Pavlovich shook my hand more firmly than usual, gave a pleasant smile—and that was that. He did not like effusiveness. I, however, felt a need for it, for I had become an enthusiastic admirer of his talent. It was already difficult for me to be on the simple terms we had been on before, and I felt myself to be an insignificant figure in the presence of a famous one. I wished I had greater stature, greater intellect than God had granted me, and so I chose my words, tried to talk about important things, and resembled a blind devotee in the presence of his idol. Anton Pavlovich noticed it and was embarrassed. For many years thereafter I was unable to restore our simple relationship, yet it was precisely this kind of relationship which Anton Pavlovich sought to have with everyone.

Moreover, I was unable to hide during this meeting the impression that some fatal change had overtaken him. His illness had accomplished its cruel work. Perhaps the expression on my face frightened him, but it was difficult for us to find ourselves alone in each other's company.

Fortunately, Nemirovich-Danchenko soon arrived and we began to discuss business. This business was that we wanted to acquire the right to stage Chekhov's *Uncle Vanya*.

"What for? Listen, I'm not a playwright," Anton Pavlovich excused himself.

Worst of all, the imperial Maly Theater was also seeking to secure this right. A. I. Yuzhin, who was so energetic in promoting the interests of his theater, was not wasting time.

In order to avoid the painful necessity of offending any of us with his refusal, Anton Pavlovich invented every kind of excuse in order not to give the play to either theater.

"I absolutely have to revise the play," he told Yuzhin, while to us he said, "I don't know your theater. I simply must see how you perform."

Chance favored us. One of the officials of the imperial theater invited Anton Pavlovich to come for negotiations. It would, of course, have been more correct for the official to take the trouble to go to Anton Pavlovich. The conversation began very strangely. To begin with, the official asked the famous writer, "What is your occupation?"

"I write," replied the surprised Anton Pavlovich.

"That is, of course, I know . . . but . . . what do you write?" the official asked, becoming confused.

Anton Pavlovich reached for his hat to leave.

His excellency then made an even more unsuccessful attempt to move directly to the business at hand. This was that the rehearsal committee, having heard *Uncle Vanya*, did not agree with the shooting episode in the third act. The finale had to be rewritten. In the protocol, the inexplicable reason for this was set out roughly as follows: it was impermissible that a university professor, a personage of such high qualifications, should be fired at with a pistol. After that, Anton Pavlovich politely took his leave, having requested that a copy of this remarkable protocol be sent to him. He showed it to us with unconcealed indignation.

After this comically dramatic incident, the question resolved itself. Nonetheless, Anton Pavlovich continued to insist, "I don't know your theater."

This was nothing but a maneuver. He simply wished to see our production of *The Seagull,* so we provided him with such an opportunity.

As our theater did not have a permanent location, we were temporarily working at the Nikitsky theater. A closed performance was announced, and all the scenery was transferred there. One would not think that an empty, damp, and dirty theater building with furnishings transported from elsewhere could provide an atmosphere suitable for the performers and their sole spectator. Nonetheless, the performance pleased Anton Pavlovich. Very probably he had sorely missed the theater during the period of his "exile" in Yalta.

With almost childish pleasure he visited the dirty dressing rooms. He loved not only the footlights, but the backstage of the theater as well. The performance pleased him, but he criticized some of the performers, including my role as Trigorin.

"You act splendidly," he said, "only that's not my character. I didn't write that."

"What's wrong?" I asked.

"He has checkered trousers and shoes with worn soles."

That was all he said in reply to my repeated questions.

"Checkered trousers, mind, and he smokes a cigar like this," he rather clumsily illustrated his words. I was able to get nothing more from him. His comments were always graphic and brief. They were striking and memorable, like charades with which you continued to wrestle until you had solved them.

This particular charade I resolved only six years later, when we staged our second production of *The Seagull.*

Indeed, why had I chosen to play Trigorin as a dandy, in white trousers and shoes *bain de mer?*[*] Was it because women fell in love with him? Was such dress typical of the Russian writer? It was not, of course, the checkered trousers, worn shoes, and cigar that mattered. Nina Zarechnaya, her head full of the pleasant but empty little stories of Trigorin, falls in love not with him, but with her own girl's dream. In this lies the tragedy of the wounded seagull. In this cruel irony lies the harshness of life. The first love of a provincial girl notices neither the checkered trousers, nor the worn shoes, nor the foul-smelling cigar. This travesty of life is recognized when it is too late, when a life has been broken, the sacrifices made, and love has turned into a habit. New illusions are needed in order to be able to continue living, and Nina looks for them in faith.

However, I have digressed.

There was one performer whom he particularly criticized to the point of harshness. It would have been hard to imagine in someone normally of such exceptional mildness. Anton Pavlovich demanded that the role be given to someone else immediately. He refused to accept any apologies and threatened to prevent any further performances of the play.

While talking of other roles, he permitted himself to make humorous comments on any faults in the performance, but no sooner did the conversation move to this unsuccessful role then Anton Pavlovich immediately changed his tone and lashed out mercilessly.

"Listen, it's quite impossible. This is a serious matter," he said.

That was the reason for his mercilessness.

These words also explained his attitude toward our theater. He pronounced neither compliments, nor detailed criticism, nor encouragement.

Thanks to the warm weather, Anton Pavlovich spent the whole of that spring in Moscow and attended our rehearsals every day. He did not interfere in our work but simply wished to be in the atmosphere of the arts and to converse with cheerful performers. He loved the theater, but could not abide triteness. It made him either cringe with embarrassment or else hastily depart.

"Excuse me, but I must go. I'm expected," and he would go home, sit down on the divan, and think.

A few days later, exactly as if it were some reflex response, Anton

[*] (Fr.) beach shoes.

Pavlovich said something unexpected by everyone, but which aptly defined the triteness which had offended him.

"I categor-r-r-rically protest," he said suddenly and collapsed in laughter. He had remembered an unbelievably long speech by someone who was not altogether Russian, but who had spoken about the poetry of the Russian countryside and used this very word.

We naturally availed ourselves of every opportunity to talk about *Uncle Vanya,* but to our questions Anton Pavlovich replied laconically, "It's all written down."

Once, however, he expressed himself quite clearly. Someone was talking of a performance of *Uncle Vanya* he had seen in the provinces. There the man playing the leading role had depicted him as a landowner who had let himself go and wore dirty boots and a peasant shirt, the traditional theatrical image of the Russian provincial landowner.

Good heavens, how Anton Pavlovich reacted to this piece of vulgarity!

"Listen, how can one do things like that? It's written clearly in the play he wears marvelous ties. Marvelous! Try to understand, landowners dress better than we do."

Here the crucial point was not the tie, but the central idea of the play. The inimitable Astrov and the poetically gentle Uncle Vanya are running to seed in the backwoods while a dull-witted professor flourishes in St. Petersburg and, together with others of his kind, governs Russia. There is the hidden meaning behind the comment on the tie.

Our production of *Uncle Vanya* was a great success. At the end of the performance the audience demanded, "Send a telegram to Chekhov!"

Anton Pavlovich spent the entire winter dreaming of a trip to Moscow, judging by his letters. Now he had become deeply attached to our theater, which he had never seen, unless one counts the improvised performance of *The Seagull.*

He began to think of writing a play for us.

"But to do that I absolutely must see your theater," he insisted in his letters.

When we learned that his doctors had forbidden him to come to Moscow that spring, we understood his hints and decided to go to Yalta, the full company and all our costumes and stage settings.

In April 1900, the entire company, together with their families and the stage scenery and costumes for four plays, set off from Moscow to

Sebastopol. We were followed by some of our audience, devotees of Chekhov and our theater, and even one famous theater critic, S. V. Vasilyev (Flerov). He went with the particular purpose of sending detailed reviews of our performances.

Our journey resembled a great migration. I particularly remember A. R. Artem, who was leaving his wife for the first time in his life. On the journey to Sebastopol he chose as his "wife" A. L. Vishnevsky, who became his energy and willpower during the trip. As we were approaching Sebastopol, Artem asked everyone whether there were any cabmen there, whether we would have to climb the mountains on foot, et cetera.

Very often, if Vishnevsky was absent for any length of time, Artem would send for him. During the entire journey the old man talked about death and was very gloomy.

Near Sebastopol, when the tunnels, cliffs, and beautiful landscapes began, the entire company went out onto the platform. The gloomy Artem also went out for the first time during the entire journey, accompanied by Vishnevsky. Vishnevsky began to console Artem in his own typical manner, "No, you won't die, Sasha! What do you want to die for? Look—seagulls, the sea, the cliffs. No, you won't die, Sasha!"

Artem, in whom the artist had been awoken by the sight of these cliffs, the sea, and the splendid twists and turns along which the train was traveling, was already looking with shining eyes at the picture around him. Then he suddenly shook his head and, turning angrily on Vishnevsky, said cunningly, "Of course I shan't die, if that's what you're after!"

Then, turning away with a gesture of annoyance, he added, "Of all the things to think of!"

The Crimea did not give us a very warm welcome. An icy wind was blowing from the sea, the sky was clouded over; in the hotels the stoves were lit, but we were cold nonetheless.

The theater was still boarded up after the winter, and the storm tore down our playbills, which no one had read.

Everyone was depressed.

But then the sun rose, the sea smiled, and we cheered up.

Some people came, took down the boards from the theater, and opened the doors. We went in. It was as cold as a cellar. Indeed it was like a basement, it would take a whole week to air, and we had to perform in two or three days. Above all we were concerned for Anton Pavlovich, who would have to sit in this musty atmosphere. Our womenfolk spent the entire day choosing the best place for him to sit, a place least exposed to draft. Our company began to gather more and more often near the theater which had become a focal point of life and bustle.

We were in festive mood—our second season, everyone dressed in new jackets and hats, everyone feeling young and happy that we were actors. At the same time, everyone was trying to be excessively correct, as if to underline that we were not some backwoods theater, but a company from the capital.

Finally a rather overdressed lady appeared. She declared she belonged to the local aristocracy, that she was a friend of Chekhov, and demanded a seat in the special box for every play. A queue formed behind her at the ticket office, and very soon all the tickets for the four advertised plays were sold out.

We were waiting for Chekhov to arrive. Knipper, who had gone to Yalta, had still not written anything from there, and that worried us. On Palm Sunday she returned with the sad news that Anton Pavlovich was not well and would probably be unable to come to Sebastopol.

This news depressed everyone. We also learned from her that it was a great deal warmer in Yalta (as always), that Anton Pavlovich was an amazing man, and that virtually all the notable figures of Russian literature had assembled there: Gorky, Mamin-Sibiryak, Stanyukovich, Bunin, Yelpatievsky, Naidenov, and Skitalets.

This news disturbed us even more. That same day everyone went to buy Easter cheesecakes and currant loaves for the forthcoming celebration away from home. At midnight the bells rang differently than in Moscow, the singing was also not like that in Moscow, but the cheesecakes and currant loaves tasted of Turkish delight.

Artem had nothing but criticism for Sebastopol, convinced that Easter should be celebrated only at home. However, a walk along the seashore after Easter breakfast and the spring morning air soon made us forget about the north. The sunrise was so fine that we sang Gypsy songs and declaimed poetry to the sound of the sea.

The following day we impatiently awaited the boat on which Anton Pavlovich was to arrive. At last we saw him. He was the last to emerge from the passenger's lounge, pale and thin. He was coughing badly. His eyes were the sad eyes of a sick man, but he tried to smile in welcome.

I felt like weeping.

Our amateur photographers photographed him on the gangway of the boat, and this photography scene appeared in the play he was then already pondering *(The Three Sisters)*.

A general lack of tact meant that he was bombarded with questions about his health.

"Fine. I'm already completely well," he replied.

He did not like fuss about his health, even from those close to him. He himself never complained about it, however ill he felt.

Soon afterwards he left for his hotel, and we did not trouble him until the next day. He stayed at Vetsel's, and not where we were staying (we were staying at Kist's). Probably he was afraid of being too close to the sea.

The next day, that is, on Easter Monday, our tour began. We had to face a double test—Anton Pavlovich, and a new public.

The whole day was spent in anxiety and bustle.

I did no more than catch sight of Anton Pavlovich in the theater. He came to look at his box and was concerned about only two questions: would he be concealed from the public and where would the "lady" be sitting?

Despite the biting cold he was wearing a light coat. A great many comments were made about it, but again he merely replied, "Listen, I'm quite well!"

It was very cold in the theater as there were cracks everywhere and no heating. The dressing rooms were heated by kerosene lamps, but the drafts annulled the warmth.

That evening we all put on our make-up in one small dressing room which was warmed by the heat of our own bodies, and the ladies, who were obliged to sport fine muslin dresses, went to a nearby hotel. There they were able to warm up and change their costumes.

At eight o'clock the public was summoned to the first performance of *Uncle Vanya* by the resounding tones of a hand bell.

We were acutely aware of the shadowy figure of the author, concealed in the director's box behind Vladimir Nemirovich-Danchenko and his wife.

The first act was given a cool reception. Towards the end stormy applause expressed the growing success of the play. The author was requested on stage. He wished desperately to avoid it, but nonetheless came out.

The following day, Artem, whose nerves were exhausted, took to his bed and did not come to the rehearsal. Anton Pavlovich, who loved to practice medicine, rejoiced at having a patient as soon as he heard of it, all the more so as the patient was Artem, of whom be was very fond. He immediately set off with Tikhomirov to see the sick man, while we watched and wondered what treatment he would use. On his way to see his patient, Anton Pavlovich called in at his hotel to get a little hammer and a tube.

"Listen, I can't manage without instruments," he said, clearly concerned.

He spent some time listening to Artem, sounding him, and then proceeded to try to convince him that he needed no treatment at all. He gave him a mint sweet, "Now, listen, eat this!"

With that the treatment came to an end, as the next day Artem was once again in good health.

Anton Pavlovich loved to come during rehearsals, but as it was very cold inside the theater, he simply looked in occasionally and spent most of the time sitting in front of the theater, in the sunlit square where the performers also came to warm themselves in the sun. He chatted happily with them, repeating every other minute, "Listen, your theater's a wonderful affair, a truly remarkable affair."

That was Anton Pavlovich's constant refrain, so to speak, at that time.

The scene was usually as follows: he would sit on the square, animated and cheerful, chatting with the actors or actresses—particularly with Andreyeva and Knipper, whom he was then courting—and would criticize Yalta at every opportunity. Already a tragic note could be heard.

"In winter the sea's as black as ink. . . ."

Very occasionally phrases would slip out which revealed restlessness and melancholy.

I recall how he spent several hours with the theater's carpenter, instructing him how to imitate a cricket.

"He chirps like this," he said, illustrating. Then he would fall silent for a few moments and again, "Tik-tik."

A certain N. N. would arrive on the square at a certain hour and begin to make quite unnecessary statements about literature. Anton Pavlovich would then immediately slip away somewhere.

The day after a performance of *Einsame Menschen,* which had deeply impressed him, he said, "What a wonderful play!"

He asserted that the theater was very important in life in general and that it was absolutely necessary to write for the theater. As far as I remember, he first said this after *Einsame Menschen*.

During these conversations on the square, he spoke about *Uncle Vanya*, was full of praise for all those taking part in it, and made just one comment to me about Astrov in the last act: "Listen, he whistles. It's Uncle Vanya who snivels, but he whistles."

Given the rather rigid views I held at the time, I simply could not reconcile myself to this. How was it possible that at such a dramatic moment someone could whistle?

Anton Pavlovich always arrived at the theater some time before the beginning of the performance. He liked to come up onto the stage and see how the scenery was being placed. During the intervals he would go around to the dressing rooms talking to the actors about this and that. He always had a great love for theatrical trifles—how scenery was lowered, how the stage was lit—and when such matters were discussed in his presence, he would stand there and listen, and sometimes smile.

When *Hedda Gabler* was being performed, he would often call in the dressing rooms during the interval and remain there even when the next act had begun. This worried us. If he was in no hurry to return to his seat, this could only mean he did not like the performance. When we asked him about it, we were surprised to hear him say, "But listen, Ibsen is no playwright!"

Anton Pavlovich did not watch *The Seagull* in Sebastopol—he had seen it earlier. Moreover, the weather changed, there were high winds and storms, his health deteriorated, and he was obliged to leave.

We staged *The Seagull* in the most dreadful conditions. The wind howled so that a stagehand stood by each stage set in the wings to make sure that a gust of wind did not bring it down on the audience. All the time we could hear the troubled calls of ships' horns and sirens coming from the sea. Our costumes fluttered in the wind blowing across the stage. It was raining.

There was also the following incident. We needed at all costs to light the stage in a way which required that half the city gardens remain in darkness. It seemed impossible to do without this effect. Vladimir Nemirovich-Danchenko sometimes displayed such uncompromising resolution: he quite simply ordered that half the city gardens be left without light.

The production of *The Seagull* was a great success. People gathered after the performance. I had only just emerged onto a stairway with my umbrella in my hand when some of the crowd seized hold of me, high-school students as I recall, but they were unable to overpower me. My situation was indeed pitiful: the students were shouting, they had lifted up one of my legs, and I was hopping on the other as they were pulling me forwards; my umbrella had been dashed from my hand, it was pouring down rain, but it was impossible to say anything as everyone was shouting "Hurrah!" My wife was running towards me from behind, frightened I would be hurt. Fortunately they soon grew tired and let me go, so I was able to reach my hotel on both my legs. However, at the very entrance to the hotel they again wanted something and brought me down on the rain-sodden steps.

The doorman came out and began to wipe me down, while the panting students continued to talk heatedly for some time, discussing how it had all come about.

We were already acquainted with all the city officials, and before leaving for Yalta we received telephone reports from all sides: "Northwest, northeast, there will be a heavy sea . . . there will not be a heavy sea," while all the sailors told us that everything would be fine, that a heavy sea would be somewhere in the region of Ai-Todor, and that here was a bend, and we would be crossing a quiet sea.

There was no bend, and we had such a stormy crossing that we are never likely to forget it. We were thoroughly shaken up. Many of us were traveling with wives and children, and some people from Sebastopol were sailing with us to Yalta. Nannies, maids, children, scenery, stage props—all were thrown into confusion on the deck of the ship. In Yalta, on the landing stage, there was a crowd of people waiting, dressed up for the occasion and carrying flowers, while at sea there was storm and wind—in a word, total chaos.

There was the sensation of some new feeling, the feeling that the crowd acknowledged us. There was happiness and awkwardness in the face of this new situation—the first embarrassment of popularity.

We barely had time to arrive in Yalta, install ourselves in our hotel rooms, wash and get our bearings, when I met Vishnevsky, who was running as fast as his legs would carry him, beside himself with enthusiasm and shouting, "I've just met Gorky—what a charming man! He's already decided to write a play for us! Before even seeing us."

The next morning the first thing we did was go to the theater. There a wall was being demolished, they were cleaning and washing—in short, the place was a hive of work. Walking around on stage among the shavings and the dust were Gorky, with a walking stick in his hand, Bunin, Mirolyubov, Mamin-Sibiryak, Yelpatievsky, Vladimir Nemirovich-Danchenko.

Having looked around the stage, they all left for breakfast in the city gardens. The entire terrace was immediately filled with our actors, and we took possession of the whole gardens. Stanyukovich sat at a separate table—he seemed to remain aloof from the whole company.

From there we all set off, some on foot, others traveling six to a carriage, to call on Anton Pavlovich. Anton Pavlovich always had the table set to receive guests, whether for breakfast or for tea. His house was still not completely finished, and around it was a rather sparse-looking garden which he had only just set out with plants.

Anton Pavlovich looked dreadfully animated, as if he had literally just risen from the dead. He reminded me—I remember this impression quite clearly—of a house which has stood empty all winter, its doors and shutters closed. Then, suddenly, with the advent of spring, it is opened up, and all the rooms are filled with light, begin to smile and sparkle. He was always on the move, his hands behind his back, and constantly adjusting his pince-nez..One moment he was on the terrace, piled with new books and journals, then, his smile not leaving his face, he would appear in the garden or the courtyard. Very occasionally he would hide away in his study, obviously taking a rest.

People came and left. One breakfast ended, and another was set. Maria Pavlovna was unable to keep pace, while Leonardovna (Knipper), like a faithful friend or future housewife, was busy helping, sleeves rolled up.

In one corner a literary argument was in progress; in the garden they were engaged, like schoolboys, in seeing who could throw a stone the farthest; while in a third group, I. A. Bunin was illustrating something with extraordinary talent. And wherever Bunin was to be found, there also was Anton Pavlovich, chuckling and helpless with laughter. No one was able to amuse Anton Pavlovich like Bunin when in a good mood.

For me, the focal point was Gorky, who had instantly captured me with his charm. In his unusual figure and face, his accented o's, his unusual gestures—shaking a fist in moments of particular fervor—in the bright, childlike smile, in the tragically moving expression which sometimes came over his features, in his now amusing, now forceful, colorful, and vivid speech, one could feel a certain mildness of temperament and gracefulness; and his figure had, despite his stoop, its own expressiveness and beauty. I often found myself admiring his pose or gesture.

The loving look which he often gave Anton Pavlovich, the way his face melted into a smile at the mere sound of Anton Pavlovich's voice, the benevolent laughter at his slightest witticism, drew us together in our common liking for our host.

Anton Pavlovich, who always liked to talk about whatever it was which was engaging his interest at that particular moment, approached first one and then another with the naiveté of a child and repeated one and the same question: whether one or another of his guests had seen our theater. "Really, its a wonderful affair. You must definitely write a play for this theater." And he tirelessly asserted that *Einsame Menschen* was a wonderful play.

The presence of Gorky, with his stories of his wandering life, of Mamin-Sibiryak and his unusually bold, at times even slapstick humor, of Bunin and his elegant humor, of Anton Pavlovich and his unexpected comments, and of Moskvin with his apt witticisms created a harmonious atmosphere and united all in one family of art. Everyone began to think that we should meet again in Yalta, and there was even talk of finding an apartment for this purpose. In short, spring, the sea, entertaining company, youth, poetry, art—such was the atmosphere in which we found ourselves in those days.

Such days and such evenings were virtually an everyday occurrence at the home of Anton Pavlovich.

At the theater ticket office a very diverse public was gathering, composed of overdressed ladies and their escorts from the two capitals, teachers and clerks from various provincial towns around Russia, local residents and consumption sufferers who, during their cheerless winter, had not forgotten about the existence of the arts.

The first performance was staged, complete with floral tributes, presents, et cetera. Despite the fact that at tragic points in the performance the band in the city gardens accompanied us with a polka or a march, we enjoyed tremendous success.

In the city gardens, near the terrace, there were heated arguments about the new trend in the arts and about the new literature. Some, even prominent writers, did not understand the most elementary things in realistic art, while others veered off in exactly the opposite direction and dreamed of seeing on stage that which is unworthy of appearing on the stage. Whatever the case may be, performances provoked arguments which could go as far as fisticuffs—and therefore they attained their goal. It was as if all the men of letters who were in Yalta suddenly recalled the existence of dramatic art, and some nursed the idea, secretly or openly, of writing a play.

What spoiled any performance for Anton Pavlovich was the inevitable request that he come out on stage in response to the demand of the audience and accept almost daily ovations. Therefore quite often he simply disappeared from the theater, and then we had no choice but to inform the audience that the author was not present. In the majority of cases he simply came backstage, going from dressing room to dressing room and enjoying life behind the scenes with its anxieties and excitement, its triumphs and failures, and that tension which inevitably brings with it a sharper sense of life.

In the mornings everyone gathered on the promenade. I joined Gorky, and during our walk he would fantasize on various themes for some future play. He was constantly interrupted by the escapades of his unusually high-spirited little boy, Maximka, who played the most unbelievable pranks.

One other episode has remained in my memory from our stay in Yalta. One afternoon I happened to approach Anton Pavlovich, and I noticed that he was furious, fierce and disheveled; I had never seen him like that before. When he had calmed down, the matter turned out to be as follows: His mother, whom he adored, had finally decided to come to the theater to see *Uncle Vanya*. For the old lady this was a momentous occasion, as she was going to see a play by Antosha. The fuss and bustle began that morning. The old lady went through all her trunks and at the bottom of one of them found a silk dress of very old-fashioned cut which she planned to wear for this memorable evening. Anton Pavlovich happened to learn of this plan and had become very upset over it. His imagination presented him with the following scene: the son had written a play, his mother was sitting in a box in the theater wearing a silk dress. The picture was so sentimental that he was prepared to leave for Moscow in order to avoid being a part of it.

In the evenings we sometimes gathered in a separate room in Rossiya Hotel. Someone would play the piano, everything was amateurishly naive, yet despite this the sound of music immediately reduced Gorky to tears.

On one occasion Gorky was carried away and described the theme of the play he proposed to write: a shelter for the homeless, stale air, bunks, a long, boring winter. The horror of their existence has driven people wild; they have reached the end of their patience and hope and, their patience gone, are tormenting each other and philosophizing. Each tries to prove to the rest that he still has his dignity. An ex-waiter is particularly proud of his cheap paper shirtfront—all that remains of his former life of bow tie and tails. One of the inhabitants of the shelter decides to pull a trick on the former waiter, finds the shirtfront, and rips it in two. The old waiter finds this torn shirtfront, and the result is a total disaster, total collapse. He is thrown into despair, for tearing the shirtfront has also torn all the links with his former life. The cursing and arguing continue far into the night but are brought to a halt by the unexpected news that the police are on their way. Hurried preparations are made for the arrival of the police; each rushes about and conceals anything which is dear to him or might compromise him. All return to their bunks and pretend to be asleep. The police arrive. Some without identity are taken away to the police station, and those in the bunks begin to fall asleep. Only one pious old man climbs down from the stove in the silence, brings out the wax stub of a candle from his pocket, lights it, and begins to pray fervently. From one of the bunks there appears the head of a Tatar, who says, "Say one for me!"

With this the first act ends.

The following acts were very roughly indicated, and therefore it was difficult to pass any judgment. In the last act, spring, sunshine, the inhabitants of the shelter were digging the soil. These weary people had come out to celebrate this festival of nature, and it was as if they had risen from the dead. Indeed, it was almost as if, under the influence of nature, they had learned to love each other. That is what has remained in my memory from what Gorky told me of his play.

The theater ended the whole series of its productions and concluded its tour with a marvelous breakfast on the vast, flat roof of Fannya Karlovna Tatarinova. I recall the hot weather, a festive awning, and the sea glittering in the distance. The whole troupe was here, the whole of the literary world, so to speak, had gathered together, headed by Chekhov and Gorky, with their wives and children.

I remember the solemn speeches, warmed by the southern sun, full of hope, endless hope.

This wonderful celebration under the open sky concluded our stay in Yalta.

The following year we staged *Snow White, Doctor Stockmann, The Three Sisters,* and *When We Dead Awaken.*

From the very start of the season, Anton Pavlovich frequently sent letters to one or another of us. He asked all of us for information about the life of the theater. These few lines from Anton Pavlovich, his constant attention, exerted, without our realizing it, a great influence on our theater which we can appreciate only now, after his death.

He took an interest in every detail and particularly, of course, in the repertoire. We, for our part, kept prompting him to write a play. From his letters we knew that he was writing about military life, we knew that some regiment or other was moving from one place to another, but from these short, disconnected phrases we were unable to guess what the theme of the play might be. In his letters, as in his writing, he was very laconic. We were able to assess these disconnected phrases, these scraps from his creative thought, only later, when we learned about the play itself.

Perhaps he was finding it difficult to write; or, on the contrary, the play had long since been completed, and he could not bring himself to part with it but had put it away in his desk to mature. Whatever the reason, he did all he could to put off sending us the play. One of his excuses was that many fine plays had appeared—that Hauptmann should be staged, that Hauptmann had written another work, that he (Chekhov) was not a playwright.

All these excuses brought us to the brink of despair, and we wrote pleading letters asking him to send his play as soon as possible, save the theater, et cetera. We ourselves did not then realize that we were forcing the creativity of a great writer.

At last one or two acts of the play arrived, written in the familiar, small handwriting. We read them avidly, but, as is always the case with any genuinely scenic work, reading could not reveal its real value. With just two acts in our hands, we could not begin work on model sets, nor on allocating the roles, nor on any scenic preparation.

Therefore we began all the more energetically to try to obtain the remaining two acts of the play. We finally received them, but not without a battle.

Finally, Anton Pavlovich not only agreed to send the play but delivered it himself.

He never read out his plays and was embarrassed and agitated if he was present while the play was being read to the performers. When the play had been read out and we began to ask Anton Pavlovich for further clarifications, he was dreadfully embarrassed and excused himself saying, "Listen, all I knew I have written down there."

Indeed, he was never able to criticize his own plays and listened with great interest, even surprise, to the opinions of others. What amazed him most of all, and what he was never, up to his death, able to accept, was that his *The Three Sisters,* and later *The Cherry Orchard,* reflected the serious drama of Russian life. He was sincerely convinced that it was a cheerful comedy, almost vaudeville. I cannot recall that he ever defended any other of his convictions as heatedly as this when, at that meeting, he first heard this comment on his play.

We, of course, availed ourselves of the presence of the author to find out all the details we needed. Here, too, however, he gave us monosyllabic answers. At the time his answers seemed vague and incomprehensible to us, and it was only later that we came to understand their unusual imagery and realize that they were characteristic both of him and of his work.

When the preparatory work got underway, Anton Pavlovich began to insist that we invite a general whom he knew. He wanted the daily life of the military to be accurate to the smallest detail. Anton Pavlovich himself, as if he were a third party, someone not involved in this affair, observed our work from the sidelines.

He was unable to help us in our work and in our search to depict the inside of the Prozorov house. We could sense that he knew this house in detail, saw it, but failed completely to notice what rooms, furniture, and objects filled it; in short, he felt only the atmosphere of each room individually but not its walls.

Such is the writer's perception of life around him. However, this is not enough for the director, who must clearly draw and order all these details.

It is now obvious why Anton Pavlovich laughed so benevolently and smiled with pleasure when the aims of the director and producer coincided with his own intent. He would look at the model scenery for a long time and then, having examined every detail, laugh good-naturedly.

One needs an experienced eye in order to judge by the model what will result, to see what it will be on the stage. This purely theatrical sense of the scenic was possessed by Anton Pavlovich, as he was a man of the theater by his nature. He loved, understood, and felt the theater —from its best side, of course. He loved to repeat the same stories, stories about how, when he was young, he had acted in various plays and about various amusing incidents from these amateur efforts. He loved the anxious mood of rehearsals and the performance, loved the work of the stagehands, loved to listen to trifles from stage life and about the mechanics of the theater, but he was particularly enthusiastic about the natural sounds on stage.

Alongside all his other anxieties about the fate of his play, he was not a little concerned about how the alarm would be conveyed in the third act, when there is a fire offstage. He wanted to illustrate to us the sound of a provincial bell tower sounding the alarm. Whenever a convenient opportunity presented itself, he would approach one of us and with his hands, with rhythm and gesture, try to inspire us with the mood of this heart-piercing provincial alarm.

He attended nearly all the rehearsals of his play but very rarely, cautiously, almost fearfully, expressed his opinion. There was only one thing he insisted on energetically; here, as in *Uncle Vanya,* he feared an exaggeration which would produce a caricature of provincial life, that the military men would be turned into the usual heel-clickers with jangling spurs and not be presented as simple, pleasant, good people dressed in worn, and not theatrical, uniforms, without any theatrical adjustments, raised shoulders, rude behavior, et cetera.

"There's none of that," he argued rather heatedly, "military personnel have changed, they have become more cultured, many of them have even begun to realize that in peacetime they should bring culture with them into remote backwaters."

He insisted on this even more as the military community of the day, having learned that the play was based on their way of life, were rather apprehensively awaiting its appearance on the stage.

The rehearsals proceeded with the participation of a general recommended by Anton Pavlovich, and who became such a part of the theater and so involved in the fate of the play that he often forgot about his actual purpose and was far more worried about the fact that one or another actor was not succeeding in presenting his role or conveying some particular scene.

Anton Pavlovich saw the whole repertoire of the theater and made his monosyllabic comments which always obliged us to ponder their unexpectedness and which were never immediately understood. It was only when some time had passed that we were able to come to terms with them. As an example of one such comment, I can refer to the remark mentioned earlier, which was that in the final act of *Uncle Vanya* Astrov whistles.

Anton Pavlovich was not even able to stay to see the dress rehearsal of *The Three Sisters,* as his worsening health obliged him to leave for the south, and he departed for Nice. From there we received notes—in scene such-and-such, after the words such-and-such, add this phrase. For example, "Balzac married in Berdichev" was one note we received from Nice.

On another occasion he suddenly sent us a short scene. These little jewels which he sent had an extraordinarily enlivening effect on the action of the play when we introduced them into our rehearsals and prompted the actors into genuinely experiencing their roles.

We also received the following instruction from abroad. In the fourth act of *The Three Sisters,* the degenerate Andrei, talking to Ferapont as no one else was willing to talk with him, describes what a wife is from the point of view of a provincial degenerate. It was a marvelous monologue about two pages long. Suddenly we received a note saying that the whole of the monologue was to be crossed out and replaced with just the phrase "A wife is a wife!"

This short phrase, if one reflects on it, covers everything that was said in the long, two-page monologue. This was typical of Anton Pavlovich, whose work was always short and succinct. Behind each word lay a whole range of diverse moods and thoughts, about which he said nothing but which came naturally to mind.

That explains why, although the play might be performed a hundred times, there was not a single performance in which I did not make new discoveries in the long since familiar text and in the emotions experienced in the role. The depth of Chekhov's works is inexhaustible for the thoughtful and sensitive actor.

How worried Anton Pavlovich was at the thought of the first performance of *The Three Sisters* can be judged by the fact that on the day before the performance he left the town where we knew his address for an unknown destination, so as not to receive any news of the premiere.

The response to the first performance was rather enigmatic.

After the first act there were loud cries of "encore," and the actors took about twelve curtain calls. After the second act they went out just once. Following the third act, just a few applauded rather timidly, and the actors could not go out on stage at all; and after the fourth act, there was one rather feeble curtain call.

We had to stretch the truth considerably to telegraph Anton Pavlovich that the play was "a great success."

It was only three years after the first performance that the public gradually came to appreciate the beauty of this fine work and began to laugh and to fall silent where the author had intended. Each act then became a triumph.

The press also did not understand the play for some time and, however strange it may seem, the first review we read worthy of the play was in Berlin, when we went there on tour.

In Moscow, during the first year of the production, the play was performed only a few times and was then taken to St. Petersburg. We also expected to find Anton Pavlovich there, but bad weather and his health prevented his coming.

On returning to Moscow, the theater began its preparations for the next season. Anton Pavlovich arrived. By that time rumors were circulating among the actors that Chekhov and Knipper were planning to marry. Indeed, it is true that they were often seen together.

On one occasion, Anton Pavlovich asked Vishnevsky to arrange a formal dinner and to invite his (Chekhov's) relatives and also, for some reason, the relatives of Olga Knipper. Everyone gathered at the appointed hour, and only Anton Pavlovich and Olga Leonardovna were missing. We waited, worried and confused, till finally we received the news that Anton Pavlovich had left with Olga Leonardovna for the church to get married, and from there they were going directly to the railway station to take the train for Samara to drink *koumiss*. *

The whole dinner had been arranged in order to collect together in one place all those who might have prevented a private wedding, without the usual noise and fuss. So little did the pomp of a wedding suit the taste of Anton Pavlovich. Vishnevsky received a telegram from Chekhov, sent en route.

The following year Anton Pavlovich was planning to spend the autumn in Moscow and leave for Yalta only during the coldest months. That autumn he did indeed arrive and live in Moscow. Somehow this period has not remained very clearly in my memory, and I shall just recall certain incidents.

I remember, for example, that Anton Pavlovich watched the rehearsals for *The Wild Duck* and was visibly bored. He did not like Ibsen. Sometimes he would say, "Listen, Ibsen just doesn't know life. In life it simply isn't like that."

Anton Pavlovich could not watch Artem in this play without smiling and saying, "I'll write a play for him. He really ought to sit on the bank of a river and catch fish."

---

* A drink of fermented mare's milk, considered good for the health.—Tr.

Then he thought for a moment and added, "And Vishnevsky will be washing and splashing next to him, wearing a bathing suit, and talking very loudly."*

And he himself roared with laughter at the combination.

At one rehearsal, when we began to insist that he write yet another play, he started to drop hints about the subject of a future play. He imagined an open window and a branch of a white, blossoming cherry tree coming from the garden into the room. Artem was already cast as the footman, and then, all of a sudden, as the steward. The master of the house or, as it sometimes seemed it might be, the mistress was always without money and in moments of crisis she would turn for help to her footman or steward, who had managed to put aside quite a large sum.

Then there appeared a group of billiard players. One of them, a devotee of the game, had only one arm, was very cheerful and lively, and was always shouting at the top of his voice. Chekhov began to visualize Vishnevsky in this role. Then there appeared a conservatory, and then this again gave way to a billiard room. However, none of these cracks through which he allowed us a glimpse of his future play gave us the slightest concept of it. We therefore began to encourage him all the more enthusiastically to write it.

His liking for Hauptmann was exactly proportional to his dislike for Ibsen. Rehearsals for *Michael Kramer* were then in progress, and Anton Pavlovich followed them eagerly.

I remember one very characteristic feature of his direct and naive response to impressions.

At the dress rehearsal of the second act of *Michael Kramer* I could sometimes hear him chuckling when I was on the stage. As the action on the stage did not suit such a response, yet, naturally, I highly valued the opinion of Anton Pavlovich, this laughter confused me unspeakably. What was more, in the middle of the act, Anton Pavlovich stood up several times and walked quickly down the middle aisle, still chuckling. This only added to the confusion of the performers.

At the end of the act, I went into the auditorium to discover why Anton Pavlovich was amused, and I saw him beaming and again running excitedly down the middle aisle. I asked him for his impression. He liked the play very much.

* A. L. Vishnevsly was then living in an apartment over the Sandunovsky baths and went every day to bathe. It was this which prompted Anton Pavlovich to make this joke. Comment by K. S. Stanislavsky.

"It's wonderful!" he exclaimed. "Marvelous, just marvelous!"

It seemed he was laughing with pleasure. Only the most spontaneous spectators are able to laugh like that.

I recalled peasants, who can also suddenly laugh at a most unsuitable point in a play from a feeling of artistic truth.

"How true to life it is!" they say at such moments.

During that season he watched *The Three Sisters* and was very pleased with the performance. However, in his opinion, we had not succeeded in capturing the sound of the alarm in the third act. He decided to arrange it himself. Obviously he wanted to work with the stagehands personally, do a little producing, work behind the scenes. We, of course, let him have some stagehands.

On the day of the rehearsal he drove up to the theater with a cab-driver, and the cab was loaded with various pans, bowls, and metal-ware. He himself placed the stagehands in position with these instruments, was very concerned to tell each how to strike what, and became confused in his own explanations. He ran several times from the auditorium onto the stage and back, but somehow it did not work.

The performance started, and Chekhov began to wait apprehensively for his alarm. The noise was unbelievable. The result was total cacophony, with everyone striking whatever came to hand, and it was impossible to hear what the actors were saying.

Next to the director's box, in which Anton Pavlovich was sitting, some spectators began to criticize first the noise, then the play and the author. On hearing such remarks, Anton Pavlovich moved further and further back in the box and finally left it and sat modestly in my dressing room.

"Why aren't you watching the play, Anton Pavlovich?" I asked.

"Just listen, they're criticizing it. It's not very agreeable."

So he sat the whole evening in my dressing room.

Anton Pavlovich loved to arrive before the start of the performance, sit opposite someone putting on his make-up, and watch the face change. He would watch silently and wholly concentrated. When some feature painted on the face changed it in a manner which suited the given role, he would suddenly grow cheerful and laugh in his deep baritone. Then he would fall silent again and watch attentively. Chekhov was, in my opinion, a wonderful physiognomist. Once, a very close acquaintance of mine called into my dressing room; he was very lively, cheerful, and generally considered to be rather dissolute.

Anton Pavlovich looked at him very closely all the time he was there and sat silently, his face very serious, not joining in our conversation. After the gentleman had left, Anton Pavlovich came up to me several times in the course of the evening and asked me all kinds of questions about the man. When I asked why he was so interested in him, Anton Pavlovich said, "Listen, he's suicidal!"

Such a combination seemed comical to me. It was with amazement that I recalled this incident a few years later, when I learned that this man had indeed poisoned himself.

Sometimes I would call to see Anton Pavlovich, sit, and talk. He would be sitting on his padded divan, coughing from time to time and tossing back his head occasionally to look at me through his pince-nez.

I had the impression that I was quite cheerful. On arriving at Anton Pavlovich's, I forgot all the disagreeable things that had happened prior to my arrival. However, during a moment when we found ourselves alone, he would suddenly ask, "Listen, you look dreadful today. Has something happened?"

Anton Pavlovich was very offended when he was called a pessimist, and his heroes neurasthenics. When he happened to come across articles by critics, who then used to attack him so venomously, he would jab his finger at the newspaper and say, "Tell him that he needs to take a water cure. He's also neurasthenic; we're all neurasthenics."

Then he would start to walk up and down the room, coughing now and again, and would repeat with a smile, but with traces of bitterness in his voice and stressing the letter *i*, "Pessimist!"

Anton Pavlovich was the most optimistic believer in the future I ever met. He would sketch with animation and faith a beautiful picture of the future life of Russia. As for the present, he related to it honestly and was not afraid of the truth. Those very people who called him a pessimist were the first to become embittered or fulminate against the present, particularly the eighties and nineties in which Anton Pavlovich found himself living. If one adds to that his serious illness, which inflicted so much suffering on him, his loneliness in Yalta, and, despite this, his ever cheerful face always full of interest in everything around him, then one can scarcely find in such data the features necessary to draw a pessimist.

In the spring of that year the theater went on tour to St. Petersburg. Anton Pavlovich, who by then was already in Yalta, very much wanted to go with us, but the doctors would not let him leave Yalta. We were then performing in the Panayevsky theater and, as I remember, were very afraid that we would not be given permission to perform *The Petty Bourgeois* by Gorky. A special performance was arranged for the censor before the opening of the season. It was attended by the Great Princes, ministers, various officials from the censorship board, et cetera. They were to decide whether or not it was permissible to stage this play. We performed it as tactfully as we could, with omissions we ourselves had decided upon.

In the end the play was passed. The censorship committee ordered us to strike out only one phrase, "In the house of the merchant Romanov . . ."

At the end of rehearsals, everyone was interested in the actor Baranov, who played the role of Teterev. B. had come to us from the choristers, accepting very low pay as long as he could avoid the choir. He was of enormous build and had a superb bass voice. For several years he had remained unnoticed, but when he was given the role of Teterev, which suited him perfectly, he immediately won fame.

I remember that Gorky concerned himself a great deal over B. at the time, but Anton Pavlovich repeatedly declared, "Listen, he's not for your theater."

Then, after the rehearsals, B. was conducted into the auditorium. Society ladies were full of enthusiasm for this man of natural talent, found him handsome, intelligent, and charming. Our talented man immediately felt in his element, became dreadfully self-opinionated, and in order to be chic, declared to someone from the royal retinue in his pompous bass, "Ah, forgive me, I did not recognize you."

The first night came. A dozen armed policemen were hidden under the stage. A large number of seats in the auditorium were occupied by members of the secret police—in short, the theater was under martial law.

Fortunately, nothing out of the way occurred. The play was a great success.

The following day, when reviews full of praise were published, B. appeared at the theater wearing a top hat. The censor, who was in the office at the time, asked to be introduced to him. After the greetings usual on introduction, there came a short pause, and then B. suddenly began to complain that there were so few newspapers in St. Petersburg.

"How fine it is to live in Paris or London—there, so they say, they publish up to sixty newspapers a day."

Thus did he naively reveal how much he liked reading flattering reviews.

Olga Knipper fell ill during the second performance. Her illness proved very dangerous, requiring a serious operation, and she was taken away to the hospital on a stretcher by an ambulance.

Telegrams began flowing between Yalta and St. Petersburg. We were obliged to engage in a partial deception with regard to Anton Pavlovich. It was clear that he was extremely worried, and his soft, gentle heart revealed itself in his anxious, concerned telegrams. However, despite all his desire to come to St. Petersburg, he was not allowed to leave Yalta.

Our tour ended, but Olga Knipper could not leave. The members of the troupe went their several ways. A week or two later, Knipper also left for Yalta. The operation had not been a success, and in Yalta she fell ill again and took to her bed. The dining room in Anton Pavlovich's house was turned into a bedroom for the patient, and Anton Pavlovich looked after her like the very best of nurses.

In the evenings he would sit in the adjoining room and read through his short stories, which he was collecting for an anthology.[38] He had completely forgotten some of the stories and on rereading them burst out laughing, finding them witty and amusing.

When I began to pester him with reminders about the new play, he said, "Here it is, here," and took out a small piece of paper covered in very small handwriting.

During this depressing time, Ivan Alexeyevich Bunin was a great comfort.

In the midst of all these worries and upsets, Anton Pavlovich nonetheless never ceased to think of leaving Yalta and moving to Moscow. Long evenings were spent in meeting his demand for a detailed, personal account of the whole life of the theater. He took such an interest in life in Moscow that he even asked about what was being built and where, and I had to tell him where, on what corner, a given house was being built, in what style, who was building it, how many floors, et cetera. He would smile and sometimes conclude by saying, "Listen, that's wonderful!"

He was always cheered by any sign of culture and good amenities. However, as a doctor, Anton Pavlovich was, it seems, not very far-sighted, as he resolved to bring his wife to Moscow when she was apparently still far from being ready to undertake such a journey.

They arrived just when the school spring examinations were in progress. These examinations took place in the building constructed by S. T. Morozov[39] on Bozhedomka Street especially for our rehearsals. The stage was almost the same size as the one in our theater, and there was a small room for spectators. Anton Pavlovich and his wife hurried here on the day of their arrival, and on the following day Olga Leonardovna fell ill again, and very seriously. She was close to death, and we already thought her case was hopeless. Anton Pavlovich never left her side day or night, himself applying poultices, et cetera. We stayed with him in turn, not for the sake of the patient, who was already well looked after, nor would the doctor permit us to go in to her, but for the sake of Anton Pavlovich himself, in order to keep up his spirits.

On one such difficult day, when the condition of the patient was particularly critical, all those close to him gathered together and discussed which famous doctor ought to be sent for. As always happens in such cases, each of us insisted on his opinion. Among those recommended was one doctor who had marred his reputation by some violation of professional ethics. On hearing this name, Anton Pavlovich declared with unusual decisiveness that if this doctor was invited, then he would have to leave for America permanently.

"Listen, I'm a doctor," he said, "for that I'll be excluded from the medical profession."

While this conversation was taking place in his house, a famous theatrical man, Gilyarovsky,[40] myself, and one of our actors stood on the street smoking, as we never allowed ourselves to do this in the apartment of Anton Pavlovich. By the house opposite, near the public bar, stood a carriage from the Iberian Chapel.[41] It was being said that a young life could come to an end. Such talk so disturbed G-sky that he broke into tears. In order to recover, he apparently began to think what he could do. Then, suddenly, he ran hatless across the street and went into the public bar; then he sat in the carriage, drank beer from a bottle, and gave the cabdriver three rubles to drive him along the boulevard. The startled cabdriver urged the horses forward. The lumbering carriage jolted heavily along the road, rolled along the boulevard, and from there G-sky gave us a friendly wave of the hand. This was that same G-sky about whom Anton Pavlovich so liked to talk.

Anton Pavlovich roared with laughter when we related this incident to him.

Anton Pavlovich loved to tell us about one of G-sky's jokes.

Once, in those troubled times when bombs were often thrown and the whole police force was on the alert, Anton Pavlovich and G-sky were driving along Tverskoy Boulevard. In his hands G-sky was holding a pumpkin and cucumbers wrapped in paper. As they were driving past a policeman, G-sky stopped the carriage, called to the policeman, and, his face serious and businesslike, gave him the wrapped pumpkin. The policeman took it. When the cabdriver set off again, G-sky shouted to the policeman, as if in warning, "It's a bomb!"

Then the pranksters were borne off along the boulevard in the handsome cab. Meanwhile the dumbfounded policeman, fearing to move from the spot, stood in the middle of the street, carefully holding the wrapped pumpkin in his hands.

"I kept looking back," said Anton Pavlovich. "I wanted to know what he would do next, but I couldn't see."

The summer holidays began and everyone departed, but the patient was no better—she was still in a critical condition.

Until that time, despite our long acquaintance, I had never felt completely at ease with Anton Pavlovich and could not converse with him on simple terms. I always remembered that I was talking to a famous person and strove to appear cleverer than was in fact the case. No doubt this artificiality embarrassed Anton Pavlovich, who liked only simple relations. My wife, who immediately succeeded in establishing with him precisely such simple relations, always felt much more at ease with him than I did. I cannot here describe their conversations, and how this light, unconstrained chatter cheered and amused the innately natural and simple Anton Pavlovich.

It was only during these long days which I spent sitting with Anton Pavlovich in the room next to the sick woman that I was first able to establish that simplicity in our relations. This period brought us together so closely that Anton Pavlovich began to turn to me occasionally with requests of an intimate nature, about which he was so sensitive. For example, having learned that I was able to inject arsenic—I had once boasted in his presence of my skill in performing this operation—he requested me to give him an injection.

Watching my preparation, he smiled approvingly and was already willing to believe in my skill and experience. However, in fact I was accustomed to do it only with new, sharp needles, and in this instance I had a needle that had already been used several times.

He turned his back to me, and I began to do the injection. The blunt needle would not penetrate the skin. I immediately lost my nerve, but was unable to admit my clumsiness and began to push in the needle with greater force, clearly causing Anton Pavlovich considerable pain. He did not even flinch but just coughed briefly once, and I recall how that cough destroyed my confidence entirely, and I began to think what I could do to extricate myself from this painful situation. However, I was unable to think of anything.

I then placed the point of the needle against his body and turned the syringe slightly to one side, to create the impression that the needle had penetrated, and simply released all the liquid out of the needle, letting it pour onto his linen.

When the operation was over and, embarrassed, I put the hypodermic away, Anton Pavlovich turned towards me, gave me a friendly look, and said, "Wonderful!"

However, he never made that request of me again, although we had agreed that I would always give him his injections.

During that period our conversations were often about our new theater being built on Kamergersky Lane. As Anton Pavlovich was unable to leave the patient, the plans and sketches were brought to his home. During his wife's illness, Anton Pavlovich himself became thin and weak. They were staying in the house over the Sandunovsky baths, the windows overlooked the street. In June the air was very bad—dusty and stifling—and it was impossible to go anywhere. Everyone had left, and there was only myself, my wife, and Vishnevsky. However, I also could stay no longer; I had to leave for the spa in order to finish the cure before the beginning of the new season. Thus poor Anton Pavlovich would be left behind alone, and so Vishnevsky, who was sincerely attached to him, decided to stay. I went abroad with my family.

During all this time Anton Pavlovich's only pleasure was one very skillful juggler at the Aquarium, whom he went to see very occasionally when the patient had recovered sufficiently to be left alone from time to time. Finally, almost at the very end of June, we received the news that, although Olga Leonardovna was already able to go out, there could be no talk of her going to Yalta. Moscow, however, was draining Anton Pavlovich of strength.

We suggested that he and his wife and Vishnevsky could stay in the wing of my mother's country house, where we usually spent the summer. It was close to Moscow, on the Yaroslavskaya railway line, at Tarasovka—the Alexeyev estate of Lyubimovka.

Shortly afterwards, Anton Pavlovich, his sick wife, a nurse, and Vishnevsky went to stay there. About their life there I know only by hearsay.

The Cherry Orchard

I had the good fortune to observe the process of the creation of Chekhov's play *The Cherry Orchard*. Once, in a conversation with Anton Pavlovich about fishing, A. R. Artem, one of our performers, illustrated how a worm is attached to a hook and how the line is thrown to lie at the bottom or float on the surface. These and other scenes were illustrated with great talent by our incomparable actor, and Chekhov was genuinely sorry that they were not seen by a large audience in the theater. Shortly after this, Chekhov was with us when another of our performers was bathing in a river, and there and then he decided, "Listen, Artem must definitely catch a fish in my play, and N. must be with him, bathing in the river. He flounders and shouts, and Artem is annoyed with him for frightening the fish."

Anton Pavlovich mentally saw them on stage—one fishing beside the bathing pool and the other bathing in it, that is, backstage. A few days later, Anton Pavlovich solemnly informed us that the bathing man had an arm amputated but nonetheless passionately enjoyed playing billiards with his one arm. The angler proved to be the old footman who had put away a little money.

Some time later, Chekhov began to imagine the window of an old country house through which came branches. Then they blossomed with snow-white flowers. Then a gentlewoman came to live in Chekhov's imagined house.

"Only we don't have an actress like that. Listen! It has to be a special kind of old lady," Chekhov pointed out. "She keeps running to the old footman and borrowing money from him."

Then a brother or uncle appeared alongside the old lady—a gentleman who had lost an arm and who loved to play billiards. He was simply an overgrown child who could not live without a footman. On one occasion the footman left without having prepared his master's trousers, and so he spent the whole day in bed.

Now we know what found its way into the play and what disappeared without trace or left only an insignificant mark.

In the summer of 1902, when Anton Pavlovich was preparing to write the play *The Cherry Orchard,* he was living with his wife, Olga Knipper-Chekhova, a theatrical actress, in our little house on my mother's estate, Lyubimovka. An Englishwoman, a governess, was living in a neighboring family. She was small and thin, with two long plaits like a girl, and wore a man's suit. Given such a combination, it was difficult to guess her sex, origin, and age straight away. She addressed Anton Pavlovich in a hail-fellow-well-met manner which he liked very much. They would meet every day and chatter about nothing at all. For example, Chekhov assured the Englishwoman that when he was young he had been a Turk, that he had a harem, that he would soon be returning to his native country and become a pasha, and then he would send for her. As if to express her gratitude, the agile, gymnastic Englishwoman jumped on his shoulders and, sitting there, greeted everyone who passed by on his behalf, that is, took his hat off his head and sketched a bow with it, saying in her broken, comical Russian, "Zdlastye! Zdlastye! Zdlastye!"*

As she spoke, she bowed Chekhov's head as a sign of greeting.

Those who have seen *The Cherry Orchard* will recognize in this original the prototype for Charlotta.

On reading the play, I immediately understood it and wrote an enthusiastic letter to Chekhov. How emotional he became! How strenuously he assured me that Charlotta must be a German, and also thin and tall—like the actress Muratova, and not at all like the Englishwoman on whom Charlotta was based.

The role of Yepikhodov was based on a number of models. The basic features were taken from a servant who lived at the country house and waited on Anton Pavlovich. Chekhov often talked with him, sought to persuade him that he needed to study, needed to be a literate and educated man. In order to achieve this, the prototype of Yepikhodov first bought himself a red tie and decided he wanted to study French. I do not know how, starting out from this servant, Anton Pavlovich finally arrived at the image of the rather stout, middle-aged Yepikhodov whom he depicted in the original edition of his play.

However, we did not have an actor who fit this description, and at the same time it was impossible to leave out of the play the talented actor I. M. Moskvin, whom Anton Pavlovich liked very much, and who was then young and thin. The role was reworked to suit him, and the young actor adapted it to himself, making use, moreover, of his own impromptu at the first actors' skit, which I will talk about further on. We thought that Anton Pavlovich would be annoyed at such a liberty, but he laughed a great deal and at the end of the rehearsal said

* *Zdravstvuite*—abbreviated to "zdraste"—is the Russian for "hello." As the English r is much softer than the Russian, this gives the impression that the r has been replaced by an *l.*—Tr.

to Moskvin, "That was precisely what I wanted to write. Listen, that's wonderful!"

I remember that Chekhov rewrote the role according to the outline created by Moskvin.

The role of the student Trofimov was also taken from one of those then living at Lyubimovka.

In the autumn of 1903, Anton Pavlovich Chekhov arrived in Moscow very ill. That, however, did not prevent him from attending almost all our rehearsals of his new play, the final title for which he still could not decide on.

One evening I was told over the telephone of Chekhov's wish that I call to see him on business. I dropped my work, hurried around to see him, and found him in a very animated mood despite his illness. It seemed he had kept this conversation on business till the end, like children keep a particularly tasty cake. In the meantime everyone was sitting around the table as usual, drinking tea and laughing, for it was impossible to be bored in Anton Pavlovich's presence. Tea ended, and Anton Pavlovich took me into his study, sat down in his customary corner on the divan, sat me down opposite him, and began, for the hundredth time, to persuade me to change some of the performers in his new play who, in his opinion, did not suit. "They're wonderful actors," he hastened to say to mitigate the blow.

I knew that such talk was merely the prelude to the main topic, and therefore I did not argue with him. Finally we came to the point. Chekhov paused for a moment, trying to be serious, but he failed, and a triumphant smile broke its way through onto his face.

"Listen, I have found a wonderful title for the play. Just wonderful!" he informed me, looking straight into my face.

"What?" I asked nervously.

"The Cherry Orchard," and he broke into happy laughter.

I did not understand the reason for his amusement and could see nothing special in the title. However, so as not to disappoint Anton Pavlovich, I had to pretend that his discovery had impressed me. What was it that so captivated him in the new name for his play? I began to inquire cautiously but again came up against that curious characteristic: Chekhov was not able to talk about his work. Instead of an explanation, Anton Pavlovich began to repeat, with every possible kind of intonation and tonal fluctuation, "The cherry orchard. Listen, that's a wonderful name! The cherry orchard. Orchard!"

From this all I could understand was that he was talking of something wonderful to which he was deeply attached: the beauty of the name was conveyed not in words, but in his very intonation. I carefully indicated this. My comment disappointed him, his triumphant smile disappeared from his face, our conversation lost its momentum, and there followed an awkward pause.

After this meeting several days or a week passed. Then, during a performance, he called into my dressing-room and sat down at my table with a triumphant smile. Chekhov loved to watch us preparing for a performance. He watched us putting on our make-up so attentively that one could tell from his face whether one was putting it on successfully or not.

"Listen, not cherry plantation but cherry orchard," and he collapsed with laughter.

At first I could not understand what he was talking about, but Anton Pavlovich continued to savor the name of his play, emphasizing the soft sound of "orchard," as if trying thereby to caress the former beautiful but now futile life which he tearfully destroyed in his play. I then grasped the nuance. A cherry plantation is a commercial undertaking which brings in a profit. Such plantations are still necessary today. A cherry orchard, however, brings no profit but preserves within itself, in its blossoming whiteness, the poetry of a former carefree life. Such an orchard grows and blossoms for pleasure, for the eyes of pampered aesthetes. It is a pity to destroy it, but it must be destroyed, as the economic development of the country requires it.

As before, this time also, during the rehearsals of *The Cherry Orchard* we had to drag out of Anton Pavlovich comments and advice about his play. His replies were like riddles which we had to resolve for ourselves, as Chekhov would disappear to avoid pestering by the producers. If someone were to see Anton Pavlovich at rehearsals, modestly sitting somewhere in the back rows, he would not believe that this was the author of the play. Whatever attempts we made to move him to the producer's table, we had no success. And if we did succeed, he began to laugh. It was impossible to discover what it was that amused him: perhaps that he had become producer and was sitting behind such an important desk, perhaps because he found the producer's table superfluous, perhaps because he was imagining how he would deceive us and conceal himself in his hideaway.

"I wrote everything down," he would then say. "I'm not a producer, I'm a doctor."

When one compares the behavior of Chekhov at rehearsals with that of other authors, one is amazed at the extraordinary modesty of this great man and the boundless self-esteem of other, far less talented writers. One of them, for example, at my suggestion that we cut down a long-worded, false-sounding, florid monologue in his play, replied with a note of offended bitterness in his voice, "Cut it down, then, only don't forget that you'll answer for it to history."

On the contrary, when we ventured to suggest to Anton Pavlovich that he cut out an entire scene—at the end of the second act in *The Cherry Orchard*—he became very depressed and paled with the pain we had caused him at that moment. However, having reflected and recovered, he replied, "Cut it out!"

And he never uttered another reproach to us about it.

I shall not describe the production of *The Cherry Orchard,* which we performed so many times in Moscow, Europe, and America. I shall just recall the facts and conditions in which the play was staged.

The production proved a difficult task; nor was this surprising: the play is a difficult one. All its charm lies in the elusive, deeply buried fragrance. In order to feel it, one has, as it were, to open up a bud and oblige its petals to unfold and blossom. However, this should happen naturally, without force; otherwise, you will crush this fragile flower and it will fade.

At the time I am talking about, our internal technique and ability to act upon the creative spirit of the performers were still primitive. We still had not learned to identify exactly the hidden doors which led into the heart of a work. In order to help the performers, to stimulate their emotional memory and inspire them with creative insight, we attempted to create for them an illusion by means of scenery, lighting, and sound effects. Sometimes this helped, and I am used to making too much use of sound and light effects.

"Listen!" Chekhov said to someone, but loud enough for me to hear, "I shall write a new play, and it will begin as follows: 'How wonderful, how quiet! One can hear no birds, no dogs, no cuckoos, no owls, no nightingales, no docks or bells, not so much as a cricket.'"

That shot was, of course, fired in my direction.

For the first time since we had been performing Chekhov, a premiere of one of his plays coincided with his own arrival in Moscow. This gave us the idea of organizing a jubilee celebration in honor of our favorite writer. Chekhov resisted, threatened to stay at home and not come to the theater. However, the temptation was too much for us, and we insisted.[42] Moreover, the first performance coincided with his name day (17/30 January).

The appointed day was drawing near, and we had to start thinking about the jubilee celebration itself and about our tributes to Anton Pavlovich. A difficult problem! I visited every shop dealing in antiques, hoping to come across something; but apart from some marvelously embroidered material worthy of a museum, I found nothing. For lack of anything better, I decorated a garland with it, and thus presented it to him.

At least—I thought to myself—it will be something artistic.

However, Anton Pavlovich then criticized me for giving him such a valuable present.

"Listen, it's absolutely wonderful, it should be in a museum," he reproached me following the jubilee celebration.

"Well, tell me then, Anton Pavlovich, what should I have given you," I replied, trying to vindicate myself.

"A mousetrap," he replied seriously, having thought for a moment. "Listen, mice need to be wiped out." Here he himself broke into laughter. "Korovin the artist sent me a marvelous present. Just marvelous!"

"What?" I asked, curious.

"Fish hooks."

Nor did any of the other presents he received please him, and some even annoyed him by their banality.

"Listen, you shouldn't give a writer a silver pen and an antique inkpot."

"So what should you give him?"

"A clyster pipe. Listen, I'm a doctor. Or socks. My wife doesn't look after me. Listen, dear, I say to her, my toe on my right foot is poking through my sock. 'Wear it on your left,' she says. But I can't do that!" he joked and again broke into cheerful laughter.

However, at the jubilee celebration he was not cheerful at all, as if he could feel the approaching end. When, following the third act, he stood at the front of the stage, deathly pale and thin and unable to stop coughing all through the speeches and presentations, we all felt our hearts contract painfully. Voices from the auditorium called out that he should sit down. Chekhov, however, frowned and stood throughout the whole of the long, wearisome ceremony of the kind which he laughed at benevolently in his works. Nonetheless, even here he could not prevent a smile. One of the writers began his speech with almost exactly the same words with which Gayev greets the old wardrobe in the first act: "Dear and much respected (in place of the word 'bookcase' the writer put in the name Anton Pavlovich), in greeting you . . ."

Anton Pavlovich glanced across at me—I played the role of Gayev—and a malicious smile flitted across his lips.

The jubilee celebration was a success, but it left an oppressive impression. It was reminiscent of a funeral. We all felt depressed.

The performance itself was moderately successful, and we condemned ourselves for not having been able, from the first performance, to bring out what was most important, wonderful, and significant in the play.

Anton Pavlovich did not live to see the real success enjoyed by his last, fragrant work.

As time passed, and the production matured, many of our actors were able once again to reveal their great talent. This was particularly true of Olga Knipper, who played the main role of Ranevskaya, and also of Moskvin as Yepikhodov, Kachalov as Trofimov, Leonidov as Lopakhin, Gribunin as Pishchik, Artem as Feers, and Muratova as Charlotta. I also enjoyed success in the role of Gayev, and during rehearsals was praised by Anton Pavlovich himself for my last exit in the fourth act.

We were moving into the spring of 1904. Anton Pavlovich's health was deteriorating. Disturbing stomach symptoms appeared, indicating tuberculosis of the intestines. A consultation of specialist doctors ordered that Chekhov be dispatched to Badenweiler, and preparations began for the journey abroad. All of us, myself included, felt drawn in those final days to visit him more frequently, but very often his health prevented him from receiving us. Despite his illness, however, his good spirits did not leave him. He took a great interest in Maeterlinck's play, then being painstakingly rehearsed. We had to keep him informed, show him the stage models of the scenery, and explain the *mise en scène.*

He himself dreamed of writing yet another play along lines completely new for him. Indeed, the subject of the play he had in mind was apparently far from Chekhovian. Judge for yourselves: two friends, both young, love the same woman. A shared love and jealousy create complex relations. It ends with both leaving on an expedition to the North Pole. The scenery in the final act depicts a huge ship lost in the ice. The finale shows the two friends seeing a white vision slipping across the snow—obviously the shade or soul of the woman they love, who has died far away in their native land

That was all I was able to learn from Anton Pavlovich about the new play he planned to write.

During the trip abroad, according to Olga Knipper, Anton Pavlovich enjoyed the cultural life of Europe. Sitting on his little balcony in Badenweiler, he watched the work going on in the post office opposite his room. People came to it from every direction, bringing their thoughts, written down in letters, and from here these thoughts were dispersed around the world.

"It's wonderful!" he exclaimed.

In the summer of 1904 we received from Badenweiler the sad news of the death of Anton Pavlovich.

"Ich sterbe"* were the last words of the dying man. His death was fine, calm and solemn.

Chekhov had died, but after his death he became even more popular at home, in Europe, and in America. Nonetheless, despite his success and popularity, he remained neither understood nor appreciated by many. In place of an obituary, I shall set out a few of my thoughts about him.

There are still those who think that Chekhov is a poet of everyday life, of gray people, that his plays are a sad page in Russian life, testifying to a spiritual inertia afflicting the country. The dissatisfaction which paralyzes any undertaking, the hopelessness which saps energy, the wide expanse enabling the development of generic Russian melancholy—such are the motifs of his theatrical works.

Yet why is it that this description of Chekhov so sharply contradicts my picture and recollections of the deceased? I see him far more frequently cheerful and smiling than gloomy, despite the fact that I made his acquaintance when his illness had already entered its serious stage. Wherever the sick Chekhov was to be found, there was joking, wit, laughter, and even pranks. Who better than he was able to make others laugh, or utter stupidities with a serious face? Who more than he hated ignorance, rudeness, whining, gossip, vulgarity, and endless tea drinking? Any new and useful undertaking—be it a young society of scholars or the design for a new theater, a library, or a museum—was for him a genuine event. Even some simple addition to the amenities of

---

* (Ger.) I am dying.

life evoked his animated interest and concern. I remember, for example, his childlike joy when on one occasion I told him about a large house being built near Krasnye Vorota in Moscow in place of a rather old, one-story private house which had been demolished. For a long time afterwards, Anton Pavlovich described this event enthusiastically to everyone who came to visit him: such was his ardent desire to see in everything a herald of the future Russian and universal human culture, and not only inner but also external culture.

The same is true of his plays: amidst the total hopelessness of the eighties and nineties, from time to time there appear bright dreams, encouraging predictions about life two hundred, three hundred, or a thousand years hence and for the sake of which we must suffer now, dreams about new inventions, thanks to which we shall fly through the air, about the discovery of a sixth sense.

Have you noticed, however, how often, during a performance of one of Chekhov's plays, there is laughter in the auditorium, and such a ringing, happy laughter such as one does not hear during the performance of other plays. When Chekhov takes up vaudeville, he expands a joke to the scale of hilarious buffoonery.

And his letters? When I read them, I, of course, do not fail to note the general mood of sadness. However, against this backdrop there shine, like cheerfully glittering stars against the night sky, witty words, amusing comparisons, hilarious descriptions. Not infrequently he even engages in tomfoolery, in the anecdotes and jokes of the born humorist, the irrepressible joker who was Antosha Chekhonte, who lived on, later in the heart of the ailing, exhausted Chekhov.

When a healthy man feels lively and cheerful, that is quite natural and normal. However, when a sick man who knows his own death sentence (for Chekhov was a doctor), who is fixed to one hated spot like a prisoner—far away from relatives and friends and seeing no ray of light ahead—is nonetheless able to laugh, engage in bright dreams, and have faith in the future, carefully gathering cultural wealth for generations to come, then such a love of life and ability to live should be recognized as extraordinary, exceptional, far above the norm.

I understand even less why Chekhov is considered to be out-of-date for our age, and why there exists the opinion that he would not have been able to understand the revolution and the new life it is creating.

It would, of course, be ridiculous to deny that the age of Chekhov was very far removed in its mood from the present age and the new generations brought up in the spirit of the revolution. In many ways they are even directly opposed to each other. It is also understandable that modern, revolutionary Russia, with its activity and energy spent in destroying the old foundations of life and creating new ones, does not accept, does not even understand, the inertia of the eighties, their passive restlessness.

Then, in the stifling, stagnant atmosphere, there was no source of revolutionary upsurge. Only somewhere, underground, forces were accumulating and making ready to deliver dreadful blows. The work of progressive people could consist only in developing a public mood, inspiring new ideas by explaining the futility of the old way of life. Chekhov was among those who carried out this preparatory work. He was able, as only a few were, to depict the intolerable atmosphere of stagnation and to ridicule the banality of the life it produced.

Time passed, eternally moving onwards. Chekhov could not march on the spot. On the contrary, he evolved with life and the age.

As the atmosphere thickened and the situation moved towards revolution, he became more resolute. They are mistaken who believe that he was weak-willed and irresolute like many of the characters he described. I have already said that he surprised us more than once with his firmness, decisiveness, and resolution.

"It's dreadful! But without that it's impossible. Let the Japanese force us into action," Chekhov said to me, agitated but firm and confident, when the smell of gunpowder reached Russia.

In the belles-lettres of the turn of the century, he was one of the first to sense the inevitability of revolution when it was still only in embryonic form and society continued to wallow in extravagance. He was one of the first to sound the alarm. Who was it if not he who began to fell the wonderful, blossoming cherry orchard, realizing that its time had passed, that the old life was ineluctably doomed to demolition?

A man who anticipated so far in advance much of what has now actually occurred would have been able to accept everything he had predicted.

Taganrog. 1860s

Taganrog. The house where Anton Chekhov was born

The Chekhov family (1874). Upper row, second on the left—Anton

The artist Isaac Levitan. 1887

Anton (left) and Nikolai Chekhov. The early 1880s

Anton Chekhov. 1888

Before leaving for Sakhalin. Spring 1890

Sakhalin. The prison in the Alexandrovsk Fort

Lika Mizinova

Anton Chekhov, Tatiana Shchepkina-Kupernik (center),
and Lidia Yavorskaya

Anton Chekhov in Melikhovo. 1897

Anton Chekhov and Maxim Gorky with the actors of the
Moscow Arts Theater. Yalta, 1900

In the garden of Chekhov's house. Yalta, 1900

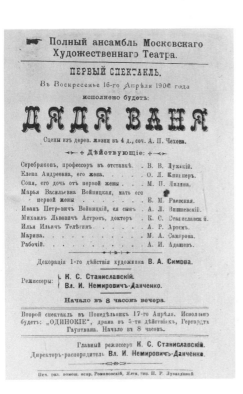

The playbill for *Uncle Varya*

A scene from *Uncle Vanya* staged by the Moscow Arts Theater. 1899

Anton Chekhov and Lev Tolstoy. 1900

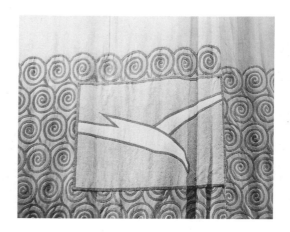

The curtain of the Moscow Arts Theater. 1953

The playbill for *The Seagull*

Konstantin Stanislavsky

Konstantin Stanislavsky as Gayev
in *The Cherry Orchard*

Vladimir Nemirovich-Danchenko

Olga Knipper as Ranevskaya in *The Cherry Orchard*. 1904

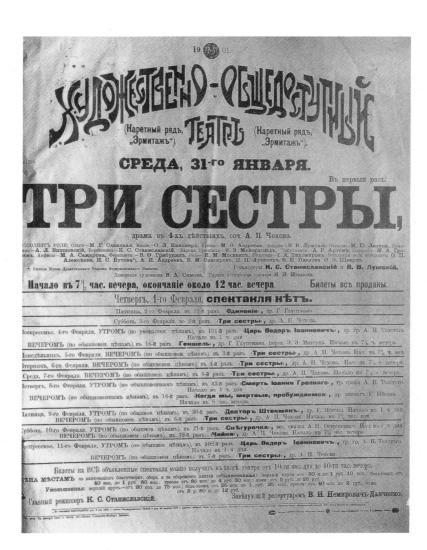

The playbill for *The Three Sisters*. 1904

Ivan Bunin

Vladimir Korolenko. 1907

Maria Pavlovna Chekhova. 1901

The Chekhov memorial house in Moscow

Anton Chekhov and Olga Knipper

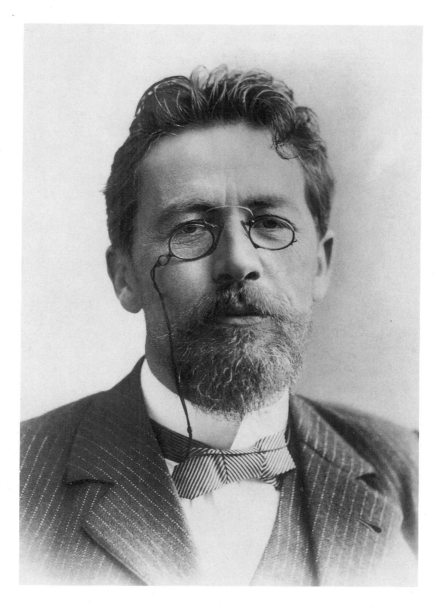

Anton Chekhov. 1903

A. P. CHEKHOV

On one occasion Chekhov invited me to visit him in the village of Kuchuk-Koi where he had a small piece of land and a white, two-story house.[43] There, showing me round his "estate," he said to me in animated tones, "If I had a lot of money, I would build a sanitarium here for sick village teachers. You know, I would have such an airy building constructed—full of light, with large windows and high ceilings. I would have a wonderful library, various musical instruments, an apiary, a vegetable garden, and an orchard; there could be lectures in agronomy and meteorology, because a teacher needs to know everything, old man, everything!"

He suddenly fell silent, coughed, glanced sideways at me, and smiled his gentle, kind smile which was always so irresistibly attractive and evoked especial and keen attention to his words.

"You find it boring, listening to my fantasies? But I like talking about this. If you knew how much the Russian village needs a good, intelligent, educated teacher! Here in Russia he needs to be given certain special conditions, and this should be done as soon as possible if we realize that without broad popular education the state will collapse like a house built of badly baked bricks! A teacher needs to be an actor, an artist, passionately devoted to his work, but in Russia he's a laborer, a badly educated man who goes to teach village children with the same enthusiasm with which he would go into penal exile. He is hungry, ignorant, frightened of losing his daily bread. Yet, he ought to be the most important man in the village, able to answer any questions the villagers put to him; so that they recognize in him a force worthy of attention and respect, and no one dares to shout at him, humiliate him as now everyone does: the village constable, the rich shopkeeper, the village priest, the local police superintendent, the local school patron, the village elder, and the official with the title of school inspector, who does not concern himself with improving school education but only with scrupulous adherence to district circulars. Is it not folly to pay a mere pittance to a man who is called upon to educate the people—you understand?—educate the people! It should not be permitted that such a man is obliged to dress in tatters, shiver from cold in damp, drafty schools, breathe in the fumes from a broken-down stove, develop laryngitis, rheumatism and tuberculosis at the age of thirty. It's a shame on all of us! Our teacher lives for eight or nine months of the year like a hermit; he has no one to talk to; he becomes dull from loneliness, lacking books and entertainment. And if he sends for his colleagues, he's accused of unreliability—a stupid word used by the crafty to frighten fools! It's all revolting—the abuse of a man who is doing enormous and terribly important work. You know, when I see a teacher, I feel embarrassed by his timidity, his shabby clothes; I have the feeling that I am somehow guilty of the fact that he is so poor—honestly!"

He fell silent, thought for a while, then gave a wave of his hand and said in a quiet voice, "What an absurd, fumbling country this Russia of ours is!"

A deep sadness veiled his handsome eyes, fine wrinkles surrounded them, deepening their gaze. He glanced around him and then laughed at himself, "You see—I've just subjected you to an entire editorial from a liberal newspaper. Come on, I'll give you some tea for being so patient."

He often behaved like that: he would talk so warmly, seriously, sincerely, and then suddenly laugh at himself and his own words. One could feel in that gentle, melancholic laughter the penetrating skepticism of a man who knew the value of words, the value of dreams. One could also feel in that laughter an attractive modesty and sensitivity.

We made our way unhurriedly to the house in silence. It was a clear, hot day, we could hear the sea, and the waves were glittering in the bright rays of the sun; below the hill a dog was yelping affectionately, content with something. Chekhov took my arm and said slowly, coughing slightly, "It's both shameful and sad, but true: there are a lot of people who envy dogs."

Then he immediately gave a laugh and added, "Today I'm talking in clichés, which means I'm growing old!"

I often heard him say, "A teacher came here, you know—ill, married. Do you think you could help him? For the moment I've fixed him up."

Or, "Listen, Gorky—there's a teacher here who'd like to be introduced to you. He can't come out because he's ill. Do you think you could call on him?"

Or, "There're some women teachers who want to know if they can be sent some books."

Sometimes I found him with this "teacher": an ordinary teacher, red with embarrassment, was sitting on the edge of a chair, choosing his words in the sweat of his brow, trying to speak more smoothly, to sound "educated," or else, with the familiarity of the painfully shy, was concentrating entirely on trying not to appear stupid in the eyes of a writer, and was subjecting Anton Pavlovich to a flood of questions which he probably had never even thought of until that moment.

Anton Pavlovich listened attentively to this clumsy speech; a smile gleamed in his sad eyes, the wrinkles on his temple twitched, and then he would begin, in his deep, soft, velvet voice, to say simple, clear words close to life itself, words which somehow immediately caused the other to become simpler: he ceased trying to appear intelligent, and immediately became more intelligent and more interesting.

I remember one teacher—tall, thin, with a yellowish, hungry face and a long, hooked, melancholic nose—sat opposite Anton Pavlovich, gazing motionlessly into his face with his dark eyes and saying in a gruff bass voice, "From such impressions of existence over the course of a pedagogical year, such a psychic conglomeration forms which absolutely suppresses any possibility of relating objectively to the surrounding world. Of course, the world is nothing other than our concept of it."

At this point he entered the field of philosophy and strode across it like a drunken man walking on ice.

"And tell me," Chekhov asked in quiet, friendly tones, "who is it in your district who beats the children?"

The teacher jumped up from his chair and waved his hands in agitation, "What are you saying! Me? Never! Beat?"

And he snorted in offense.

"Don't take offense," continued Anton Pavlovich with a soothing smile, "was I talking about you? But I recall—I read it in the newspapers —that someone beats them, and in your district."

The teacher sat down, wiped the perspiration from his face, and with a sigh of relief, said in his gruff bass, "It's true! There was such a case. It was Makarov. You know—it isn't surprising! It's dreadful, but it can be explained. He's married, has four children, his wife is ill—and he himself has consumption. His pay is twenty rubles, and the school is like a cellar, and the teacher has one room. In such conditions you'd flog an angel for nothing, and the pupils are far from being angels, I can assure you!"

And this man, who had only a moment before been overwhelming Chekhov with his learned vocabulary, suddenly, his head with its hooked nose swaying menacingly, began to speak in simple words, heavy as stones, illuminating the dreadful truth about life in the Russian countryside.

On taking his leave, the teacher took Chekhov's small, dry hand with its fine fingers into both of his, shook it and said, "When I came to see you, I thought it would be like talking to the authorities. I felt timid and apprehensive, puffed out my chest like a cockerel, and wanted to show you that I also know a thing or two. But now I feel as if I'm leaving a fine, close friend who understands everything. That's a wonderful thing—to understand everything! I'm very grateful to you! I'll go now, and I'll take away with me a fine, good thought: outstanding people are simpler and understand more easily, and are closer to us than all these wretches among whom we live. Good-bye! I shall never forget you."

His nose quivered, his lips formed a good-hearted smile, and he unexpectedly added, "But to speak the truth, wretches are also unhappy people—devil take them!"

Anton Pavlovich watched him depart, laughed and said, "A fine lad. He won't be a teacher much longer."

"Why not?"

"They'll make his life a misery, drive him out."

Then, after a moment's thought, he added quietly and gently, "In Russia an honest man is a bit like the chimney sweep with which nannies frighten little children."

It seems to me that all those who found themselves in Anton Pavlovich's company inevitably felt the desire to be simpler, more honest, more themselves; and more than once I noticed how people threw off the colorful vesture of bookish phrases, fashionable terms, and all those cheap little trinkets with which the Russian, desirous of imitating the European, seeks to beautify himself—rather like a savage putting on a necklace of shells or fish's teeth. Anton Pavlovich did not like fish's teeth and cock's feathers. When men dressed themselves up in the garish, the jangling, and the alien simply to "look important," Anton Pavlovich was embarrassed; and I noticed that every time he saw in front of him a man decked out in this fashion, he was consumed with the desire to free him from all this cumbersome and unnecessary trumpery, which distorted the true face and living soul of his companion. All his life Anton Chekhov lived on his inner wealth; he was always himself, possessed inner freedom, and never took account of what some expected from Anton Chekhov and what others, more vulgarly, demanded from him. He did not like conversation on "elevated" themes, conversation with which our nice Russian fellow strenuously consoles himself, forgetting that it is perhaps amusing but not at all witty to discuss velvet suits in the future when one does not have even a decent pair of trousers today.

Himself attractively simple, he loved all that was simple, genuine, sincere, and he had his own particular way of making others simpler.

Once he was visited by three very elegantly attired ladies; having filled his room with the rustling of silken skirts and the scent of strong perfume, they sat down ceremoniously opposite their host, pretended to be very interested in political matters, and began to "put questions."

"Anton Pavlovich! How do you think the war will end?"

Anton Pavlovich coughed, thought, and gently replied in a serious, affectionate tone, "Very probably—with peace."

"Well, yes, of course! But who will win? The Greeks or the Turks?"

"It seems to me that the stronger will win."

"And who, in your opinion, is the stronger?" the ladies continued to question, vying with each other.

"Those who are better fed and better educated."

"Oh, how witty!" one of the ladies exclaimed.

"And which do you prefer—the Greeks or the Turks?" asked the other.

Anton Pavlovich gave her an affectionate look, and replied with a timid, friendly smile, "I like marmalade. And how about you?"

"Awfully," the lady exclaimed enthusiastically.

"It has such a rich taste!" the other confirmed weightily.

And all three began to talk with animation, revealing on the matter of marmalade considerable erudition and profound knowledge of the subject. It was obvious that they were very happy not to have to wrack their brains and pretend to be seriously interested in Turks and Greeks, to whom they had never given a thought till then.

On leaving, they cheerfully promised Anton Pavlovich, "We shall send you some marmalade!"

"You had a marvelous conversation," I commented when they had left.

Anton Pavlovich laughed quietly and said, "Each person needs to speak in his own language."

On another occasion I found him with a young, good-looking assistant prosecutor. He was standing in front of Chekhov, shaking his curly-haired head and saying in lively tones, "Your story 'The Miscreant,' Anton Pavlovich, has placed me in a very difficult position. If I admit that Denis Grigoryev is motivated by ill will and acted knowingly, then I must, without further argument, send him to prison as required by the interests of society. However, he is a savage, he did not appreciate the criminality of his action, and I feel sorry for him! But if I treat him as a subject who acted without understanding and give way to my feeling of sympathy, how can I guarantee society that Denis will not unscrew the bolts on a railway line again and cause a catastrophe? That's the question! What is to be done?"

He fell silent, leaned back, and fixed his penetrating gaze on the face of Anton Pavlovich. He was wearing a new brand uniform, and the buttons on his chest glittered with the same self-confidence and stupidity as the eyes in the clean face of this young zealot for the law.

"If I were a judge," Anton Pavlovich replied seriously, "I would find Denis not guilty."

"On what grounds?"

"I would say to him, 'You, Denis, have still not matured into a deliberate criminal—go your way—and mature!'"

The lawyer laughed, but then immediately reassumed his aspect of solemn seriousness and continued, "No, my dear Anton Pavlovich, the question which you have raised can be resolved only in the interests of society, the life and property of which I am called upon to protect. Yes, Denis is a savage, but he is also a criminal—and that is the truth!"

"Do you like the gramophone?" Anton Pavlovich suddenly asked gently.

"Oh, yes! Very much! A wonderful invention!" the young man responded with enthusiasm.

"And I cannot abide gramophones!" Anton Pavlovich admitted regretfully.

"Why not?"

"Because they talk and sing without feeling anything. Everything they produce resembles a caricature, lifeless. Are you interested in photography?"

It turned out that the lawyer was keenly interested in photography: he immediately began to talk about it warmly, showing not the slightest interest in gramophones, despite his resemblance to this "wonderful invention" which Chekhov had so unerringly noted. Once again I saw how there appeared from beneath the uniform a living, and quite amusing human creature who still felt himself in real life like a puppy on a hunt.

Having seen the young man to the door, Anton Pavlovich said rather gloomily, "There's the kind of blisters you get sitting in court and deciding people's future."

Then, after a short pause, he added, "Public prosecutors love fishing. Particularly ruff."

Anton Pavlovich possessed the art of finding and highlighting crudeness everywhere—art, which is accessible only to those who make rigorous demands of life and is born exclusively of the burning desire to see people become simple, beautiful, full of harmony. In him any vulgarity found a sharp, harsh judge.

Someone once related in his presence that the publisher of a popular journal, a man who was ever discussing the need for love and compassion, had quite gratuitously insulted a railway conductor, and that he was a man who in general was very rude with those who were dependent upon him.

"Well, of course," said Anton Pavlovich, laughing darkly, "he's an aristocrat, after all, educated . . . he went to high school! His father wore bast shoes, and he wears patent leather."

These words were spoken in such a tone that they immediately reduced the "aristocrat" to someone worthless and comical.

"A very talented man!" he said of one journalist. "He always writes so nobly, so humanely . . . like lemonade. He calls his wife a fool in front of others. His servant's room is damp, and his maids always end up with rheumatism."

"Anton Pavlovich, do you like N. N.?"

"Yes, very much. A pleasant fellow," Anton Pavlovich agreed, coughing. "He knows everything, reads a great deal. He appropriated three books of mine. He's absent-minded; today he'll tell you that you are a wonderful chap, and tomorrow he'll inform someone that you stole the silk socks—black, with dark blue stripes—of your mistress's husband."

Someone once complained in his presence that the "serious" sections in the large journals were boring and made heavy reading.

"Then don't read those articles," Anton Pavlovich advised him resolutely. "It's the literature of friends. It's composed by Krasnov, Chernov, and Belov.* One writes an article, the other objects, and the third reconciles their contradictions. It's as if they were playing cards with an idiot. As for what interest it has for the reader—that's something none of them asks himself."

On one occasion he was visited by a rather stout but attractive lady, full of health and well dressed, who began to talk a la Chekhov.

"Life is very boring, Anton Pavlovich! Everything is so colorless: people, the sky, the sea, even flowers seem colorless. One doesn't feel any desire for anything at all—melancholy of the soul—as if one had fallen ill."

"It is an illness," Anton Pavlovich replied with conviction. "It is an illness. In Latin it is called *morbus pritvorialis*."**

Happily, it seemed that the lady did not understand Latin or perhaps hid the fact that she did.

"Critics are like gadflies which prevent the horse from plowing the soil," he said, laughing his knowing laugh. "The horse is working, its muscles as taut as the strings of a double bass, and then a gadfly settles on its crupper, stinging and buzzing. One has to shake the straps and wave one's tail. What is it buzzing about? Even the gadfly doesn't know. It just has a restless character and wants to be noticed, as if to say, 'I live here as well! You see—I can even buzz, buzz about everything!' I have been reading critics writing about my stories for twenty-five years, and I can't remember a single useful comment, haven't heard a single piece of good advice. There was just one occasion when Skabichevsky impressed me; he wrote that I would die drunk, under a fence."[44]

There was almost always a gentle glint of humor in his gray, sad eyes, but sometimes these eyes became cold, sharp and harsh; at moments like that his warm, modulated voice sounded harder, and then I had the impression that this gentle, modest man, if he ever

* (Rus.) Mr. Red, Mr. Black, and Mr. White.—Tr.

** A simulated illness.—Tr.

thought it necessary, could stand up firmly, resolutely, against any force hostile to him and would not give way before it.

Sometimes it seemed to me that in his attitude towards others there was a feeling of hopelessness close to cold, quiet despair.

"The Russian is a strange creature!" he said once. "He lets everything through, like a sieve. In his youth he avidly fills his soul with everything that comes his way, and then, after thirty, all that remains is some gray waste. In order to live a good, humane life one needs to work! Work with love, with faith. But that's something we are unable to do. Having built two or three fine houses, the architect becomes a card player, plays for the rest of his life, or else spends it sitting backstage in the theater. A doctor, if he has a practice, stops following medical science, reads nothing except *What's New in Therapy*, and at the age of forty is quite convinced that all illnesses have their origins in a cold. I have never met a single official who had just the slightest understanding of his work: usually he sits in the capital or a provincial town, composes directives, and sends them to Zmiyev and Smorgon★ to be carried out. As for who will be denied freedom of movement in Zmiyev and Smorgon—to this the official gives as little thought as the atheist to the torments of hell. Having made for himself the reputation of a successful defense lawyer, this same lawyer ceases to concern himself with defending the truth, and defends only the right to property; he bets on horses, dines on oysters, and imagines himself to be an expert in all the arts. Having given a tolerable performance in two or three roles, the actor no longer learns any roles but puts on a top hat and thinks he is a genius. The whole of Russia is a country of avaricious and lazy people: they eat far too much, drink far too much, love to sleep during the day, and snore in their sleep. They marry for the sake of domestic order and have a mistress for social prestige. They have the psychology of a dog: if you beat them, they whine softly and hide in their kennel; if you pat them, they roll on their backs, their paws up, and wave their tail."

There was melancholic, cold contempt in these words. However, he not only despised but also pitied, and if you happened to criticize someone in his presence, he would immediately intervene: "Now why say that? He's an old man, already over seventy," or, "He's still very young, it's just foolishness."

★ Small provincial towns.—Tr.

And when he spoke like that, I saw no look of disgust on his face.

When one is young, vulgarity seems merely amusing and insignificant; but gradually one is surrounded by it, it penetrates with its gray mist into the brain and the blood like poison and fumes, and one comes to resemble an old, rusty sign—something would seem to be depicted on it, but what it is one cannot tell.

In his very first stories Anton Chekhov was able to reveal the tragically black humor in the dull sea of vulgarity; one need only read carefully his "humorous" tales to realize how much cruelty and ugliness the author sadly noted and hid for shame behind amusing phrases.

He possessed a kind of virginal modesty which would not permit him to proclaim loudly and openly, vainly hoping that they would themselves perceive the crying need to be so, "May you be more decent!" Detesting everything that was vile and base, he described the baseness of life in the noble language of a poet, with the gentle irony of the humorist; and the fine facade of his tales all but conceals the bitter reproach directed at their content.

The honorable public reads "Daughter of Albion," laughs, and barely notices in this story the base abuse by a rich baron of a lonely, alienated person. In every humorous story by Anton Chekhov I can hear the soft, deep sigh of a pure, truly humane heart, the hopeless sigh of compassion for those who are unable to respect their own human dignity and who, offering no resistance to crude force, live like slaves, believe in nothing except the need to consume each day as much food as possible, and feel nothing except the fear that someone strong and insolent may strike them.

No one understood so clearly and so shrewdly as Anton Chekhov the tragedy of the trifles of life; no one before him had been able to draw such a mercilessly honest picture of dull, shameful lives in the gray chaos of middle-class prosiness.

His enemy was vulgarity; he battled against it all his life. He ridiculed it, depicted it with his sharp, dispassionate pen, and was able to find the mold of vulgarity even there where, at first glance, it seemed that everything was well ordered, even elegant. And vulgarity took its revenge on him with a vile trick, laying his corpse—the corpse of a poet—in a railway car for "oysters."

The dirty-green stain of that railway car is, for me, like the broad, triumphant smile of vulgarity at a weary foe; and the innumerable "reminiscences" in the popular press are a hypocritical grief behind which I feel coldness, the foul-smelling breath of that same vulgarity, secretly content at the death of its enemy.

The stories of Anton Chekhov summon up a melancholic day in late autumn, when the bare trees, crowded buildings, and gray people are starkly outlined in the clear air. Everything appears so strange—lonely, still, and powerless. The deep, dark-blue horizon is empty, and when it merges with the pale sky, it breathes a melancholy coldness over the earth covered with frozen mud. The mind of the author, like the autumn sun, illumines with harsh clarity the pitted roads, twisting streets, and the crowded, dirty houses in which small, pitiful people suffocate from boredom and idleness, filling their homes with mindless, semi-somnolent bustle. In "The Darling," a kind, timid woman capable of loving so much, so slavishly, darts about fearfully like a gray mouse. You can strike her on the face, and she will not even venture to cry out, a submissive slave. Next to her stands the sad figure of Olga from *The Three Sisters:* she also loves deeply and submits without murmur to the whims of the base, dissolute wife of her idle brother. She watches the lives of her sisters being destroyed before her eyes, and she weeps, unable to help anyone, totally incapable of a single living, powerful word of protest.

Then come the weepy Ranevskaya and the other former proprietors of *The Cherry Orchard*—as selfish as children and decrepit as old men. They have overstayed their time and languish, seeing nothing of the world around them, understanding nothing—parasites lacking the strength to re-attach themselves to life. The worthless student Trofimov pronounces fine words about the need to work—and does nothing, amusing himself out of sheer boredom by making fun of Varya, who works tirelessly for the benefit of good-for-nothing idlers.

Vershinin dreams of how wonderful life will be in three hundred years' time, and lives his life without noticing that all around him is decaying, that before his very eyes Solyony is ready, out of boredom and stupidity, to murder the pitiful baron Tusenbach.

Before the eyes of the reader there passes an endless parade of men and women who are slaves to their love, their stupidity and idleness, their avid desire for the pleasures of this world; slaves to a dark fear of life, they live in troubled apprehension, pouring out incoherent speeches about the future and sensing that there is no place for them in the present.

Sometimes a shot can be heard within their gray mass: Ivanov and Treplev have realized what it is they ought to do—and have shot themselves.

Many of them have fine dreams of how wonderful life will be in two hundred years' time, and not one of them asks the simple question: who will create this wonderful life if we do nothing but dream?

A great man, intelligent and attentive to everything around him, walked past this gray, depressing mass of powerless people, looked at these boring inhabitants of his native land, and with a sad smile, with a gentle but profound note of reproach, with hopeless melancholy on his face and in his heart, said in his fine, honest voice, "You live wretched lives, gentlemen!"

A high temperature for five days, but I don't feel like taking to my bed. A gray, Finnish rain is sprinkling the ground in a fine dust. The cannon are roaring on Fort Inno; they're finding the range. At night the long tongue of the searchlight licks the clouds: a repulsive picture, for it does not allow you to forget that devilish delusion—war.

I have been reading Chekhov. If he had not died ten years ago, the war would no doubt have killed him, having first poisoned him with hatred for people. I recalled his funeral.

The coffin of the writer so "tenderly loved" by Moscow was delivered in a green railway car with the words "For Oysters" written in large letters on its doors. A part of the small crowd, which had gathered at the station to meet the writer, followed the coffin of General Keller, which had been brought from Manchuria, and were very surprised that Chekhov was being buried to the accompaniment of an orchestra playing military music. When the mistake was discovered, people began to grin and giggle. About a hundred people, no more, followed Chekhov's coffin;[45] I clearly remember two lawyers, both wearing new boots and colorful ties—like two grooms. Walking behind them, I heard one of them, V. A. Maklakov, talking about the intelligence of dogs; and the other, who was unknown to me, was praising the amenities of his country house and the beauty of the surrounding countryside. A lady in a lilac-colored dress and walking beneath a lace umbrella was saying to an elderly man in horn-rimmed glasses, "Oh, he was unbelievably nice and so witty."

The old man coughed doubtfully. It was a hot, dusty day. In front of the procession there rode a plump police officer majestically astride a plump white horse. All of this, and much else besides, was cruelly vulgar and incompatible with this major and talented writer.

In one of his letters to the aging A. S. Suvorin, Chekhov wrote, "There is nothing more depressing and unpoetic, so to speak, than the prosaic battle to survive, which robs you of the joy of life and harries you into apathy."

These words express a very Russian mood which, in my opinion, was not at all typical of Anton Pavlovich. In Russia, which has a lot of everything, but whose people do not like to work, such is the opinion of the majority. The Russian admires energy, but has little faith in it. A writer of energetic outlook—Jack London, for example—is impossible in Russia. Although the works of Jack London are very popular with the Russian public, I see no sign of their arousing the Russian to action; they simply irritate his imagination. Chekhov, however, is in that sense not very Russian. For him, even while he was still young, the "battle to survive" became an unattractive, colorless sequence of petty cares connected with earning his daily bread, and not only for himself but a large loaf. These joyless concerns took all the strength of his youth, and one can only be amazed that he preserved his sense of humor. He saw life only as the boring desire for a full stomach and rest; its great dramas and tragedies were concealed from him beneath the thick layer of everyday existence. It was only when he no longer needed to worry so much about providing for those around him that he was able to turn his penetrating gaze onto the essence of these dramas.

I never saw a man who felt the significance of work as the basis of culture as profoundly and comprehensively as Anton Pavlovich. This revealed itself in every trifle of domestic life, in his selection of things, and in that noble love for things which, while completely excluding any desire to accumulate them, never ceases to admire them as the product of man's creative spirit. He loved to build, to plant gardens, to beautify the earth; he felt the poetry of work. With what moving concern he would watch growing in his garden the fruit trees and decorative bushes he had planted! When he was arranging for his house to be built in Autka, he said, "If each man did all he could on his own plot of land, how beautiful this earth of ours would be!"

When I had begun writing the play *Vaska Buslayev*, I read the boastful monologue by Vaska:

Oh, if I had more strength!
I would breathe fire and melt the snow,
I would circle the globe and plow
and sow.
I would travel five score years—build
cities
And churches, and cover the earth
with gardens!
I would adorn the earth like a maid,
I would embrace the earth like a
bride,
I would press the earth to my
breast,
I would lift it up and take it
to the Lord.
"Look, oh Lord, at the earth,
See how Vaska has adorned it!
You set it as a stone in the
heavens,
And I have turned it into emerald!
Look, oh Lord, and rejoice.
How it gleams green in the sun!
I would present it to you as a gift.
But it will set me back a
lot—it's dear to me!

Chekhov liked this monologue; coughing emotionally, he said to me and Doctor Alexin, "It's good. Very true, real, human! That is precisely the 'meaning of all philosophy.'[46] Man has made the earth habitable; he will make it comfortable for himself." Then, having obstinately nodded his head, he repeated, "He will!"

He asked me to read Vaska's boast again, listened, looking through the window, and advised me, "The last two lines you can leave out. Impudence, it's not necessary."

About his own literary work he said very little and reluctantly—I feel like saying "chastely"—with that same caution with which he spoke of Lev Tolstoy. Only very occasionally, if he was feeling cheerful, would he laughingly describe a subject, always a humorous one.

"You know, I'll write about a teacher, an atheist. She adores Darwin and is convinced of the need to fight against prejudice and popular superstition, but at twelve o'clock at night she boils a black cat in her bath in order to get a 'bow'—the little bone which makes a man fall in love with you—there is such a little bone."

He spoke of his plays as if they were "lighthearted," and it seemed he was sincerely convinced that he wrote lighthearted plays. It was no doubt on the basis of Chekhov's own words that Savva Morozov obstinately insisted that "Chekhov's plays should be staged as lyrical comedies."

In general, however, he took a perceptive interest in literature, movingly so when it was the work of "debutant writers." He showed amazing patience in reading the copious manuscripts of B. Lazarevsky, N. Oliger, and many others.

"We need more writers," he would say. "Literature is still a newcomer in our lives, and 'for the elect.' In Norway there is a writer for every two hundred and twenty-six people, but in Russia one for a million."

His illness sometimes made Chekhov a hypochondriac, and even misanthropic. On such occasions he became fractious in his arguments and difficult in his relations with others.

Once, lying on the divan and coughing dryly as he played with a thermometer, he said to me, "To live in order to die is not very amusing, but to live knowing that you will die before your time is completely ridiculous."

On another occasion, sitting at an open window and gazing into the distance, towards the sea, he suddenly said angrily, "We are used to living on hopes for fine weather, for a good harvest, for a pleasant affair, the hope of becoming rich or being promoted to chief of the city police, but I have never noticed that anyone lives on the hope of becoming wiser. We think: under the new tsar life will be better, and two hundred years from now, better still, and no one does anything to make that better life begin tomorrow. Life is becoming more complicated with every day and seems to be moving somewhere of its own accord, while people are becoming noticeably more stupid, and more and more of them are taking no part in life."

He thought for a moment, frowned, and added, "Just like crippled beggars during a religious procession."

He was a doctor, and illness in a doctor is always worse than in his patients; the patients only feel, but the doctor also knows something about how his body is degenerating. This is one of those cases when knowledge can be said to bring death closer.

He had fine eyes when he laughed, somehow femininely affectionate, gentle and soft. His laughter, almost soundless, was somehow especially fine. When he laughed, he enjoyed laughing, exulted; I do not know who else could laugh so—shall I say—"from the soul."

He was never amused by crude anecdotes.

Laughing gently, genuinely amused, he said to me, "Do you know why Tolstoy is so changeable towards you? He is jealous, he thinks that Sulerzhitsky prefers you to him. Yes, yes. Yesterday he said to me, 'I can't be sincere with Gorky, I don't know why, but I can't. I even find it disagreeable that Suler lives in his house. That's bad for Suler. Gorky's a malicious man. He's like a seminary student who's been forcibly made to take the tonsure, and it's made him bitter towards everyone. He has the soul of a spy; he has come from somewhere or other to the land of Cana'an, alien to him; he observes everything, notes everything, and reports on everything to whomever his god is. And his god is an ugly being, like a forest gnome or water spirit that village women believe in.'"

While he was recounting this, Chekhov laughed till there were tears in his eyes. Then, wiping away the tears, he continued, "I say 'Gorky's kind-hearted,' but he replies, 'No, no, I know. He has a nose like a duck, and only the miserable and the malicious have noses like that. Women don't like him, and women, like dogs, know a good man. Now take Suler—he has the truly invaluable gift of unselfish love for men. In that he is a genius. If you know how to love, then you can do anything.'"

Having paused for breath, Chekhov repeated, "Yes, the old man is jealous. What a surprising man he is."

When he spoke about Tolstoy, Chekhov always had a particular, barely detectable, affectionate and bashful smile in his eyes. He would lower his voice as if talking of something spectral, mysterious, something requiring mild and cautious words.

He often expressed his regret that Tolstoy did not have an Eckermann, someone who would carefully note down the penetrating, unexpected, and often contradictory ideas of the old sage.

"Now if you would do that," he tried to persuade Sulerzhitsky. "Tolstoy is very fond of you, talks so much and so well with you."

About Suler, Chekhov said to me, "He's a wise child."
That was very well put.

On one occasion Tolstoy expressed in my presence his admiration for a story by Chekhov—if I remember correctly, "The Darling." He said, "It's like lace woven by a maid. There used to be such spinster lace-weavers in the past, old maids. They put their whole life, all their dreams of happiness, into the pattern. They dreamed of their beloved in patterns, and they wove all their misty, maidenly love into the lace." Tolstoy was deeply moved and there were tears in his eyes.

That same day Chekhov had a high temperature. He was sitting and carefully wiping his pince-nez, his head bowed, his cheeks covered with red blotches. For a long time he said nothing, then he sighed and finally spoke, his voice quiet and embarrassed, "There are printing errors in it."

One can write a great deal about Chekhov, but one should write very scrupulously and clearly, which I am unable to do. It would be wonderful to be able to write about him as he wrote "The Steppe," an aromatic tale, light, and with a typically Russian pensive sadness. A tale for one's own sake.

It is a fine thing to be able to remember such a man. A feeling of cheerfulness immediately returns to your life, a clear sense of purpose invests it once again.

Man is the pivot of the world.

And—some will say—his vices and failings?

We are all starving for love towards man, and when one is hungry even badly baked bread tastes sweet.

I saw, however, how once, sitting in his garden, Anton Chekhov was trying to catch a ray of the sun with his hat, and then tried—quite unsuccessfully—to put it on together with his hat. And I saw that this failure irritated our sunbeam catcher; his face became more and more angry. Finally he slapped his hat against his knee disconsolately, then abruptly put the hat on and pulled it down over his eyes, pushed away the dog Tuzik bad-temperedly with his foot, glanced up at the sky through wrinkled eyes, and set off towards the house. Then, seeing me on the porch, he said with a short laugh, "Hello. Have you read Balmont's 'The Sun Smells of Grass?'[47] Stupid. In Russia the sun smells of Kazan soap, and here—of Tatar sweat."

He once also tried long and hard to put a thick, red pencil into the neck of a tiny chemist's bottle. He was clearly seeking to defy some law of physics. He gave himself to this attempt seriously, with the obstinate persistence of a man performing an experiment.

I. A. BUNIN

CHEKHOV

I

I made his acquaintance in Moscow, at the end of 1895. Some of his
characteristic phrases have remained in my memory.

"Do you write a lot?" he once asked me.

I replied that I wrote very little.

"You're wrong," he said almost gruffly in his low, deep voice. "One
should work, you know. All the time . . . all one's life."

Then, after a short silence and without any obvious link, he added,
"In my opinion, when you have written a story, you should cross out
its beginning and end. That is where we, the belletrists, most often lie.
And one should be brief, as brief as possible."

After Moscow we did not see each other again until the spring of
1899. That spring I went to Yalta for a few days, and I met him one
evening on the promenade.

"Why don't you call to see me?" he said. "You must definitely come
tomorrow."

"When?" I asked.

"In the morning, about eight o'clock."

Then, having no doubt noticed the surprise on my face, he explained,
"We get up early. And you?"

"I do as well," I said.

"Well, then come as soon as you get up. We'll have a cup of coffee.
Do you drink coffee? In the morning one should drink coffee, not
tea. A marvelous beverage. When I'm working, I make do with coffee

and clear soup until evening: in the morning, coffee, at midday, broth."

We then walked along the promenade in silence and sat on a bench in the square.

"Do you like the sea?" I asked.

"Yes," he replied. "Only it's very desolate."

"That's precisely what's good about it," I said.

"I don't know," he replied, looking somewhere into the distance and obviously engrossed in his own thoughts. "I think it must be fine to be an officer, a young student, sitting somewhere where there are lots of people, listening to cheerful music."

And then, in his characteristic manner, having paused for a moment and without any obvious link, he added, "It's very difficult to describe the sea. Do you know what description of the sea I read recently in a student notebook? 'The sea was big.' And that was all. Brilliantly put, in my opinion."

In Moscow I saw a man of middle age, tall, slim, light of movement; he was friendly, but so simple that I mistook this simplicity for coldness. In Yalta I found him very changed: he had grown thin, his face was darker, his movements slower, and his voice sounded more muted. In general, however, he was virtually the same as in Moscow: he was friendly but restrained, spoke in fairly animated tones, but even more simply and laconically, and throughout the conversation was constantly thinking of something else, leaving his companion to guess for himself the shifts in the concealed flow of his thoughts, and forever looking at the sea through the glass of his pince-nez, his face raised slightly. On the morning after our encounter on the promenade, I went to his house. I remember very clearly that sunny morning which we spent in his garden. From then on I began to call on him more frequently and finally became a constant visitor at his house. Along with this, his attitude towards me changed, became warmer, simpler.

The white stone house in Autka, its small garden which he, always so fond of flowers and trees, cultivated with such care, his study, whose only ornamentation was two or three pictures by Levitan and a large, semi-circular window which looked out onto the Uchan-Su valley with its gardens and the blue triangle of the sea—those hours, days, sometimes even weeks which I spent in that house have remained forever in my memory.

When we were alone together, he often laughed his infectious laugh; he loved to joke, to invent all sorts of trifles and comic nicknames; as soon as he felt just a little better, he was inexhaustible in his invention. He loved to talk about literature. When he spoke about it, he often expressed his admiration for Maupassant and Tolstoy. He referred to them very often indeed, and also to *Taman* by Lermontov.

"I cannot understand," he would say, "how, when he was only a boy, he could do something like that! If one could write something like that, and a good vaudeville as well, then one could die content!"

He would often say, "No one should read their work before it is printed. One should never listen to anyone else's advice. You make a mistake, you lied—let the mistake be yours alone. In one's work one needs to be bold. There are large dogs and there are small dogs, but the small dogs should not be put off by the existence of large ones: they are all supposed to bark—and to bark in the voice God gave them."

Of nearly all writers who have died it is said that they rejoiced over the success of others, that ambition was alien to them. He, however, did indeed rejoice at any talent and was unable not to: on his lips the word "mediocrity" sounded as a condemnation. As for his own literary successes, he viewed them with concealed bitterness.

"Yes, Anton Pavlovich, we'll soon be celebrating your jubilee!"

"I know these jubilees! They tear someone to pieces for twenty-five years, and then present him with a miserable aluminum pen and talk enthusiastic nonsense about him all day with tears and kisses!"

"Have you read it, Anton Pavlovich?" you would ask him, having seen somewhere an article about him.

He would look down at you mischievously from over his pince-nez, "My grateful thanks! They write a thousand lines about someone, and below they add, 'And there is also a writer called Chekhov—a moaner.' Am I a moaner, I ask you? Am I a 'gloomy fellow,' 'cold-blooded' as the critics call me? Am I a 'pessimist'? Of all my stories, my favorite is 'The Student.' And what an unpleasant-sounding word, 'pessimist.'"

And sometimes he would add, "When you, dear sir, are criticized somewhere, then think of us sinners more often: we were drubbed like schoolboys by the critics for the smallest flaw. One critic predicted that I would die under a fence; for him I was like a young man expelled from high school for drunkenness."

"You should sit down to write only when you feel as cold as ice," he once said.

"Skorpion[48] writes carelessly about their book," he wrote to me after the publication of the first almanac *Severniye tsvety.* "They exhibit me first, and when I read that announcement in *Russkiye Vedomosti,* I swore I would never again have anything to do with scorpions, or crocodiles, or grass snakes."

He had, on my insistent request, sent one of his early stories ("Out at Sea") to the Skorpion almanac. Later he regretted doing so.

"No, all this new Moscow art is rubbish," he said. "I remember, I saw a sign in Taganrog which said '*artificial* mineral waters.' This is just the same. The new is only what is talented. Only the talented is new."

One of my last recollections of him dates from the early spring of 1903, Yalta, Rossiya Hotel. It was already late evening. Suddenly the telephone rang. I took the receiver and heard, "Dear sir, take a good cabdriver and come to my house. We'll go for a drive."

"For a drive? At night? What's the matter, Anton Pavlovich?"

"I'm in love."

"That's fine, but it's already past nine o'clock. And you may catch cold."

"Young man, stop arguing!"

Ten minutes later I was in Autka. In the house where he spent the winter alone with his mother there was, as always, silence, darkness, with two candles burning feebly in the study. As always my heart contracted at the sight of that study where he spent so many lonely winter evenings.

"What a wonderful night!" he said with a gentleness unusual for him and with a kind of sad joyfulness as he met me. "But at home— what boredom! The only joy is that the telephone suddenly rings, and someone asks me what I'm doing, and I answer, 'I'm catching mice.' Let's go to Oreanda."

It was a warm, quiet night with a clear new moon and light, white clouds. The cab drove along the white road; we sat in silence, looking at the sparkling, flat expanse of the sea. Then came a forest with a delicate pattern of shadows, and beyond that black clusters of cypresses rising up to the stars. When we halted the cab and walked quietly beneath them, past the ruins of a palace, bluish-white in the moonlight, he stopped and said, "Do you know for how many more years I'll be read? Seven."

"Why seven?" I asked.

"All right, seven and a half."

"You're sad today, Anton Pavlovich," I said, looking at his face, pale in the moonlight.

He had lowered his eyes and was pensively digging with the end of his walking stick in the pebbles, but when I said that he was sad, he gave me a joking look.

"It's you who are sad," he replied. "And you're sad because you had to pay for the cab."

Then he added seriously, "All the same, they'll read my work for only seven years, and I have even less left to live: six. Only say nothing of this to the Odessa reporters."

He lived not another six years, but only just over one year.

I received one of my last letters from him in January of the following year in Nice:

> Hello, my dear I. A. A happy New Year! I received your letter, thank you. Here in Moscow everything is going well, there is nothing new (except the New Year) even on the horizon, my play has not been staged yet, and no one has any idea when it will be. . . . It's quite possible that I'll come to Nice in February. . . . Give my regards to the dear warm sun, the quiet sea. Enjoy yourself to the full, don't concern yourself about anything, write more often to your friends. . . . Good health, good cheer and happiness, and don't forget your northern brown-bear compatriots suffering from indigestion and poor spirits. My affectionate greetings.
>
> *1904*

II

Once he said (unexpectedly, as was his wont), "Do you know what once happened to me?"

Then, having looked me in the face for a while through his pince-nez, he began to laugh, "You see, I was once going up the main staircase in the Moscow Assembly of the Nobility, and by the mirror, his back to me, there stood Yuzhin-Sumbatov, holding Potapenko by one of his buttons and saying insistently, even through his teeth, 'Try to understand, you are now the first, the leading writer in Russia!' Then he suddenly saw me in the mirror, blushed, and quickly added, indicating me over his shoulder, 'And him.'"

It may seem strange to many, but it is true: he did not like actresses and actors, and said of them, "They are seventy-five years behind the development of Russian society. They are vulgar people, wholly eaten up by self-importance. I remember, for example, Solovtsov."

"Just a minute," I said, "don't you remember the telegram you sent to the Solovtsov theater after his death?"

"And what does one not have to write in letters and telegrams? What does one not say sometimes so as not to cause offense?"

Then, after a short silence, with a fresh burst of laughter, "And about the Arts Theater . . ."

In his notebook there is something which I heard from him personally. He asked me more than once, for example (each time forgetting that he had already said it, and each time laughing heartily), "Listen, do you know the kind of lady who makes you think, when you look at her, that she has gills beneath her corset?"

More than once he said, "In nature, the nasty caterpillar turns into a beautiful butterfly. But with people it's the other way round: out of a beautiful butterfly there comes a nasty caterpillar."

"It's awful to dine every day with someone who stammers and talks rubbish."

"When a mediocre actress eats pheasant, I feel sorry for the pheasant, which was a hundred times more intelligent and gifted than the actress."

"However much they may admire her, Savina was on the stage what Victor Krylov was among playwrights."

Sometimes he would say, "A writer should be poor, should be in such a position that he knows he'll die of hunger if he doesn't write, if he indulges his idleness. Writers should be sent to convict labor gangs, and there obliged to write by being put in the punishment cell, by flogging, beating. . . . Oh, how grateful I am to fate that I was so poor when I was young! How I admired Davydova![49] Mamin-Sibiryak would sometimes call on her, 'Alexandra Arkadyevna, I haven't a penny, let me have at least fifty rubles in advance.' 'Even if you were dying, I wouldn't. I'll let you have an advance only if you agree to let me lock you up this moment in my study, send you ink, a pen, paper, and three bottles of beer, and let you out only when you knock and tell me that you've written a story.'"

But sometimes he would say something quite different, "A writer should be fabulously rich, so rich that he could set off on a trip around the world at any moment aboard his own yacht, equip an expedition to the source of the Nile, to the South Pole, to Tibet and Arabia, purchase the whole of the Caucasus or the Himalayas. . . . Tolstoy says that a man needs only three *arshins*★ of land. Rubbish—it's a corpse that needs three arshins of land, but the living need the entire globe. And particularly the writer."

Speaking of Tolstoy, he once said, "What I particularly admire about him is his contempt for all of us other writers or, more accurately, not contempt, but rather that he views all of us other writers as nothing. He sometimes praises Maupassant, Kuprin, Semyonov, myself. Why? Because he sees us as children. Our stories, tales, novels are for him children's games; and therefore, in effect, he sees both Maupassant and Semyonov through the same eyes. Now Shakespeare—that's something else. Shakespeare is an adult and irritates him because he doesn't write a la Tolstoy."

Once, reading the newspapers, he raised his face and said, unhurriedly and without intonation, "It's always the same: Korolenko and Chekhov, Potapenko and Chekhov, Gorky and Chekhov."

Now he is separate. However, even now he is not, in my opinion, properly understood: he was too original, too complex, his inner world was hidden.

There is a remarkable line in his notebook: "Just as I will lie alone in my grave, so, in fact, I also live alone."

The same notebook contains the following thoughts:

> How willingly people deceive themselves, how they love prophets, oracles, what a herd!
>
> For every intelligent man there are one thousand fools; for one intelligent word there are one thousand stupid ones, and these thousand muffle.

He was muffled for a long time. Until "Peasants," far from his best work, the broad public read him eagerly, but saw him simply as an entertaining storyteller, the author of "The Screw" and "Book of Complaints." Men of "ideological principle" took little interest in him: they acknowledged his talent, but did not view him seriously. I remember how some of them laughed at me in all sincerity when, still young, I ventured to compare him to Garshin, Korolenko, while there were

★ *Arshin*—about two feet.—Tr.

those who said that they would never read a man who had begun to write under the name of Chekhonte. "One cannot imagine," they said, "that Tolstoy or Turgenev would decide to change his name for such a vulgar nom de plume."

Genuine fame came to him only when his plays were staged by the Arts Theater. No doubt he was no less pained by that than by the fact that he was only discussed after "Peasants." His plays are, after all, far from being the best of his works; and, moreover, this meant that it was the theater which had attracted attention to him, that his name appeared a thousand times on theater billboards, that they remembered "twenty-two misfortunes," "dear and much respected bookcase," "they've forgotten me."[50]

He himself often said, "What kind of playwrights are we! The only true playwright is Naidyonov: a born playwright with the undeniably dramatic spring within. Now he should write another ten plays, have nine failures, and with the tenth have such a success again that you can only gasp in surprise!"

Then, after a pause, he suddenly collapsed in merriment, "You know, I recently went to see Tolstoy in Gaspra. He was still in bed, but had a lot to say about everything, and also about me. Finally I stood up and said good-bye. He kept hold of my hand and said, 'Kiss me,' and, having done so, suddenly put his lips to my ear and said with a quick, senile burst of energy, 'But nonetheless I cannot abide your plays. Shakespeare wrote badly, but you're even worse!'"

For a long time he was known only as the "gloomy" writer, the "proponent of somber moods," "a sick talent," a man who looked at everything with hopelessness and indifference.

Today the exaggeration is in exactly the opposite direction: "Chekhovian gentleness, melancholy, warmth," "Chekhovian love for man." I can well imagine what he himself would have felt on reading about his "gentleness"! Even more repugnant to him would have been "warmth" and "melancholy."

When talking about him, even talented people sometimes adopt the wrong tone. Take, for example, Yelpatyevsky: "I met good and gentle people at Chekhov's, neither demanding nor imperious, and he was attracted to such people. He was always attracted by quiet valleys with their shadow, their misty dreams and quiet tears." Korolenko describes his talent with such pitiful words as "simplicity and sincerity," ascribing to him "sorrow for specters." One of the best articles about him was written by Shestov, who calls him the most pitiless of talents.[51]

He was precise and laconic even in his everyday life. He placed great value on the word and reacted sharply to the pompous, false, or bookish; he himself had a fine command of language—always in his own style, clear and correct. There was no echo of the writer in his speech; he rarely used similes or epithets, and if he did use them, then nearly always simple ones, and never for display, never savoring his own well-turned phrase.

He felt intense dislike for "elevated" words. There is a wonderful passage in one collection of reminiscences about him: "Once I complained to Anton Pavlovich, 'Anton Pavlovich, what should I do? I'm a prey to reflection!' Anton Pavlovich replied, 'Then drink less vodka.'"

True, as a result of this dislike for "elevated" words and careless use of language—typical of many poets, particularly today—he rarely enjoyed poetry.

"That's worth the whole of Urenius," he once said, recalling *The Sail* by Lermontov.

"Who's Urenius?" I asked.

"Isn't there a poet by that name?"

"No."

"Well, Uprudius[52] then," he said seriously.

"As soon as Tolstoy dies, everything will go to the devil," he kept repeating.

"You mean literature?"

"Literature as well."

Of the Moscow "decadents," as they were then called, he once said, "What decadents? They're large, hefty fellows! You could send them to serve in convict labor gangs."

Of Andreyev he also said, not very flatteringly, "I read one page by Andreyev, and then I have to take a stroll for a couple of hours in the fresh air."

It sometimes happened that people from very diverse ranks of society would gather at his house: he was the same with everyone, showed no particular preference, wounded no one's pride by making him feel ignored or superfluous. And he invariably kept all of them at a certain distance.

He had a great sense of his own dignity and independence.

"I'm afraid only of Tolstoy. Just think, it was he who wrote what Anna[53] herself felt, saw, her eyes shining in the dark! Seriously, I am afraid of him," he said, laughing and apparently enjoying this fear.

On one occasion he took almost an hour to decide which trousers to wear to visit Tolstoy. He tossed his pince-nez aside, looked years younger, and mixing the humorous and the serious together as was his custom, kept coming out of his bedroom first in one pair of trousers, then another. "No, these are indecently narrow! He'll think: scribbler!" Then he went to change, and came out again, laughing, "And these are as wide as the Black Sea! He'll think: insolent fellow."

Once he went with a small group of close friends to Alupka and breakfasted there in a restaurant. He was cheerful and joked a great deal. Suddenly one of those sitting at a neighboring table stood up with a glass in his hand, "Gentlemen! I propose a toast to Anton Pavlovich, who is here with us, the pride of our literature, a proponent of somber moods."

Chekhov turned pale, got up, and walked out.

I lived for some time in Yalta, and spent nearly every day at Chekhov's house. Often I left late in the evening, and he would say, "Come tomorrow, as early as you can."

He lisped certain letters, his voice was rather low, and he often spoke without intonation, as if mumbling: sometimes it was difficult to know whether or not he was speaking seriously, and I sometimes did not try. He would take off his pince-nez, put his hand on his heart with a barely visible smile on his pale lips, and repeat slowly and carefully, "Well, I most urgently request you, Marquis Bukishon! If you are bored with this old, forgotten writer, sit with Masha, with Mother, who is in love with you, with my wife, the Hungarian Knipshiz. We'll talk about literature."

I would go to see him, and it sometimes happened that we sat in his study all morning and said nothing, looking through the newspapers, of which he received a large number. He said, "Let's read the newspapers, and extract from this provincial chronicle subjects for dramas and vaudevilles." Sometimes we came across something about me, usually something very unintelligent, and he hastened to soften it,

"About me they wrote even more stupidly, even more maliciously, and sometimes said nothing at all."

Sometimes it was I who "was in a Chekhovian mood." He would liven up, even become agitated, and exclaim with mild annoyance, "Oh, how stupid it is! Oh, how stupid! I was also plagued with 'Turgenevian notes.' You and I are as alike as a borzoi and a hound. You, for example, are a great deal sharper than I am. You write 'the sea smells of watermelon.' That's wonderful, but I would not have put it like that. Now about the girl student—that's another matter."

"What girl student?"

"Don't you remember, we thought of a story: hot weather, the steppe beyond Kharkov, a very long mail train. And you added a girl student: she is wearing a leather belt, standing by a window in a third-class coach, and shaking wet tea leaves out of a teapot. The tea is caught by the wind and flies into the face of a fat gentleman who is leaning out of another window."

Sometimes he would suddenly lower his newspaper, take off his pince-nez and begin to laugh with quiet enjoyment.

"What have you just read?"

"Babkin, a Samara merchant," he replied in a reedy voice, laughing, "left all his money for a memorial to Hegel."

"You're joking?"

"No, it's quite true, to Hegel."

Another time he would lower his newspaper and ask suddenly, "What will you write about me in your memoirs?"

"It's you who'll be writing about me. You'll outlive me."

"You're young enough to be my son."

"Just the same. You have the blood of the common folk in you."

"And you have the blood of the aristocracy. Peasants and merchants degenerate with frightening speed. Read my story 'Three Years.' And then, you're bursting with health, only very thin like a borzoi. If you take drops for your appetite, you'll live to be a hundred. I'll write out a prescription for you now, I'm a doctor, after all. Nikodim Palych Kondakov came to me personally, and I cured his hemorrhoids. But in your reminiscences of me, don't write that I was a 'likable talent and a man of crystalline purity.'"

"That was written about me," I said. "They wrote about me that I was a likable talent."

He began to laugh with that tortuous enjoyment with which he laughed when something particularly pleased him.

"Just a minute, wasn't it Korolenko who wrote that about you?"

"Not Korolenko—Zlatovratsky. About one of my first stories. He wrote that this story 'would be worthy of an even greater talent.'"

He laughed, bent over till his head touched his knees, then put on his pince-nez, gave me a piercing, cheerful look, and said, "Even so, it's better than what they wrote about me. The critics tore strips off us every Saturday. And quite rightly. I began writing like some unutterable wretch. I'm a proletarian, after all. When I was a child, I sold tallow candles in our little shop in Taganrog. Oh, how cold it was there! Yet I enjoyed wrapping this icy candle in a piece of cotton. And the outhouse was on a vacant plot of land, a whole verst away from our house. Sometimes you would run there at night and find some rogue bedded down for the night, and we'd frighten each other to death! Only here's my advice," he suddenly added, "stop being a dilettante and become at least a little of a craftsman. It's very unpleasant to have to write as I did, for a piece of bread, but to some extent one has to be a craftsman and not always wait for inspiration."

Then, after a pause, "But Korolenko ought definitely to be unfaithful to his wife—so he can begin to write better. As it is, he's far too noble. Remember how you told me that he was in tears of admiration once for some verse in *Russkoye bogatstvo* by some Verbov or Vetkov or other about the 'wolves of reaction' surrounding the minstrel, the poet of the people, in the field in a dreadful snowstorm, and how he plucked so melodiously on the strings of his lyre that the wolves took fright and ran off? Were you telling the truth?"

"Honestly, the truth."

"And by the way did you know that in Perm all the cabdrivers resemble Dobrolyubov?"[54]

"You don't like Dobrolyubov?"

"I *do* like him. They were decent people. Not like Skabichevsky, who wrote that I would die from drink under a fence because I don't have 'the divine spark.'"

"You know," I said, "Skabichevsky once said to me that he had never in all his life seen rye growing and had never talked to a peasant."

"There you are, and all his life he wrote about the people and about tales from popular life. Yes, I don't even like to remember what they wrote about me! And that I'm cold-blooded—remember my story 'Cold Blood'?—and it's decidedly all one to me what I depict: a dog or a drowned man, a train or a first love. I was saved by my *Gloomy*

Folk—those stories were considered worth something, after all, because they described the reaction of the eighties. And another story, 'Nervous Breakdown'—there an 'honest' student goes mad at the very thought of prostitution. And I can't tolerate Russian students—they're idlers."

Once, when he began to pester me jokingly about what I was going to write about him in my memoirs, I replied, "First of all, I'll write about how and why I made your acquaintance in Moscow. That was in 1895, in December. I didn't know you'd come to Moscow, but there I was, sitting with a poet in the Bolshaya Moskovskaya, drinking red wine and listening to an organette, and the poet was reading his verse with increasing enthusiasm. We left very late, and the poet was already so carried away that he continued to read his verse on the stairway. He was still reciting as he looked for his coat in the cloakroom. The doorman said to him gently, 'Permit me, sir, I'll find it myself.' The poet snapped back, 'Quiet, don't interfere!' 'But sir, that is not your coat.' 'What, you wretch? You mean I'm taking someone else's coat?' 'Exactly so, sir, someone else's.' 'Silence, wretch, it's my coat.' 'But no, sir, it's not your coat!' 'Then tell me this minute whose it is.' 'Anton Pavlovich Chekhov's.' 'You're lying, I'll strike you down on the spot for such a lie!' 'That's as you will, but the coat belongs to Anton Pavlovich Chekhov.' 'You mean he is here?' 'He always stays with us.' And so we nearly rushed off to meet you, at three o'clock in the morning. Fortunately, however, we restrained ourselves and came the next day, but the first time we did not find you in—we only saw your room, which was being cleaned by a maid, and your manuscript on the table. It was the beginning of 'Women's Kingdom.'"

He was doubled up with laughter and he said, "I can guess who the poet was. Balmont, of course. But how did you know what manuscript was lying on the table? So you sneaked a look at it, did you?"

"Forgive me, old friend, we couldn't stop ourselves."

"It's a pity you didn't call that night. It's so agreeable to go somewhere at night, unexpectedly. I love restaurants."

He was extraordinarily pleased on one occasion when I told him that once, at my father's birthday dinner, our village deacon ate about two pounds of caviar to the last grain. He used that story to begin his "In the Gully."

He was very fond of saying that if a man did not work, did not live constantly in an artistic atmosphere, then even if he was Solomon the Wise he would feel empty, mediocre.

Sometimes he would take his notebook out of his desk, raise his head, the glass of his pince-nez sparkling, and wave the notebook in the air, "Exactly one hundred subjects! Yes sir! The young are no match for me! I'm a worker! Would you like me to sell you a couple?"

Sometimes he permitted himself evening strolls. Once we were returning rather late from such a walk. He was so tired he was having to force himself on—he had coughed up a lot of blood over the previous few days—and he said nothing, his eyes partly closed. We passed a balcony, and behind the awning there was a light and women's silhouettes. Suddenly he opened his eyes and said in a very loud voice, "Did you hear? How dreadful! Bunin has been killed! In Autka, in the house of a Tatar woman!"

I stopped in amazement, but he whispered to me quickly, "Quiet! Tomorrow the whole of Yalta will be talking about the murder of Bunin."

A writer was complaining, "I'm so ashamed I could weep over how badly I've begun to write!"

"Oh, come now, come now," he exclaimed. "It's wonderful to begin by writing badly! Don't you realize that if a debutant writer begins splendidly, it's the end of him, you can say he's failed."

Then he began to argue heatedly that only able people, that is, those who are not original, who are, in fact, without any talent, mature early and quickly because ability is knowing how to adapt oneself, and "one has an easy life," whereas talent suffers, seeking to reveal itself.

A great many Turks and Caucasians worked along the coast of the Black Sea. Knowing of that ill will mixed with contempt which we feel for those of alien race and culture, he never lost an opportunity to speak with admiration of their industriousness and honesty.

He ate very little, slept very little, and liked everything to be neat and tidy. His rooms were amazingly clean, and his bedroom resembled that of a young girl. However weak he was at times, he never let himself be careless as regards clothes.

His hands were large, dry, pleasant.

Like almost all those who think a great deal, he often forgot what he had already said more than once.

I recall his silence, his cough, his half-closed eyes, his thoughtful face, calm, sad, almost with an air of importance—only not "melancholy" nor "warmth."

A winter's day in the Crimea, gray, cool, sleepy thick clouds on the Yaila: in Chekhov's house all was quiet, with the steady tick of the alarm clock coming from the room of Yevgenia Yakovlevna. He was sitting at his desk in his study, without his pince-nez, and unhurriedly, accurately writing something down. Then he stood up, put on his hat, coat, and short leather galoshes, and went out somewhere where there was a mousetrap. He returned, holding a live mouse by the end of its tail, went out onto the porch, and slowly crossed the garden as far as the fence, on the other side of which was a Tatar cemetery on a stony hillock. He carefully tossed the mouse into the cemetery and then, looking attentively at the young trees, went to the bench in the middle of the garden. A crane and two little dogs ran behind him. Having sat down, he carefully played with his walking stick with one of the dogs, which had rolled onto its back at his feet, fleas crawling on its pink belly, and he laughed. Then, leaning back against the back of the bench, he looked out into the distance, towards the Yaila, his face raised, thinking about something. He sat there for an hour or an hour and a half.

Was there in his life at least one great love? I think not.

"Love," he wrote in his notebook, "is either what is left of something which is decaying and which was once very large, or else part of that which in the future will develop into something very large, but in the present it does not satisfy, gives far less than one expects."

What did he think about death?

Many times he strenuously asserted that immortality, life after death in any form, is pure nonsense. "It's superstition. Any superstition is dreadful. One should think clearly and boldly. We'll talk seriously about that some time. I'll prove to you, like two times two is four, that immortality is rubbish."

But then several times he said just the opposite even more firmly, "It's impossible that we should just disappear without trace. We shall most definitely live on after death. Immortality is a fact. Just wait, and I'll prove it to you."

Towards the end he often mused out loud, "How nice it would be to be a vagabond, a wanderer, go on pilgrimage to the holy places, stay in a monastery in the middle of a forest by a lake, sit in the summer evening on a bench by the monastery gates."

His "Bishop" passed unnoticed—unlike *The Cherry Orchard* with its large paper flowers blooming in unbelievably thick blossoms behind the theatrical windows. Who knows what may have become of his fame were it not for "The Screw," "Peasants," and the Arts Theater!

"A month later, a new bishop was appointed, and no one remembered the Reverend Pyotr. Then he was forgotten completely. Only an old woman, the mother of the deceased, now living in a small provincial town, when she went out towards evening to bring her cow home and met other women in the pasture, began to talk about her children and grandchildren and how her son had been a bishop. She spoke timidly, fearing she would not be believed. And indeed not everyone believed her."

I received my last letter from him from abroad in the middle of June 1904, when I was living in the country. He wrote that he was feeling reasonably well, had ordered a white suit, and was depressed only over Japan, a "wonderful country," which would, of course, be defeated and crushed by Russia. On 4 July, I rode on horseback into the village to collect my letters and newspapers and then turned into the blacksmith's to have my horse shoed. It was a hot, sultry day typical of the steppe, with a dull sky and a hot southern wind. I opened the newspaper while sitting on the step of the blacksmith's—and it was as if an icy razor had slashed my heart.

His death was brought on by a cold. Before leaving Moscow to go abroad, he had gone to the baths and had then dressed and left too quickly: he had met Sergeyenko in the dressing room and had fled from his tiresome chatter.

It was that same Sergeyenko who had pestered Tolstoy for many years *(How Tolstoy Lives and Works),*[55] and whom, because he was thin, tall, with black hair, and invariably wearing a black suit, Chekhov had nicknamed "the upright hearse."

1914

Supplement

We were sitting as usual in Anton Pavlovich's study, and for some reason began to talk about our godfathers.

"Your godfather was General Sipyagin, but mine was the merchant brother Spiridon Titov. Have you heard of such a title?"

"No."

And Anton Pavlovich handed me his birth certificate. I read it and asked, "May I copy this?"

"Of course."

The record is in the register of births at the Taganrog cathedral church:

> 1860, in the month of January, born on the 17th day and on the 27th christened Anton, his parents: Taganrog merchant of the third guild Pavel Georgiyevich Chekhov and his lawful wife Yevgenia Yakovlevna, godparents: Taganrog merchant brother Spiridon Titov, and the wife of Taganrog merchant of the third guild, Dmitry Safyanopulo.

"Merchant brother! What an extraordinary title! Never heard of it!"

The birth certificate shows that Chekhov was born on 17 January. In a letter to his sister, however, Anton Pavlovich wrote (16 January 1899), "Today is my birthday, thirty-nine years. Tomorrow my name day, and the local young ladies and matrons (who are known as *antonovka**) will send and bring presents."

A difference in dates? No doubt the church deacon made a mistake.

I asked Yevgenia Yakovlevna (Chekhov's mother) and Maria Pavlovna, "Tell me, did Anton Pavlovich ever cry?"

"Never in his life," both replied decisively.

Remarkable.

Chekhov said more than once to my friends the Yelpatyevskys, "I never broke the fourth commandment."[56]

In the spring of 1900, when the Arts Theater was on tour in the Crimea, I also went to Yalta. There I met Mamin-Sibiryak, Stanyukovich, Gorky, Teleshov, and Kuprin. The theater had brought

---

* A large, slightly sour apple very popular in Russia.—Tr.

four plays: *The Seagull, Uncle Vanya, Einsame Menschen* by Hauptmann, and *Hedda Gabler* by Ibsen. They performed first in Sebastopol and then in Yalta.

Everyone was full of high spirits and excitement. Chekhov felt fairly well. In the morning we would go to the city theater, walk around on the stage, where everyone was busily preparing for the performance, and then we would all set off for Chekhov's, where we spent most of our free time.

At the time Chekhov was full of enthusiasm for *Einsame Menschen,* talked about it a great deal, and believed that the Arts Theater should stay with such plays.

Yes, in January 1901 I was still living with the Chekhovs. I have even kept a record I made of those days:

> Crimea, winter 1901, at Chekhov's house.
>
> The seagulls are like cardboard, like eggshell, like floats alongside the bobbing boats. The foam is like champagne.
>
> Breaks in the clouds—up there is some wonderful, unearthly country. The cliffs are lime-gray, like bird droppings. Cormorants. Suuk-Su. Kuchuk-Koi. Noise below, a sunny field in the sea, a dog is barking hollowly. The sea is grayish-lilac, mirror-like, rising up very high. Hail, clouds are gathering.
>
> The beautiful Berezina!

The first performance of *The Three Sisters* was on 31 January, and of course Maria Pavlovna and "mamasha," as we all called Yevgenia Yakovlevna, were very excited. A telegram from the theater was to be sent to Sinani.[57] And they had sent their servant, Arseny, to see him. Maria Pavlovna asked him to telephone from town.

About twenty minutes later, Arseny informed us in excited tones: "Enormous success!"

Guests gathered: V. K. Kharkeyevich, the head of the local high school, S. P. Bonye, the Sredins; of course, we all had a drink to celebrate.

At the beginning of February, Maria Pavlovna left for Moscow, and I remained till Anton Pavlovich arrived with his mother, with whom I was on very close terms and who told me a great deal about Antosha.

In every word she said, one could feel that she idolized him.

In the middle of February—as I now see from the letters—Anton Pavlovich returned home. I moved into the hotel Yalta, where I spent a very unpleasant night—next to my room lay the corpse of a dead woman. Chekhov, appreciating what I had lived through during that night, had teased me about it.

He insisted that I come every morning to spend the day with him. During that period we became especially close, although without crossing beyond a certain point—we were both rather reserved but were already very fond of each other. I was never as close to any other writer as I was to Chekhov. During all this time there was not the slightest hostility. He was invariably reserved with me, gentle, friendly, like an elder brother—I am almost eleven years younger than he—but at the same time he never made me feel his superiority and always enjoyed my company. I can say this now, as it is confirmed by his letters to his friends, "Bunin has left, and I'm alone."

In the morning we would drink a cup of excellent coffee. Then we would sit in the garden, where he always found something to do in the flower bed or by the fruit trees. We would talk about the country-side. I depicted peasants and landowners, described my life in Poltava, spoke of my interest in Tolstoy's philosophy, and he spoke of his life in Luka, on the Lintvarev estate, and we both expressed our admiration for Little Russia (as the Ukraine was then called). We had both been to the Svyatogorsk Monastery and to the places associated with Gogol.

In my company he often laughed his infectious laugh. He loved to joke, to think up all sorts of things, silly nicknames; as soon as he felt a little better, he was inexhaustible in his inventions.

Sometimes we thought up stories together about some shabby despotic official, or a sentimental story with heroines called Eire, Australia, Neuralgia, Hysteria—all names of that kind. He had a great supply of wit. Sometimes I acted the drunkard. In an amateur photograph —I do not recall who took it—we are sitting in his study, he in an armchair and I on the arm of the chair. He has a smiling face, and I an angry, torpid one—I am depicting a drunk.

Sometimes I read him his old stories. He was preparing them for publication at the time, and I often saw how he reworked his stories, virtually rewriting them.

Once I selected and began to read "The Crow," a story he had written many years earlier, in 1866.

At first Anton Pavlovich frowned, but then, as the action developed, he became more and more favorably disposed, began to smile a little, even laugh. True, I was very good at imitating drunks.

On another occasion, as evening fell, I read "Gusev," praising it madly, believing it to be first-class, but he was upset and silent. I read the last paragraph of the story again to myself, "And meanwhile, up above, where the sun is setting, clouds are gathering, one like a triumphal arch, another like a lion, and third resembling scissors." "How he loves to compare clouds to things," I thought to myself. "From behind the clouds comes a broad green ray and stretches to the very middle of the sky, then shortly afterwards a golden ray lies alongside it, and then a rosy one. . . . The sky becomes a soft lilac. Looking at this magnificent, enchanting sky, the ocean at first frowns, but then itself soon acquires caressing, joyous, vibrant colors difficult to name in words."

"Will I ever see it?" I thought to myself. The Indian Ocean had attracted me since my childhood.

Then suddenly there came a flat, quiet voice, "You know, I'm getting married."

And then he immediately began to joke that it was better to marry a German than a Russian because she would be more orderly, and the child would not crawl about the house and beat on a metal bowl with a spoon.

I already knew, of course, about his attachment to Olga Leonardovna Knipper, but I was not sure that it would end in marriage. I was already on friendly terms with Olga Leonardovna and realized that she came from a completely different milieu than the Chekhovs. I knew that it would not be easy for Maria Pavlovna when Olga Leonardovna became mistress of the house. True, Olga Leonardovna was an actress, and it was unlikely she would leave the stage, but nonetheless there would inevitably be a great change. Relations between the sister and the wife would be difficult, and all this would affect the health of Anton Pavlovich, who, of course, as happens in such cases, would suffer acutely on behalf of one or the other, or even both at the same time. "It's suicide!" I thought to myself. "Worse than Sakhalin." But, of course, I said nothing.

At dinner and supper he ate very little. He almost always got up and walked back and forth in the dining room, stopping beside his guest and pressing food upon him, always with a joke and an apt comment. He would also stop beside his mother, take a knife and fork, begin to cut up the meat into very small pieces, always smiling and silent.

Gradually, I came to know more and more about his life, began to realize how varied was his experience, compared it to my own, and began to understand that beside him I was still a boy, a puppy. "A Dreary Tale," "Typhus," and other works that amazed with the experience they revealed had been written before he was thirty years old.

I see Chekhov more often cheerful and smiling than frowning and irritated, despite the fact that I came to know him in the four years of our close friendship during a bad period in his illness. Wherever the sick Chekhov was, there was joking, laughter, and even pranks.

I never saw him in a dressing gown. His dress was always neat and fresh. He had a pedantic love of order—inherited, like persistence, inherited as is didacticism.

On 9 September, Anton Pavlovich wrote to his wife, "Now I am well. Bunin calls to see me every day."

Again our endless conversations began. When I arrived, he felt rather ill.

Anton Pavlovich spoke a great deal about the koumiss spa where he had recovered, and then, after returning to Yalta, he "fell ill again, began to cough, and in July even coughed blood." He was full of enthusiasm for the steppe, the horses, the native inhabitants; but society there was very uninteresting, and absolutely no amenities! Koumiss tastes rather similar to kvass and is not unpleasant, but, of course, one grows weary of it.

A few days later he was feeling better. In September he decided to go to Moscow, no doubt already missing his wife.

At the time he was reading his old stories, some of which he virtually wrote again as, in his opinion, they were rather feeble.

Before my arrival, Doroshevich[58] had been living in Yalta, a man whose intellect Chekhov admired, and also the actor Orlenev, whom Chekhov considered to be talented but dissolute; Orlenev was still there when I arrived.

Chekhov complained about the newspaper *Kurier*, "They write all kinds of scurrilous lies about me in almost every issue."

He wanted to go to Moscow before rehearsals of *The Three Sisters* in order to give a few instructions and, perhaps, make a few changes.

I still think that, although Chekhov had already become a prominent literary figure, already occupied a place of his own, he never appreciated his own value.

In the evenings guests sometimes gathered for supper: Teleshov, Gorky, Nilus.[59] After supper Yelpatyevsky called in, and sometimes I was asked to read a story by Chekhov. Teleshov recalls, "Anton Pavlovich frowned at first; it seemed embarrassing to listen to his own composition, but then he began to smile despite himself, and then, as the story proceeded, he literally shook with laughter in his armchair, but silently, trying to restrain himself."

Having listened once to a "fragmentary" story, Anton Pavlovich said, "It's easy now for you to write stories; everyone has gotten used to it, but it was I who pioneered the short story, and how I was berated for it. They demanded I write a novel, or else I could not be called a writer."

We were all happy that Tolstoy was getting well again. In short, we were in the best of moods. Then suddenly a telegram arrived saying that Olga Leonardovna had fallen ill in St. Petersburg.

Telegrams came every day. For five days we awaited her arrival, and finally, on the first day of Easter, 10 April, she was carried from the ship to Chekhov's house with a temperature of 39°C under the armpit.

Nilus, of course, had to stop painting the portrait, and soon we all left.

At the beginning of December, Anton Pavlovich arrived in Moscow. I was also there—Naidyonov[60] and I were preparing for our trip abroad. I called every evening to see Chekhov and sometimes stayed till three or four in the morning, that is, until Olga Leonardovna returned home.

In most cases she left for the theater, but sometimes for a charity concert. Nemirovich would call for her, wearing tails and smelling of cigars and expensive eau de cologne. She, wearing an evening dress, perfumed, beautiful, young, would go up to her husband and say, "Don't be bored without me, darling. In any case, you always enjoy Bukishonchik's company. Good-bye, dear." She turned to me. I kissed her hand and they left. Chekhov would not let me go until she returned. I particularly treasure those nighttime vigils.

I tried to entertain him, telling him about myself and asking about his family. He talked a great deal about his brothers Nikolai and Alexander. Alexander he thought a great deal of and felt extremely sorry for him because he had bouts of drinking—he explained this as being the reason why he had not succeeded in making anything of himself, though he was very talented.

Alexander was a man of rare erudition: he had graduated from two faculties, the natural sciences and mathematics,[61] and also knew a great deal about medicine. He was well versed in philosophical systems and knew many languages. He was unable, however, to decide which field to work in. And how brilliantly he wrote letters! Quite amazing! He was also good with his hands and made a clock. At one time he had worked as the editor of a fire brigade journal. Over his bed there hung a fire bell so he should always know when there was a fire. He was an eccentric and wrote only with quills. He liked to breed fowl and built amazing hen coops—in short, he was a man of rare intelligence and originality. He had a good sense of humor, but of late he had become rather difficult: when he was sober, he tormented himself over his behavior when he was drunk, and when he was drunk he was indeed difficult.

I asked Anton Pavlovich, "Does he perhaps torment himself because you have eclipsed him as a writer?"

He smiled his agreeable smile and replied, "Not at all, because he writes only now and then, to earn extra money. I don't even know what interests him most: literature, philosophy, science, or poultry breeding. He's too gifted in many fields to devote himself just to one. My brother Mikhail also worked in the financial department, then left, and is now working in the book business with Suvorin. He writes stories but makes no effort whatsoever to become a real writer. We don't have that ambition typical of many writers today. We all love whatever it is we are working on at the time."

Anton Pavlovich questioned me about the first performance of Gorky's play *The Lower Depths*,[62] about the supper which cost eight hundred rubles, and what we had been served for such a price.

Imitating Gorky, I replied, "Fish first, and something, devil take it, more like horse than fish."

Chekhov laughed heartily, particularly at the comment by Professor Klyuchevsky,[63] who was calmly carefree and quietly cheerful, fresh and spruce in a buttoned frock coat, and who, his head inclined slightly to one side and his glasses and wily eyes sparkling—we were standing next to each other—said softly, "Horse! That's very well as regards the size. However, it's a little discomforting. Why horse, necessarily? Are we all draymen?"

By the end of December, Naidyonov and I were already about to leave. Chekhov told me about his trip to Nice, about M. M. Kovalevsky and the consul Yurasov, gave me advice on my health, and as always, assured me that I would live to a ripe old age as I was a "robust fellow." And yet again he insisted that I write every day, drop my "dilettantism," and approach writing "professionally."

It never occurred to me during those days that they might be the last time we would see each other.

At about four o'clock, and sometimes just before dawn, Olga Leonardovna would return, smelling of wine and perfume.

"Why aren't you asleep, darling? It's bad for you. And you're still here, Bukishonchik? Well, of course, he wasn't bored in your company!"

I would get up quickly and say good night.

Chekhov's face changed every year.

Chekhov's nobleness lay in flowers, animals, the nobility of human behavior.

He was the same with everyone, whatever their status in society.

O. L. Knipper-Chekhova

About A. P. Chekhov

Sometimes in life there are important and festive high points. One such high point in my life is the year 1898—the year I graduated from the drama school of the Philharmonic Institute in Moscow, the year of the opening of the Arts Theater, the year when I met A P. Chekhov. A number of the following years were a continuation of that high point. They were years of happy creativity and work, full of love and dedication, years of excitement and strong faith.

My path to the stage was not without obstacles. I grew up in a family which never knew need. My father, a technical engineer, was for some time the director of a factory in the former Vyatka Gubernia where I was born. My parents moved to Moscow when I was two years old, and here I spent the rest of my life. My mother had a great gift for music, a fine voice, and played the piano well, but on my father's insistence, and for the sake of the family, she did not go onto the stage, nor even to the conservatory. After my father's death and the loss of a relatively comfortable life, she became a teacher and professor of singing at the school of the Philharmonic Institute, sometimes performed in concerts, and accepted with difficulty her thwarted artistic career.

After finishing a private girls' school, I lived, according to the ideas of the time, the life of a young lady: I studied languages, music, and drawing. My father had dreamed of my becoming an artist—he even showed my drawings to Vladimir Makovsky, whose family we knew—or a translator. When still a young girl I had translated fairy tales and stories, and had been interested in translation. I was the only daughter in the family, and I was pampered but isolated from life. A friend of my elder brother, a medical student, told me about higher courses for women, about a free life (sometimes seeing my depressed condition); and when they noticed how avidly I listened to these accounts, how my eyes glowed, the nice young student was for a while forbidden entry, and I was left with my dream of a free life.

As children we had performed plays every year; we made our own stage in the drawing room, performed at home and at the houses of our friends, and took part in charity evenings. However, when I was already over twenty years old and we began to talk seriously about the creation of a drama group, my father, seeing my enthusiasm, gently but firmly and categorically cut across these dreams, and I continued to live as if in mist, occupying myself with first this, then that, but with no goal in view. The stage beckoned me, but in those days it seemed unthinkably cruel to break up the family which surrounded me with care and love, to leave—and leave for where? Obviously I had little resolution and faith in myself.

The dramatic change in our position after the unexpected death of my father put things in their place. We had to think about earning a living as we had nothing left except an apartment we were renting in a large house, five servants, and debts. We moved, dismissed the servants, and began to work with unbelievable energy, as if inspired. We set up a "commune" with my mother's brothers (one was a doctor, another served in the army), and we worked well and industriously together. Mother gave singing lessons, I gave music lessons, my younger brother, a student, was a coach, while my elder brother was already working as an engineer in the Caucasus.

This was a time of great inner transformation. I changed from a "young lady" into a free individual who earned her own living and was seeing life for the first time in all its diversity.

However, my former, long-standing desire to go on stage grew stronger. It was further stimulated by the fact that, following my father's death, I spent two summer seasons at the Linen Factory on the entailed estate of the Goncharovs, with whom we and our parents were on friendly terms. Having discovered in archive documents that a small house, in which at the time there was an alehouse, had once been connected, albeit very indirectly, with Pushkin (his wife came from this same family), we begged that the house be handed over to us, and our whole life was focused around it. We erected a stage and began to collect the repertoire for a popular theater. We performed Ostrovsky, vaudevilles with songs, and recited at concerts. Our little troupe was joined by workers and clerical staff from the Goncharov paper factory. When, in 1898, we performed *Tsar Fyodor* at the opening of the Arts Theater, I received a moving address with a long list of signatures from workers at the Linen Factory, and I was extremely happy, as the Linen Factory had left on my memory an indelible impression which stayed with me for the rest of my life.

Slowly but surely the stage became my conscious and longed-for goal. I could imagine no other life than that of an actress. Without my mother knowing, I with difficulty prepared to enter the drama school of the Maly Theater. I was received very pleasantly and studied there for a month. Then suddenly we were informed that there would be a "test," after which I was asked to leave the school, though I was told I still had the right to enter again the following year. That seemed only to add insult to injury. As I later found out, I was the only one of the four new girl students who had no patron, and now they had to take another student with a very influential patron who could not be refused. Therefore I was asked to leave.

It came as a dreadful blow, as the theater was then for me a matter of life or death. When she saw how depressed I was, my mother, despite the fact that until then she had strongly opposed my decision to go on the stage, arranged through her acquaintances among the directors of the Philharmonic Society for me to enter the drama school, although enrollment had ended a month earlier.

I spent three years in the class of V. I. Nemirovich-Danchenko and A. A. Fedotov, while running from lesson to lesson, teaching music, in order to be able to pay for my studies and have money to live on.

In the winter of 1897–98, when I was finishing the course at the drama school, there were already vague but exciting rumors that some new, "free" theater was to be opened in Moscow. The picturesque figure of Stanislavsky, with his gray hair and black brows, had already appeared inside the school, together with the characteristic silhouette of Sanin; they had already watched a rehearsal of *La Bottega di Caffè*,[64] during which my heart had contracted deliciously with excitement. By the middle of winter our teacher, Nemirovich-Danchenko, had already told M. G. Savitskaya, myself, and some of my other fellow students that we would be asked to stay with the theater, and we carefully guarded our secret. Winter stretched on, our hopes sometimes strengthened, sometimes seemed to vanish altogether as the negotiations continued. Then the third year class began to talk about Chekhov's

The Seagull. Vladimir Ivanovich had already infected us with his sensitive love for it, and wherever we went we had with us the little yellow volume of Chekhov's work. We read and reread it, were unable to understand how it could be performed, but it cast an ever stronger, more profound spell over us; we were in love with it, as if we had a presentiment that it would soon become a part of our very lives, inseparable from us, our very own.

We all loved Chekhov the writer and found his work exciting, but on reading *The Seagull* we were, I repeat, at a loss as to how it could be staged. It was totally unlike any play being performed in the other theaters.

Vladimir Ivanovich Nemirovich-Danchenko spoke about *The Seagull* with enthusiastic emotion and wanted to stage it as our graduation performance. When we discussed the repertoire of our debutant theater, he again declared with heartfelt conviction that we should stage *The Seagull*. We all became excited about the play, and drawn along by Vladimir Ivanovich, we were all anxiously enamored of it. However, the play seemed so fragile, gentle, and fragrant that it was frightening to approach it and seek to embody all these images on stage.

Our graduation examinations, which were held on the stage of the Maly Theater, were over. I had finally reached my goal, I had achieved my dream, I was an actress, and moreover, with a new and unusual theater.

On 14–26 June 1898, the troupe of the new theater gathered together in Pushkin: members of the Society of Art and Literature headed by K. S. Stanislavsky, and we students who had graduated from the school of the Philharmonic, headed by our teacher, V. I. Nemirovich-Danchenko. Then began the unforgettable summer in Pushkin, where we rehearsed plays for our opening performance. For our rehearsals we were offered a summer house built in the park of some friends of K. S. Stanislavsky, with a stage and one row of chairs. We began work on *Tsar Fyodor Ioannovich, Shylock, Hanneles Himmelfahrt,* and then, as autumn approached, we rehearsed *The Seagull*.

We began work full of admiration and anxiety, and with great love for the play, but it was frightening! Only recently the poor *Seagull* had broken its wings in St. Petersburg, in a first-class theater, and now we, unknown actors of an unknown theater, were boldly and in faith undertaking this play by our favorite writer. Maria Pavlovna, Anton Pavlovich's sister, arrived and anxiously inquired who these courageous people were who had decided to perform *The Seagull* after it had caused Chekhov so much suffering. She asked out of concern for her brother.

Meanwhile we continued to work, to agonize, losing heart, and then our hopes would soar. Another problem was that we did not know each other all that well, had only just made each other's acquaintance. Somehow Konstantin Sergeyevich could not at first get the feel of the play, but Vladimir Ivanovich, with his characteristic ability to "infect," infected Stanislavsky with love for Chekhov and for *The Seagull*.

I stepped onto the stage filled with the conviction that nothing would ever separate me from it; all the more so as in my personal life I had experienced a tragedy which had disillusioned my youthful feelings. It seemed to me that the theater alone should satisfy every aspect of my life.

However, on the very threshold of that life, as soon as I began the work I had so long dreamed of, as soon as I started out on my life as an actress, together with our newborn theater, that same theater and that same life brought me face to face with something which I saw as an "apparition" on the horizon, and which obliged me to think and seriously reappraise—I met Anton Pavlovich Chekhov.

Anton Pavlovich Chekhov in the last six years of his life—such was the man I knew: the Chekhov who was weakening physically, but growing stronger in spirit.

The impression of those six years is one of restlessness and rushing about, just like a seagull flying over the ocean and not knowing where to land: the death of his father, the sale of Melikhovo, the sale of his works to A. F. Marks, the purchase of some land just outside Yalta, setting the house and garden in order; and at the same time Chekhov's strong desire to go to Moscow, to be involved in his new, theatrical undertaking; trips back and forth between Moscow and the now prison-like Yalta; the wedding, the search for a small plot of land not far from our beloved Moscow, and a dream almost realized—the doctors permitted him to spend the winter in central Russia—dreams of taking a trip along the northern rivers, to Solovki, to Sweden and Norway, to Switzerland; and the last and strongest wish of all, in Schwarzwald, in Badenweiler, just before his death, the dream of returning to Russia through Italy, which beckoned with its colors, its vitality, and, most of all, with its music and flowers. All these dreams ended on 2/15 July 1904, with his own words, "Ich sterbe" (I am dying).

During these six years our inner life was extraordinarily full, rich, interesting, and complex, so that the superficial disorder and inconveniences were blunted. Nonetheless, when I look back over those six years, they seem to be made up of a series of painful separations and joyous reunions.

"If we are not together now, it is neither you nor I who are responsible, but the demon who infected me with this bacillus and you with love for art," Anton Pavlovich once wrote.

It would seem very easy to resolve the problem: leave the theater and go to be with Anton Pavlovich. I lived with this thought and battled with it, because I knew and felt how this rupture in my life would affect and weigh on him. He would never have agreed to my voluntary departure from the theater, in which he also took such a keen interest, and which linked him to the life he so loved. A man with a very sensitive soul, he well understood what it would mean for both him and me if I left the stage, for he knew how difficult it had been for me to reach it.

We met for the first time on 9/21 September 1898—a portentous and unforgettable day. I still remember it in the smallest detail, and it is difficult to put into words the deep excitement which took hold of me and all of the performers at the new theater when we first met our beloved author, whose name we had, under the influence of Nemirovich-Danchenko, learned to speak with awe.

I shall never forget that fluttering perturbation I felt the day before, when I read Vladimir Ivanovich's notice to the effect that the following day, 9 September, A. P. Chekhov would attend our rehearsal of *The Seagull*. Nor shall I forget that unusual state of mind in which I went on that day to "Okhotnichy Klub" (Hunter's Club) on Vozdvizhenka, where we were rehearsing until our theater on Karetny Ryad was ready, nor that moment when I first saw A. P. Chekhov face to face.

We were all captivated by the extraordinarily delicate charm of his character, his simplicity, his inability to "lecture" or "demonstrate." We did not know what to say. He looked at us, now smiling, now very serious, as if embarrassed, pulling at his beard and suddenly putting on his pince-nez, and then carefully looking at the "antique" urns for the play *Antigone*.

When someone asked him a question, Anton Pavlovich would reply somehow unexpectedly and as if not to the point, as if in general terms, and we did not know how to take his remarks—seriously, or as a joke. However, that was just the first impression, and then one felt that these apparently casual remarks were beginning to sink into one's mind and heart, and that this barely detectable but characteristic little feature was beginning to shed light on the very essence of the man.

One of the actors, for example, asked Anton Pavlovich to describe the kind of writer depicted in *The Seagull,* to which came the reply: "But he wears checkered trousers." It took us some time to become accustomed to being spoken to in this manner by the author, and a great deal remained unclear and incomprehensible, particularly when we grew heated over it; later, however, when we calmed down, we penetrated to the core of the remark.

From this meeting onwards, the fine, complex threads of my life began to draw together.

Chekhov came a second time when we were rehearsing *Tsar Fyodor* at the Hermitage, in our new theater where we were planning to perform that season. We were rehearsing in the evening, in a damp, cold building still far from ready, without a floor, with candle ends in bottles in place of lighting, and wrapped up in coats. We were rehearsing the scene where Shuisky is reconciled with Godunov, and the sound of our own voices seemed so strange in this dark, damp, cold space with its sad, enormous, creeping shadows, where we could see neither ceiling nor walls. We were happy to feel that there, in the dark, empty parterre, there sat a "soul" we all loved and who was listening to us.

The following day, rainy and damp, Chekhov left to go south, to the warmth, to the Yalta he already did not like.

On 17 December 1898, we performed *The Seagull* for the first time. Our little theater was not completely filled. We had already performed *Fyodor* and *Shylock,* and although we had received praise, although it was said that the scenery and costumes were unusually life-like and the crowd played exceptionally well, nonetheless "the actors do not stand out as yet," even though Moskvin was wonderful and played Fyodor with great success. Now we were performing *The Seagull,* in which there was neither scenery nor costumes—only the actors. We all prepared literally as if for an assault. The mood was serious; we avoided talking to each other, avoided each other's eyes, and were silent, filled with love for Chekhov and for our young new theater, as if afraid to squander these two loves, and we bore them with joy and apprehension and hope. Vladimir Ivanovich was too nervous even to go into the director's box during the first act, and instead wandered up and down the corridor.

The first two acts were over. We could not understand what was happening. During the first act we could sense incomprehension in the audience, restlessness, even protests—everything seemed new and unacceptable: the darkness on stage, the fact that the actors sat with their backs to the audience, and the play itself. Everyone waited for the third act. Then, when it came to an end, silence for several seconds, and then something happened—just as if a dam had suddenly burst. At first we did not even realize what it was, and then there began a kind of madness in which you cease to feel that you have legs, a head, a body. Everything fused into one mad exultation, the auditorium and the stage seemed to be one, the curtain did not drop, we all stood as if drunk, tears flowing down all our faces, we embraced, kissed each other, and voices in the audience rang out emotionally, saying something, demanding that a telegram be sent to Yalta. *The Seagull* and Chekhov the dramatist had been rehabilitated.

How had we succeeded? As actors we were all, with the exception of Stanislavsky and Vishnevsky, inexperienced and were not performing *The Seagull* with particular brilliance. However, it seems to me that these two loves—for Chekhov and for our theater—which filled us to overflowing, and which we had taken with such joy and apprehension onto the stage, could not but transmit themselves to the audience. It was these two loves which gave us the joy of victory.

The following performances of *The Seagull* had to be canceled because of my illness—the first performance I had given with a temperature of 39°C and severe bronchitis, and the following day I had to take to my bed. My nerves gave way, and during the first days of my illness no one was permitted to see me; I lay in tears, furious at my illness. My first great success—and I could not perform!

In Yalta, poor Chekhov, having received the telegrams of congratulations and then the news that *The Seagull* had been canceled, decided that again it had been a complete failure, that Knipper's illness was merely an excuse in order not to worry him, himself an ailing man, with the news of yet another unsuccessful production of his play.

By the New Year I was better, and we performed *The Seagull* for the rest of the season with unbroken success.

In the spring, Chekhov came to Moscow. We, of course, absolutely wanted to perform *The Seagull* for the author, but we did not have our own theater. The season ended, and with the beginning of Lent our lease on the theater also ended. We rehearsed wherever we could, renting a private theater on Bronnaya Street. We decided to rent for one evening the Paradise Theater on Bolshaya Nikitskaya, where touring theaters from abroad always performed in Moscow. The theater was unheated, the scenery was not ours, and the situation was oppressive after all that was new and "ours," linked to us.

At the end of the fourth act, expecting, after our winter success, praise from the author, we suddenly saw Chekhov, the mild, tactful Chekhov, walking on the stage. With a watch in his hand, pale and serious, he declared decisively that this was all very well, but "I would ask you to end my play with the third act, I will not permit the fourth act to be performed." He disagreed with a great deal, above all with the tempo, was very agitated, and averred that this act was not from his play. It was true that this time our performance had not gone smoothly. Vladimir Ivanovich and Konstantin Sergeyevich spent some time calming him down, arguing that the reason for our unsuccessful performance was that we had not performed for some time (the whole of Lent), and all the actors were a little green, and affected by the unfamiliar, inconvenient surroundings of this gloomy theater. Later, of course, this impression was forgotten, everything was sorted out, but I have never forgotten that occasion when Chekhov protested so decisively and so untypically because something indeed displeased him.

Then came a happy, marvelous spring, full of excitement: the creation of our new theater, an assessment of the first season, the successes and failures of some productions, our extraordinary unity and shared concern and trepidation before each performance, the extraordinarily great success of *The Seagull,* our acquaintance with Chekhov, the happy awareness that we had our "own" author who was close to us and of whom we were so fond—all of this filled us with happy excitement. We were photographed with the author—the performers who played in *The Seagull* and, in the center, Chekhov, apparently reading his play. There was already talk of staging *Uncle Vanya* in the next season.

That spring I came to know Chekhov and his dear family more closely. I had first met his sister, Maria Pavlovna, that winter, and we had somehow immediately taken a liking to each other. I remember how A. L. Vishnevsky brought Maria Pavlovna to see me in the dressing room during a performance of *The Seagull.*

I recall the sunny spring days, the first day of Easter, the merry ringing of the bells filling the spring air with something joyous, full of anticipation. And on that first day of Easter, Chekhov suddenly called to see us, Chekhov, who never went visiting.

On such a sunny spring day we went to an art exhibition to see paintings by Levitan, his friend, and witnessed the fact that the public did not understand and laughed at his wonderful picture "Dusk: the Haystacks," which seemed so new and incomprehensible.

Chekhov, Levitan, and Tchaikovsky—these three names are linked together as if by one and the same thread, and indeed they were all exponents of Russian lyricism, the voice of an entire stratum of Russian society.

It was Chekhov who, in his works, vindicated the existence of the simple, superficially insignificant man with his sorrows and joys, his dissatisfaction, and his dreams of the future, of another, "unbelievably wonderful" life.

During his life Chekhov displayed extraordinary love for and attention to each of the so-called unimportant of this world and found spiritual beauty in each. People were lovingly attached to him and went to see him, even though they did not know him, in order to see and hear him; and he became exhausted, was sometimes tormented by these visits, and did not know what to say when people asked him how they should live. He could not and did not like to lecture. I asked these people why they came to see Anton Pavlovich, for he was not a preacher, nor yet a good speaker; and they replied, with timid, gentle smiles, that when they sat beside Chekhov, even though in silence, they then departed renewed.

I recall how, when I was bringing the body of Anton Pavlovich from Badenweiler to Moscow and the train was standing at a remote, abandoned, unknown station which stood alone in the middle of an endless expanse, two shy figures approached, their eyes full of tears, and with timid care attached some simple wild flowers to the rough iron bars of the sealed goods wagon in which lay the coffin with Chekhov's body. These, of course, were not "heroes," but people of the kind who came to "sit" beside him, and after their silent visit departed with their faith in life renewed.

I cannot but relive in my memory the first and last visit to the studio of Levitan (he died shortly thereafter); I cannot but remember the tranquillity and charm of those few hours when he showed Maria Pavlovna and myself his pictures and sketches. Very agitated (he suffered from a heart complaint), pale, with glowing, beautiful eyes, Levitan spoke of the sufferings he had experienced during six years, until he was finally able to convey on canvas a moonlit night in central Russia—its calm, its translucence, its lightness, its expanse, a knoll, two or three delicate birch trees. And indeed this was one of his most remarkable pictures.

I spent three wonderful, sunny spring days in Melikhovo, the Chekhovs' small country house just outside Serpukhov. Everything there breathed comfort, a simple, healthy life. One could feel the happy, affectionate atmosphere of family life: Anton Pavlovich's enchanting mother, a quiet Russian woman with a sense of humor, of whom I was very fond, Anton Pavlovich, so cheerful and happy. He showed me his "estate": a pond with carp of which he was very proud—he was a keen angler—a kitchen garden, and flower garden. He was very fond of gardening, loved everything which came from the soil. The sight of cut or plucked flowers depressed him, and when, as it sometimes happened, ladies brought him flowers, he would silently carry them out to another room a few moments after they had left. Everything there captivated me absolutely: the house, and the wing where *The Seagull* was written, the garden and the pond, the blossoming fruit trees, the calves and the ducks, and the village woman teacher walking with the teacher along the path—as if it were Masha walking with Medvedenko. I was enchanted with their cordiality, their affection, comfort, their conversations full of jokes and wit.

These were three days full of a wonderful presentiment, full of joy and sunshine. "Our feelings were like beautiful, delicate flowers."[65]

The season ended, and I went for a holiday in the Caucasus, where my brother lived with his family in a house near Mtskheta. This is the period when our correspondence began. When I was still in Moscow I had promised to go from the Caucasus to the Crimea, where Anton Pavlovich had bought a plot of land and was building a house. By letter we agreed to meet on the boat in Novorossiisk around 20 July, and we traveled together to Yalta, where I stayed with the family of Dr. L. V. Sredin, friends of my family. Anton Pavlovich was staying on the promenade, in the hotel Marino, from where he went every day to the site of the house he was having built in Autka. He did not eat enough, as he never thought of food and grew tired; and however hard Sredin and I tried to invite him on various pretexts in order to ensure that he ate normally, he came very rarely. Anton Pavlovich did not like "paying visits," and avoided dining away from home, although he liked the Sredins. At their house everything was always simple and welcoming, and all those from the world of art, literature, and music who came to Yalta always visited the Sredins (Gorky, Arensky,[66] Vasnetsov,[67] Yermolova[68]).

The site which Anton Pavlovich had chosen for his house was some distance from the sea, from the promenade, from the town and was, in the true sense of the word, an empty spot with just a few pear trees. However, thanks to Anton Pavlovich's efforts, his great love for everything born of the earth, this empty spot gradually became a wonderful, luxurious, and varied garden.

Anton Pavlovich personally supervised the building of the house, traveling to the site and watching the work in progress. In town one could often see him on the promenade, in the bookshop owned by I. A. Sinani, with whom Anton Pavlovich was on very amicable terms, as also with his family. Isaac Abramovich was very devoted to Anton Pavlovich and had, with a kind of reverence, helped him with negotiations to acquire Kuchuk-Koi and the plot of land outside Yalta, watching, offering advice, and touchingly fulfilling every request.

Near the shop was a bench, a famous bench where all the "celebrities" who came to Yalta would gather, meet, sit, and talk: writers and singers, artists and musicians. In his shop Isaac Abramovich had a book in which all these "illustrious" persons left their signature (and he was proud of the fact that they gathered by his shop); in his shop and on the bench one could learn all the latest news, everything that was happening in the small world of Yalta and the larger world beyond. One was drawn as if by a magnet to the blindingly white, sun-filled promenade to breathe in the warm, tingling smell of the sea, wrinkle one's eyes, and smile, looking at the azure fire of the water's surface; one was drawn to say hello and exchange a few words with the friendly proprietor, look at the shelves of books to see if there was anything new, learn of any new arrivals, listen to the innocent gossip.

In August, Anton Pavlovich and I went together to Moscow and rode in a horse-drawn carriage as far as Bakhchisarai via Ai-Petri. It was wonderful to sway on the soft springs, to breathe the air full of the scent of pine trees, to chatter in Chekhov's affectionate, humorous tone, and drowse when the southern sun became particularly hot and exhausting. It was wonderful to drive across the picturesque valley of Kokoz, filled with some special enchantment and charm.

Our route passed by a provincial hospital situated some distance from the road. On the terrace there stood a group of people waving desperately towards us and apparently shouting. We were riding along, absorbed in some conversation, and although we saw these agitated figures, it nonetheless did not occur to us that they were trying to attract our attention, and we decided that they were lunatics. It later turned out that they were not lunatics at all, but a group of doctors we knew from Yalta who had been at the hospital for consultations and had tried to get us to stop. This incident then became a source of laughter and all kinds of anecdotes.

Anton Pavlovich stayed for a short while in Moscow and then, at the end of August, went back to Yalta, and on 3 September our correspondence began again.

In the season 1899–1900 we performed *Uncle Vanya*.

With *Uncle Vanya* things were not as successful. The first performance came close to being a failure. What was the reason? I think it lay in us. It is very difficult to perform the plays of Chekhov; it is not enough to be a good actor and to perform one's role with skill. One needs to love, to feel Chekhov; one must be filled with the atmosphere of that particular period, and, most important of all, one must love one's fellow men as Chekhov loved them and live the life of his characters. If one finds what is living and eternal in Chekhov, then however often one may thereafter play that role, one always finds in it something new, something still not used.

In *Uncle Vanya* not all of us at first grasped the images, but the more we performed, the more we penetrated into the essence of the play; and over the course of many years, *Uncle Vanya* became the most popular play in our repertoire. In general, Chekhov's plays did not evoke immediate enthusiasm but slowly, step by step, embedded themselves deeply and firmly in the hearts of both the performers and the spectators and captivated with their charm. Sometimes we did not perform certain plays for several years, but when we returned to them, neither the actors nor the directors had the feeling of dressing up the old. We approached each revival happily, rehearsed the play as if it were new, and found again and again something new within it.

At the end of March the Arts Theater decided to go to the Crimea with the plays *The Seagull, Uncle Vanya, Einsame Menschen,* and *Hedda Gabler.* I arrived on Passion Week, together with Maria Pavlovna, and how comfortable and warm it seemed in the new house which that summer had still been under construction and uninhabited. Everything was of interest, every trifle: Anton Pavlovich loved to walk, to show, to talk about what still had not been done and what should be done with time; above all he was occupied with the garden and the planting of fruit trees.

With the help of his sister, Maria Pavlovna, Anton Pavlovich himself drew up the plan of the garden, indicated the position of each tree, where a bench was to be placed, sent to every part of Russia for trees, bushes, and fruit trees, and arranged the pear and apple trees in rows. And the result was indeed truly marvelous: peaches, apricots, cherries, apples, and pears. He carefully nurtured a birch tree, which reminded him of our northern landscape, cultivated the long-stemmed roses, in which he took such pride, and a eucalyptus beside his favorite bench. Neither the eucalyptus nor the birch, however, survived for long: a storm blew up, the wind snapped the fragile white tree which, of course, could not prove strong and hardy in alien soil. The avenue of acacias grew with incredible speed. Long and flexible, they quivered, bent, and stretched pensively in the slightest breeze, and there was something fantastic in these movements, something restless and sad. Anton Pavlovich would always gaze at them out of the large Italian window in his study. There were also Japanese miniature trees, a spreading plum tree with red leaves, an enormous black currant bush, and also vines, almond trees, and a pyramid-shaped poplar tree. All of these took root and grew with amazing rapidity thanks to the loving eye of Anton Pavlovich. There was just one problem—a constant shortage of water until Autka was finally linked up to Yalta and it became possible to install a water pipe.

In the morning Anton Pavlovich usually sat in the garden, together with his ever-present adjutants—two mongrel dogs which had appeared from somewhere or other and quickly made themselves at home thanks to the affection which Anton Pavlovich bestowed upon them, and two cranes with clipped wings which were always to be found in human company but which would not allow themselves to be touched. These cranes were very attached to Arseny (the janitor and gardener combined) and missed him badly when he went away for a while. The whole house knew when Arseny had returned from town by the cries of these gray birds and the strange movements with which they expressed their joy—something akin to a waltz.

Gorky, who was then rising to fame quickly and powerfully like a rocket, was also in Yalta at the time. He used to visit Anton Pavlovich and give wonderful, interesting, colorful accounts of his travels. Both he himself and the stories he told seemed so new, so fresh, and we sat for a long time silently in Anton Pavlovich's study and listened.

Passion Week, a week of rest, passed quietly, pleasantly, and quickly, and it was time to go to Sebastopol, where the Arts Theater troupe had arrived. I recall the feeling of loneliness which took hold of me when, for the first time in my life, I stayed in a hotel room, moreover on the eve of Easter, and after the affection and homeliness of Chekhov's family. However, preparations for our performances had already begun,

Anton Pavlovich came, and life became hectic. A kind of spring celebration began. We came to Yalta, and the celebration became even more festive; we were literally showered with flowers. This celebration ended with a fantastic performance on the roof of the house of the hospitable F. K. Tatarinova, who displayed such love for our young theater and who did not know how and with what to express her admiration for Stanislavsky and Nemirovich-Danchenko, its creators. The actors often went to see Anton Pavlovich, dined with him, wandered around the garden, sat in his pleasant study; and this pleased Anton Pavlovich so much—he so loved a dynamic, active life, and we were then full of hope, enthusiasm, joy.

We were sorry to leave the south and the sun, Chekhov and the festive atmosphere, but we had to return to Moscow to rehearse. Shortly afterwards Anton Pavlovich also arrived in Moscow, it seemed empty to him in Yalta after the life and bustle our theater had brought with it, but in Moscow he did not feel well and soon returned south.

At the end of May, I went with my mother to the Caucasus and was surprised and happy when, in the train from Tiflis to Batum, I met Anton Pavlovich, Gorky, Vasetsov, and Doctor Aleksin, who were traveling to Batum. We traveled together for about six hours, as far as Mikhailovo, where my mother and I changed to the Borzhom line.

In July, I again visited the Chekhovs in Yalta.

Our correspondence had begun again when I left for Moscow, at the beginning of August, and ended with the arrival of Anton Pavlovich in Moscow with the play *The Three Sisters*.

When Anton Pavlovich read *The Three Sisters* to us, the performers and directors who had long awaited a new play from our favorite writer, there was perplexity and silence. Anton Pavlovich gave a confused smile and paced up and down among us, coughing nervously. Then came individual attempts to pass some comment, and one could hear: "It's not a play, just the outline." "It can't be performed, there aren't any roles, only the suggestion of them." It was hard work, and we had to dig deeply into our hearts.

Several years passed, however, and we asked ourselves in amazement how it was possible that this, our favorite play, so full of emotions, so profound, so significant, so able to reach the deepest and finest qualities of the human heart, had once appeared to us to be not a play but only an outline, and we had been able to say that it contained no roles.

In 1917, after the October Revolution, one of the first plays we performed was *The Three Sisters*, and we had the feeling that previously we had performed it without thinking, not appreciating the significance lodged in the thoughts and emotions, and—above all—in the dreams. It was as if the entire play sounded different, and one could feel that these were not just dreams but presentiments, and that indeed "something huge will overwhelm us" and a strong storm will sweep away "the idleness and complacency in our society, the prejudice against work and the stagnant boredom."[69]

In the middle of December, Anton Pavlovich left for the south of France, for Nice, where he lived for about three months and was very concerned about the progress being made at the theater with the production of *The Three Sisters*.

In Moscow he watched *When We Dead Awaken*. Anton Pavlovich seemed to view Ibsen with mistrust and a smile, seeing him as complex, difficult, and philosophizing. Anton Pavlovich also felt no particular sympathy for the production of *Snow White;*[70] he said that we should not stage such plays for the moment, but stay with plays like *Einsame Menschen*.

Our renewed correspondence continued from 11 December 1990 to 18 March 1901. At the beginning of April, I went to Yalta for a short stay, and from the middle of April (to the middle of May) we exchanged letters again.

Such were the external facts. Within, however, a feeling was growing and strengthening which required definite decisions, and I decided to unite my life with that of Anton Pavlovich, despite his weak health and my own love for the stage. I had faith that life could and should be wonderful, and it became so, despite our sad separations—for they always ended in the joy of reunion. It seemed to me that life with such a man would not be frightening or difficult: he had such an ability to push aside the weeds, all the trifles of life, all that was unnecessary, darkening and soiling the very essence and charm of life.

In the middle of May 1901, Anton Pavlovich came to Moscow. On 25 May, we were married and then went down the Volga, Kama, and Byelaya to Ufa, and thence by train for about six hours to the Andreyevsky sanitarium, near the Aksyonovo railway station. En route we visited Gorky in Nizhny Novgorod, where he was under house arrest.

We had to stay at the Pyany Bor landing stage (the Kama) for a whole day and night, and we spent the night on the floor of a simple cabin a few versts from the landing stage, but we were unable to sleep as we did not know when the boat to Ufa might arrive. During the night and at dawn we had to go out several times to see if a boat had appeared. This night, spent cut off from the civilized world, a majestic night memorable for its calm seriousness, awesome beauty, and quiet dawn, made a powerful impression on Anton Pavlovich; and in his notebook, in which he noted down all his thoughts and impressions, there is a comment on Pyany Bor.

In Aksyonovo, Anton Pavlovich liked the scenery, the long shadows on the steppe after six, the snorting of the horses in the herd, the flora, the Dema (Aksakovskaya) River, where we once went fishing. The sanitarium stood in a beautiful oak forest, but it was very primitive, and the lack of amenities made living there very inconvenient. I even had to go to Ufa for pillows. At first Anton Pavlovich liked the taste of koumiss, but soon he began to weary of it, and before the six weeks were over we left for Yalta via Samara, along the Volga to Tsaritsyn and Novorossiisk. We stayed in Yalta till 20 August, and then I had to return to Moscow: work at the theater had recommenced.

Again came separations and meetings, only parting became even more painful, and after a few months I began to think seriously of whether I ought to leave the stage. However, this raised another question: did Anton Pavlovich need simply a wife cut off from the outside world? I sensed in him a solitary man who, perhaps, would find such an upheaval in his and another's life burdensome. Moreover, he greatly valued the link through me with the theater which had aroused his most lively interest.

I could not but recall with particular sharpness all these questions when, many years later, with the publication of his correspondence, I read the words he wrote to A. S. Suvorin in 1895: "Please, I shall marry if that is what you want. But my conditions: everything must be as it was before, that is, she must live in Moscow, and I in the country (he was then living in Melikhovo), and I will go to see her. A happiness which continues from day to day, from morning to morning, is one I cannot support. I promise to be an excellent husband, but give me a wife who, like the moon, will not appear in my sky every day."

At the time I knew nothing of these words but felt that he needed me to be as I was. Nonetheless, after my serious illness in 1902, I talked seriously with our directors about leaving the theater but met strong resistance. Anton Pavlovich also protested, although he refrained from any final decision. I understood the reason for his restraint, but we never expressed it in words, never spoke of that which prevented us from uniting our lives completely, and it was only in my letters that there appeared implication, suspicion, and occasionally irritation.

So life flowed on—in bursts, and with an even more frequent exchange of letters during our separation.

From this time on, the life of Anton Pavlovich was divided more than ever before between Moscow and Yalta. Frequent meetings and farewells at the Kursk Railway Station in Moscow and at a railway station in Sebastopol began. He had to live in Yalta, but was "drawn" constantly to Moscow. He wanted to be closer to life, to observe it, feel it, take part in it; he wanted to be with people, and although they sometimes wearied him with their conversation, yet nonetheless he could not live without them: it was not in his power to refuse a man who had come to see and talk to him.

He was attracted to Yalta at first purely by the building of his house, the laying out of the garden, and the organizing of his life there; later he grew accustomed to it, although he called it his "warm Siberia." He was constantly drawn to Moscow to be closer to the theater, to be among the actors, attend rehearsals, chat, joke, watch performances. He loved to walk along Petrovka, along Kuznetsky, looking at the shops and the crowds. However, he was unable to be in Moscow during its most animated period. It was only in the winter of 1903–1904 that the doctors allowed him to stay in Moscow, and he was so happy and so savored the snowy, truly Moscow winter, happy that he was able to attend the rehearsals, happy as a child over his new fur coat and beaver hat.

That winter we looked for a plot of land with a house near Moscow so that Anton Pavlovich could in the future spend the winter close to his dearly beloved Moscow (it did not occur to anyone that the end was so near). So, one sunny February day we went to Tsaritsyno to look at a small house which had been proposed to us. On the way back (either we had missed the train, or else it had not come), we had to cover about thirty versts in a horse-drawn sledge. Despite the quite bitter frost, Anton Pavlovich so enjoyed the sight of the flat expanse of white glittering in the sun and the crackle of the runners over the firmly packed snow! It was as if fate had decided to indulge him and had given him in the last year of his life all those joys which he so treasured: Moscow, and winter, and the staging of *The Cherry Orchard,* and the people he so loved.

Work on *The Cherry Orchard* was difficult, I would even say painful.

The directors and the author could not understand each other or reach agreement.

All's well that ends well, however, and after all the obstacles, difficulties, and sufferings amidst which *The Cherry Orchard* was born, we have performed it from 1904 to the present day without ever removing it from our repertoire, whereas other plays have been left to rest for one, two, even three years.

We first performed *The Cherry Orchard* on 17/30 January 1904, on Anton Pavlovich's name day. This first performance was a day of tribute to Chekhov by men of letters and friends. It exhausted him; he did not like demonstrative celebrations and even refused to come to the theater. He was very anxious over the production of *The Cherry Orchard,* and came only when he was fetched.

The first performance of *The Seagull* was a triumph in the theater, and the first performance of his last play was also a triumph. But how different these two triumphs were! There was a restless mood, something menacing in the air. I do not know, perhaps these events are now colored by all that followed, but that there was no note of pure joy on that evening of 17 July is a fact. Anton Pavlovich listened very attentively, very seriously to all the greetings, but from time to time he tossed back his head in a characteristic gesture, and it seemed that he viewed all that was happening from the height of a bird in flight, that he was purely a spectator. His face was illuminated by his gentle, radiant smile, and the familiar wrinkles appeared by his mouth—he had doubtless heard something amusing, which he would later recall and at which he would certainly laugh with his childlike laugh.

Anton Pavlovich was extraordinarily fond in general of anything amusing, of anything in which one could feel humor. He loved to listen to amusing stories, and he would sit in his corner, his hand supporting his head, plucking at his beard and laughing so infectiously that I would myself often stop listening to the story teller and perceive the story through Anton Pavlovich. He was very fond of magicians and clowns. I recall how once, in Yalta, we stood for a long time, unable to tear ourselves away from the inexhaustible flow of tricks performed by trained fleas. He loved to invent—easily, elegantly, and very amusingly, a feature of the Chekhov family as a whole. At the beginning of our acquaintance, for example, a major role was played by "Nadenka," the supposed wife or fiancée of Anton Pavlovich, and this Nadenka figured everywhere, in all our relations—she even found her way into our letters.

Just a few hours before he died he made me laugh with a story he invented. This was in Badenweiler. After three anxious, weary days, he felt better towards the evening. He sent me to get some fresh air in the park, as I had never left his side during those three days; and when I returned, he worried about the fact that I was not going to supper, to which I replied that the gong had not yet sounded. It turned out later that we had simply not heard it, but Anton Pavlovich began to invent a story in which he described an extremely fashionable resort with its many prosperous, plump bankers, healthy, food-loving, red-cheeked Englishmen and Americans, and how, on returning from an excursion, from skating, from a walk—in short, from all sides—they gathered in the hope of eating well and amply after the physical tiredness of the day. Then, suddenly, it turns out that the chef has left, and there is no supper at all—and how this blow to the stomach affected all these spoiled people. I was sitting curled up on the divan after the anxieties of the previous three days and shaking with laughter. It could never have crossed my mind that only a few hours later I would be standing before mortal remains!

In the last year of his life, Anton Pavlovich had the idea of writing a play. It was still not clear, but he told me that the hero of the play, a scholar, was in love with a woman who either did not love him or was unfaithful to him, and the scholar left for the Far North. He imagined the third act as follows: there is a boat surrounded by ice, the Northern Lights, the scholar is standing all alone on the deck, silence, the calm and majesty of the night, and against the background of the Northern Lights he sees the shade of the woman he loves.

Anton Pavlovich passed away peacefully. He awoke in the early hours of the night, and for the first time in his life himself requested that the doctor be sent for. The sensation of something tremendous approaching lay over everything I did, an extraordinary calm and precision, as if someone were confidently guiding me. I remember only a horrific moment of confusion: the sensation of the proximity of a crowd of people in the large, sleeping hotel, and at the same time the feeling of being totally alone and helpless. I recalled that some Russian students we knew were staying in this very hotel—two brothers—and I asked one of them to run for the doctor, and myself went to break up some ice to lay on the heart of the dying man. I can still hear, as if it were now, in the oppressive stillness of a dreadfully stifling July night, the sound of steps receding over the crunching sand.

The doctor arrived and ordered champagne. Anton Pavlovich sat up and loudly informed the doctor in German (he spoke very little German), "Ich sterbe."

He then took a glass, turned his face towards me, smiled his amazing smile and said, "It's a long time since I drank champagne," calmly drained his glass, lay down quietly on his left side, and shortly afterwards fell silent forever. The dreadful silence of the night was disturbed only by a huge black moth which burst into the room like a whirlwind, beat tormentedly against the burning electric lamps, and flew confusedly around the room.

The doctor left, and in the silence and heat of the night, the cork suddenly jumped out of the unfinished bottle of champagne with a terrifying bang. It began to grow light, and as nature awoke, the gentle, melodious song of the birds came like the first song of mourning, and the sound of an organ came from a nearby church. There was no human voice, no bustle of human life, only the beauty, calm, and majesty of death.

Awareness of grief, of the loss of such a man as Anton Pavlovich, came only with the first sounds of awakening life, with the arrival of people; and what I experienced and felt, standing on the balcony and looking now at the rising sun, now at nature melodiously awaking, now at the fine, peaceful face of Anton Pavlovich, which seemed to be smiling as if he had just understood something—that, I repeat, still remains for me an unresolved mystery. There had never been such moments as those before in my life, and there never will be again.

1921–1933

K. A. Korovin

First published in *Russia and Slav Culture,* Paris, No. 33, 1929.
Konstantin A. Korovin (1861–1939)—one of a whole pleiad of major
Russian artists at the turn of the century. He studied at the Moscow
College of Painting, Sculpture, and Architecture, together with the
brother of the writer, Nikolai Chekhov, and the later famous landscape painter Isaac Levitan (1860–1900). He became a close friend of
the Chekhov family.

    1. A mistake: Nikolai Chekhov lived on the ground floor, and Anton, a
student at the medical faculty of Moscow University, often went there to
study.
    2. Also inaccurate: Levitan did not receive the large silver medal, but
only the small in 1877 and 1882.
    3. These final examinations took place in 1884.
    4. One of the leading Russian newspapers in Moscow (1863–1918),
liberal in tone.

V. G. Korolenko

First published in the journal *Russkoye bogatstvo,* No. 7, 1904.
Vladimir G. Korolenko (1853–1921)—Russian writer who had connections with the student revolutionary movement in his youth and
spent several years in exile in Siberia. Later he became active in public life, and more than once took up the defense of people subjected
to arbitrary police action under the autocracy. The literary critics of
the day often compared him to his junior contemporary, Chekhov,
sometimes preferring one, sometimes the other. This, however, did not
affect the friendship between the two writers.

    5. *Tales of Melpomene* was published in 1884, and *Motley Stories* in 1886
under the pseudonym A. Chekhonte. Some of the editions of the second

contained a vignette written, however, not by Chekhov but by F. O. Shekhtel, then a famous architect who had studied with Nikolai Chekhov.

6. Alexander S. Suvorin (1834–1912)—publicist, belletrist, and dramatist, who began writing in the 1860s in a liberal spirit, but gradually moved to the right, particularly when he began to publish the newspaper *Novoye Vremya,* which Saltykov-Shchedrin acidly named "What do you want?" He quickly recognized the talent of Chekhov, invited him to cooperate in his newspaper, and acted as his patron. Chekhov valued his intelligence and support and was on friendly terms with him for a long time. They conducted an active correspondence, but, as can be seen from a number of published letters, he did not hesitate to express his sharp disagreement with a number of Suvorin's views and the general position of *Novoye Vremya.*

7. Dmitry V. Grigorovich (1822–1899)—famous Russian writer who wrote Chekhov a letter full of admiration for his talent, which raised him "far above the circle of writers of the new generation."

8. Nikolai K. Mikhailovsky (1842–1904)—Russian sociologist, publicist, literary critic, and populist.

9. Gleb I. Uspensky (1843–1902)—Russian writer and publicist.

10. Sergei N. Yuzhakov (1849–1910)—Russian publicist and economist, and liberal populist.

11. Alexei N. Pleshcheyev (1825–1893)—Russian poet. He had a warm regard for the young Chekhov and did all he could to assist the publication of his works in *Severny vestnik.*

12. The stories "The Clever Janitor" and "At the Barber's" (1883).

13. Later Chekhov left this story out of the collection of his works. However, it contains absolutely no "cynical notes."

14. Lines from the poem "The Railway" by Nikolai Nekrasov (1821–1877/78).

15. Vsevolod M. Garshin (1855–1888)—Russian writer. Not long before his death he responded enthusiastically to Chekhov's "The Steppe." In the story "Nervous Breakdown," Chekhov describes a man of Garshin's type, a man who reacts with particular sensitivity to any form of injustice.

16. A reference to their joint decision to leave the Academy of Sciences (The Imperial Academy of Sciences), after the annulment of Maxim Gorky's election as an honorary academician.

17. A novel by the German writer Wilhelm Polenz.

T. L. Shchepkina-Kupernik

First published in the collection *A. P. Chekhov,* Leningrad, 1925; extensively revised for the second edition published in 1952.

Tatiana L. Shchepkina-Kupernik (1874–1952)—writer and translator, great-granddaughter of the famous actor M. S. Shchepkin. She first met Chekhov in 1893.

18. Today the house has been reconstructed.

19. Anatoly F. Kony (1844–1927)—Russian lawyer and public figure.

20. Nikolai M. Yezhov—belletrist and satirist with the newspaper *Novoye Vremya*.

21. Chekhov completed the first variant of *The Seagull* in November 1895.

22. Play written by the Russian author Bolislav Markevich.

23. This refers to relations between L. S. Mizinova and I. N. Potapenko.

24. Melikhovo was sold in August 1899.

V. I. Nemirovich-Danchenko

Published for the first time in V. I. Nemirovich-Danchenko, *From the Past,* Moscow, Academia, 1936.

Vladimir I. Nemirovich-Danchenko (1858–1943)—Russian writer, dramatist, and theater director who, together with Stanislavsky, created the Moscow Arts Theater, which virtually opened up Chekhov's plays for the spectator. Engraved on the badge which Chekhov presented Nemirovich-Danchenko were the words: "You gave life to my Seagull. Thank you!"

25. To the publisher A. F. Marks.

26. The opening lines of a poem by Afanasy Fet (1820–1892), which was considered to be a classic example of "art for art's sake."

27. Lines from a poem "The Sowers" (1876–1877) by N. A. Nekrasov, and "Forwards Without Fear Or Doubt" (1846) by A. N. Pleshcheyev.

28. Nemirovich-Danchenko is mistaken: both vaudevilles were written after *Ivanov,* in 1888.

29. The play was not a success, in part because of the novelty of the form, which the author had still not fully mastered, and in part because of theatrical intrigues.

30. Alexander N. Ostrovsky (1823–1886)—Russian dramatist and creator of a realist dramatic repertoire for the Russian theater.

31. Judging by the entries in Suvorin's diary for 11 February 1897, Lev Tolstoy identified "autobiographical features" in Trigorin's monologue.

M. M. Chitau

First published in *Zveno,* Paris, No. 201, 1926.
Maria M. Chitau (1860–1935)—an actress with the St. Petersburg Alexandrinsky Theater (1878–1900). From 1900 she was engaged in pedagogical work. Chitau was the first to perform the role of Masha in *The Seagull,* which opened at the Alexandrinsky Theater on 17 October 1896.

M. M. Kovalevsky

First published in *Birzheviye Vedomosti,* No. 15185, 2 November 1915. Maxim M. Kovalevsky (1851–1916)—lawyer, historian, and sociologist. Dismissed in 1887 from his post as a professor at Moscow University for his "free thinking," he left for France. He delivered lectures in Paris and Brussels. In 1901 he founded the Russian High School of Social Sciences in Paris.

32. Characters in *The Refuge of Mon Repos* (1878–1879) by Saltykov-Shchedrin who epitomized the predatory bourgeoisie.
33. A mistake: Chekhov's work was not published in this newspaper.

K. S. Stanislavsky

First published in *The Yearbook of the Moscow Arts Theater, 1943,* Moscow, 1945. In part—the chapter *"The Cherry Orchard"*—in K. Stanislavsky, *My Life in the Arts,* Moscow, 1925.
Konstantin S. Stanislavsky (1863–1938)—Russian actor, director, and producer. With V. Nemirovich-Danchenko, he founded the Moscow Arts Theater and produced plays; he was also manager and leading actor of the company; he is best known for his innovative "method" system of acting.

34. They probably met on 3 November 1888, in Moscow, at the opening ceremony of the Society of Arts and Literature.
35. F. O. Shekhtel.
36. A reference to Chekhov's telegram to the Moscow Arts Theater: "Sitting in Yalta like Dreyfus on Devil's Island" (the island to which Dreyfus had been exiled).
37. Leopold A. Sulerzhitsky—writer, artist, one of the directors of the Moscow Arts Theater.

38. A reference to the collected works to be published by A. F. Marks.

39. Savva T. Morozov—manufacturer and one of the managing directors of the Moscow Arts Theater.

40. Vladimir A. Gilyarovsky (1853–1935)—writer and journalist.

41. A carriage from the Iberian Chapel on Red Square from which the icon of the Iberian Madonna was taken to people's homes for a prayer service.

42. A mistake: Chekhov knew nothing about the planned celebration (in connection with twenty-five years of literary activity) and simply left for the theater towards the end of the third act, when people came for him and told him that the play was clearly a success.

Maxim Gorky

First published in the *Nizhegorodsky Sbornik*, Znaniye, St. Petersburg, 1905. Supplement in the book: M. Gorky, *Notes from a Diary, Recollections,* Berlin, 1942.
Maxim Gorky (real name Alexei M. Peshkov, 1868–1936)—Russian Soviet writer and public figure, the author of many novels, tales, short stories, plays, and other works.
Late in October 1898, Gorky sent Chekhov his first two books, *Sketches and Stories* (Vols. 1 and 2), and his first letter. Thus began their correspondence. Personal acquaintance took place in Yalta on 19 March 1899.

43. This house was acquired by Chekhov in 1898, before the house in Yalta was built, and was later given to his brother Ivan.

44. Chekhov is exaggerating slightly the meaning of a review of *Motley Stories* written by a critic in 1886.

45. A mistake or, perhaps, a satirical exaggeration: shortly after Chekhov's funeral, Gorky wrote to his wife about the "crowd" waiting to meet the coffin, "perhaps three to five thousand."

46. From the poem "Thoughts and Dreams" by Heine (translation into Russian by P. Weinberg).

47. A quotation from the poem "The Fragrance of the Sun" by the Russian symbolist poet K. D. Balmont (1867–1942).

I. A. Bunin

First published (part 1) in the almanac of the *Znaniye* fellowship for 1904, Book 3, St. Petersburg, 1905. The second part, written in 1914, was first published in the collected works of I. A. Bunin (Vol. 6, 1915). The supplements are taken from the book *About Chekhov* by Bunin (New York, 1955).

Ivan A. Bunin (1870–1953)—Russian writer, winner of the Nobel prize (1933), author of the novel *The Life of Arsenyev* (1930), a number of tales and dramatic novellas about love, and memoirs. Bunin made the acquaintance of Chekhov on 12 or 14 December 1895. Their next meeting was in 1898 or 1899 in Yalta. They became close during the years from 1900 to 1904. Bunin emigrated in 1920.

48. *Skorpion*—a publishing house in Moscow which issued the latest West European literature and books by Russian symbolists. Chekhov is referring to the almanac *Severny tsvety* published by Skorpion.

49. Alexandra A. Davydova (1848–1902)—publisher of the journal *Mir Bozhi*.

50. Phrases from *The Cherry Orchard*.

51. From the article about Chekhov entitled "Creativity out of Nothing" in the book *Beginnings and Ends* (1908) by the Russian philosopher L. Shestov.

52. Possibly Chekhov was thinking of the symbolist poet I. I. Oreus.

53. In the novel *Anna Karenina* (part II, chapter IV).

54. Nikolai A. Dobrolyubov (1836–1861)—Russian literary critic, journalist, and revolutionary democrat.

55. The name of a book by P. Sergeyenko.

56. "Honor thy father and thy mother."

57. Isaac A. Sinani—owner of a bookshop in Yalta.

58. Vlas M. Doroshevich—a well-known journalist.

59. A portrait of Chekhov by the artist Nilus hangs in the memorial house of A. P. Chekhov in Moscow.

60. Sergei A. Naidyonov (real name Alexeyev)—a writer and playwright.

61. A mistake: he did not complete the mathematics course.

62. The premiere of *The Lower Depths* by Gorky took place in the Arts Theater on 17 December 1902.

63. Vasily O. Klyuchevsky (1841–1911)—a prominent Russian historian.

O. L. Knipper-Chekhova

First published in *The Yearbook of the Moscow Arts Theater, 1949–1950,* Moscow, 1952.

Olga L. Knipper-Chekhova (1869–1959)—an actress with the Moscow Arts Theater from its foundation, and the wife of A. P. Chekhov.

64. *La Bottega di Caffè* (1753)—a comedy by K. Goldoni.
65. Words spoken by Nina Zarechnaya in the fourth act of *The Seagull*.
66. Anton S. Arensky—a composer.
67. Victor M. Vasnetsov—an artist.
68. Maria N. Yermolova—an actress at the Maly Theater.
69. The words of Tusenbach in the first act of *The Three Sisters*.
70. A play by A. N. Ostrovsky.

LETTERS

*All his life Anton Chekhov lived on his
inner wealth, he was always himself,
possessed inner freedom, and never took
account of what some expected from Anton
Chekhov, and others, more vulgarly,
demanded from him.*

MAXIM GORKY

To Alexander P. Chekhov[1]

Dear Brother of Quality, Alexander Pavlovich,

First off let me congratulate you and your better half on the successful outcome and arrival, and the town of Taganrog on its newest citizen. May she live (cross yourself!) for many years and enjoy a superabundance (cross yourself!) of beauty of body and soul, a superabundance of wealth, eloquence, and sense. May she catch a husband of valor in time (cross yourself, you fool!), having first slain all the gymnasium boys!

Now that I have congratulated you, I shall get right down to business. Nikolka[2] just thrust your letter at me. For lack of time let us leave aside the question of the right "to read it or not." Had the letter solely concerned Nikolka's person I would content myself with congratulations, but your letter immediately raises several highly interesting questions, which I would like to take up. In passing I shall answer all the previous messages you have sent. Unfortunately, I do not have time to write much, as I ought. For the sake of plausibility and thoroughness I shall fall back on a framework, a system: I intend to pick your letter apart, thread by thread, from A to Z inclusive. I am a critic and your letter is a work of literary interest. I have the right, as a reader. Take the perspective of an author, and everything will be fine. Speaking of which, it would not hurt us writers to try our hand at criticism. A word of warning is in order: the questions cited above are the whole point; I shall try to ensure that my exposition contains nothing of a personal nature.

1) That Nikolka is wrong is not worth pursuing. Your letters are not the only ones that go unanswered: he does not even reply to business letters. I know of no one who is more discourteous in this respect. For a year now he has been getting ready to write Lentovsky,[3] who is looking for him; a letter from one upstanding individual has been lying on a shelf for half a year, lying unanswered, and the only reason it was written was to elicit an answer. It would be hard to find a more happy-go-lucky individual than our dear brother. And worst of all, he is incorrigible. You moved him to pity with your letter, but I do not think he found the time to write back. That is not the point, though. I shall start with the form of the letter.

I remember how you used to laugh at Uncle's manifestos. You were laughing at yourself. Your manifestos contend with Uncle's in their mawkishness. They have everything: "embrace," "lacerated soul." All that remained was for you to shed a few tears. If Uncle's letters are to be believed, he should have cried his eyes out long ago. (The provinces!) You weep from the beginning of the letter to the end. In all your letters and, come to think of it, all your writings—from the sound of it, you and Uncle are two big tear ducts. I am not trying to be funny or exercise my wit. I would not have brought up the tearfulness, the shortness of breath brought on by joy or grief, the lacerated souls, et cetera, if they weren't so inopportune and baneful. Nikolka (as you well know) is lollygagging; a fine, powerful, Russian talent is going to ruin, and all for nothing. Another year or two and our artist will be done for. He will fade into that bar crowd, those base Yarons[4] and other scum. You have seen his recent work. What is he doing? He is doing banal, trivial stuff, while a marvelous painting stands unfinished in his room. Russky Teatr[5] offered to let him illustrate Dostoyevsky. He gave his word but he will not keep it, and those illustrations would have made his name and put bread on the table. What is there to say? You saw him half a year ago and have not forgotten, I hope. But now, instead of encouraging our talented, good-natured brother, giving him heart with a fine, uplifting message that would have been invaluable to him, you write pitiful, mournful words. You depressed him for half an hour, crushed him, debilitated him, and that was all. By tomorrow he will have forgotten your letter.

You are a superb stylist. You have read much, written much. You understand things as well as anyone else. It would not have been hard for you to write our brother something good. Not a lecture, though! If, instead of weeping, you had talked to him about painting he would doubtlessly have gotten down to work and answered you in all likelihood. You know how to influence him. "You've forgotten. . . . I'm writing for the last time." That is silly, that is not the point. That is not what you need to emphasize. You, who are strong, educated, mature, should emphasize what is vital, what is eternal, what touches true human feeling, not petty feeling. You can do it. After all, you are witty, you are realistic, you are an artist. If I were God I would forgive you all your sins of word and deed, consciously made or not, for your letter describing the church service on the piles (with Hatteras ice).[6] (Apropos: when Nikolka read your letter he had a tremendous urge to draw the piles.)

In your writings, too, you emphasize things of little consequence.

But you were not born a subjective hack. It is not innate, but something you have acquired. Renouncing that acquired subjectivity is as easy as pie. All you need is a little more integrity: remove yourself every time, do not inject yourself into the characters of your novel, forgo yourself for at least half an hour. You have a story[7] where newlyweds spend an entire dinner doing nothing but kissing, pouting, and chattering. Not one word of consequence, just *contentment!* You were not writing for the reader. You wrote it because you enjoy that twaddle. You should describe the dinner, how they eat, what the cook is like, how trite your hero is, smug in his indolent happiness, how trite your heroine is, how funny she is in her love for that full, goose-sated fellow with the napkin around his neck. Everyone likes to see sated, content people, it is true, but depicting them requires more than reporting what *they* said and how many times they kissed. You need to do something else: get away from the impression newlywedded bliss makes on every grouch.

Subjectivity is a terrible thing. One of its chief drawbacks is that it gives the poor author away lock, stock, and barrel. I will bet that all the priest's daughters and female dabblers in writing who have read your works are in love with you, and if you were a German you would be treated to beer on the house at all the beer halls where it is sold by German women. Were it not for that subjectivity, that Chmyrevism,[8] you would be one of the most valuable writers. You are so good at poking fun, stinging, deriding; you have such a well-rounded style; you have had a lot of experiences and seen an awful lot. Oh, good material is going to waste. If you had at least put it in your letter, encouraged Nikolka's imagination. Solid goods could be fashioned out of your material, not manifestos. You could be so beneficial! Try writing Nikolka once, twice something of consequence, something honest, good—after all, you are a hundred times smarter than he—write him and you shall see. He will reply, no matter how lazy he is. But do not write pitiful, debilitating words: he is debilitated as it is.

"It does not take much," you continue, "to see that by leaving I cut myself off from the family and condemned myself to oblivion." In other words, we have forgotten you. The fact that you yourself do not believe what you write is not even worth going into. There is no reason to lie, my friend. You could not have written that knowing the petulant disposition of Mother and Nikolai, who remembers the whole world and kisses it when drunk. Were it not for your tear ducts you would never have written that.

"I got what I expected. . . ." You want to get through to—you need to get through, you really do, but you will not with words like that. They are taken straight from "Little Sister,"[9] but you have more worthwhile things that you could quote to good effect.

2) "Father wrote that I have not lived up to expectation," et cetera. That is the hundredth time you have written that. I do not know what you want of Father. He is a sworn enemy of tobacco smoking and unlawful cohabitation—do you want to make him a friend of them? You can pull that off with Mother and Aunt, but not with Father. He is just as hardhearted as the schismatics, quite their match, and you will not get him to budge. That may well be his strength. However sweetly you write him, he will sigh, write you the same thing over and over again, and worst of all, suffer. As though you did not know him. Strange.

Forgive me, dear brother, but I think another significant factor is at work here, and a pretty unsavory one at that. You are not flying in the face of general opinion—you seem to be trying to ingratiate yourself with it. Why should you care how your cohabitation is regarded by one or another schismatic? Why are you making up to him, what are you looking for? Let him think as he pleases. It is his schismatic business. You know you are right—stand your ground, no matter what they write or how they suffer. An (uningratiating) protest is the whole point of life, my friend. Everyone has the right to live with whomever he chooses and however he chooses—that is the right of a mature individual, but you must not believe that if you find it necessary to send emissaries to the Pimenovnas and Stamatichs.[10] What is your cohabitation from your point of view? It is your nest, your warm weather, your grief and joy, your poetry, but you are treating that poetry as though it were a watermelon you had stolen—giving everybody suspicious looks (what does he think?), sticking it under everybody's nose, whining, moaning. If I were your family I would feel hurt, to say the least. You would like to know what I think, what Nikolai thinks, what Father thinks? What business is it of yours? They will not understand you, just as you did not understand "the father of six children," just as you did not understand Father's feelings. They will not understand, no matter how close they are, and there is no reason for them to do so.

Live your life and be done with it. It is impossible to feel for everybody at once, and you want us to feel for you. As soon as you see indifference on our faces, you start to moan. Lord, you are an odd one! If I were you and had a family, I would not even allow understanding to be expressed, let alone other opinions. It would be *mine,* my department, and no sisters would have the right (in the normal course of things) to stick their empathizing noses into my affairs! I would not write letters about the joy of fatherhood, either. They will not understand, and a manifesto will just make them laugh—and they will be right. You have gotten Anna Ivanovna thinking your way. Back in Moscow when she met us she shed bitter tears and asked, "Is thirty really too late?" As though we had asked her. It is our business what we thought; it is not yours to give us explanations. I would rather smite myself than allow my wife to cringe before my brothers, no matter how lofty those brothers were. There. It would make a good subject for a novel. There is no time to write one.

3) "I do not have the right to demand anything of our sister, she has not had time to form an unsullied opinion of me. And she does not yet know how to look into the heart of another. "Looking into the heart of another," does that not remind you of the village constable "reading hearts"?[11] You are right. Our sister loves you, but she does not have the slightest notion of you. The scenery you write about has only made her *afraid* to think about you. Quite naturally! Think, have you ever once talked to her normally? She is a big girl now. She has enrolled in higher education courses, taken up a serious science, become serious, but have you said or written one serious word to her? It is the same story as with Nikolai. You keep silent, so it is no wonder that she does not know you. Outsiders have done more for her than you, her own kin, have. She could gain much from you, but you are stingy. (You will not impress her with love, for love without good works is stillborn.)

She is going through a struggle right now, and such a desperate one, too! It is a wonder to watch! Everything that threatened to become her life's work has crumbled.[12] She could match any Turgenev heroine now. I am not exaggerating. You could not ask for more fertile ground! Instead you dash off all that sentimental stuff and then get angry that she does not write you! What would she write you? Once she sat down to write. She thought and thought and then wrote about Fedotova.[13] She wanted to write something else, but no one would assure her that her words would not come under the scrutiny of Tretyakov and Company[14]

I confess that I am too irritable when it comes to the family. I am irritable in general, frequently rude and unfair, but why does our sister tell me what she would never tell any of you? Probably because I have not regarded her merely as an "ardently loved sister," because I have not denied that she, like Mishka,[15] is a person who *needs* to be talked to. After all, she is a person, really and truly a person. You are trifling with her: you gave her a promissory note, bought a table on credit, bought a clock on credit. A fine example! Our parents shall not answer for it in the other world. It is not their doing.

"I shall pass over Anton in silence. You alone remained. . . ."

From the point of view of chivalry, I should keep silent and disregard this. But at the start of my letter I said I would not allow personal feelings to interfere. I shall avoid them here, too, and latch onto "the issue" alone. (It is awful how many issues there are!) There is in this world a nasty disease of which no writer, not one, can boast of being ignorant! *[The following passage is crossed out: They are many and we are few. Our camp is too small. It is sick. The people of one camp do not want to understand each other.]* I got carried away! I will have to do some crossing out. And you are familiar with it. It is Kicheyevism[16]—the unwillingness of people who belong to the same camp to understand each other. A vile disease! We are one of a kind, we share the same thoughts and ideals, we are kindred spirits, and all the same, we have the pettiness to write, "I shall pass over in silence!" How declamatory! There are so few of us that we must stick together—well, *vous comprenez!* However much we may have sinned against each other (and we have not sinned so very much!), we must respect whosoever is the least "like the salt of the earth."

We, I, you, the Tretyakovs, our Mishka are superior to thousands, not inferior to hundreds. We have a common task and it is clear: to think, to have a head on our shoulders. Whoever is not with us is against us. And we are disclaiming each other! Grumbling, whining, sulking, gossiping, spitting each other in the face! Think of how many Tretyakov and Company have spit on! They drank Bruderschaft with "Vasya"[17] and relegated the rest of mankind to the status of the unenlightened! I am stupid, I have not learned how to blow my nose, there is much I have not read, but I pray to your god—that is enough to make me worth my weight in gold to you! Stepanov is a fool, but he has a university education and he is a thousand times superior to Semyon Gavrilovich and Vasya, but he was forced to strike his temple against the edge of the piano after a cancan! It is disgraceful! A fine understanding of people, and a fine use of them! I would be a fine fellow if I put the dunce cap on Zembulatov[18] because he does not know about Darwin! He is a sworn enemy of serfdom though he was raised on it, and for that reason alone I love him! But if I were to start disavowing A, B, C . . . G, one person, a second, a third, I would wind up all alone!

We newspapermen have a disease—envy. Instead of rejoicing over your good fortune, you are envied and carp, carp! Meanwhile, everyone to a man prays to the same god, works towards the same end. Pettiness! Ill breeding of some kind. And how it all poisons life!

I need to get down to work, so I shall stop here and finish some other time. I have written this in a spirit of friendship, honestly; no one has forgotten you, no one has anything in particular against you, and there is no reason for me not to be friendly.

My respects to Anna Ivanovna and one Ma.[19]

Do you get *Oskolki?* Let me know. I sent you the confirmation of Leikin[20] himself.

And finally my regards,

A. Chekhov

Would you like some story ideas by any chance?

I certainly got carried away with this letter! About twenty rubles' worth! More, in fact.

TO NIKOLAI A. LEIKIN

MOSCOW, 21–24 AUGUST 1883

Dear Nikolai Alexandrovich;

The enclosed is not one of my successful efforts. The sketches are pallid, while the story is unpolished and terribly shallow. There are better topics, and I would have written more and produced something good, but fate was against me this time. The conditions I have for writing are the worst possible. Before me lies my nonliterary work, rapping my conscience mercilessly; in the next room a kid of a relative who has come to visit is screaming; in another room my father is reading "The Sealed Angel"[21] aloud to my mother. Somebody has wound up the music box and I can hear *Lovely Yelena.* I would like to go off to the dacha, but it is already one o'clock in the morning. Worse conditions for writing would be hard to imagine. My bed is occupied by a visiting relative who comes up every so often and starts a conversation about medicine. "My daughter must be screaming because she's got colic." I have the misfortune to be a physician, and there is not one individual who does not feel the need to "discuss" medicine with me. Whoever gets tired of discussing medicine, turns the conversation to literature.

The situation is without compare. I curse myself for not having gone off to the dacha where I probably would have caught up on my sleep and written you a story and, most importantly, medicine and literature would have been left in peace.

I shall take off for Voskresensk in September, weather permitting. Your last story delighted me greatly.

The kid is bawling! I vow never to have children. The French have few children, probably because they prefer to spend their time in their studies, writing stories for *Amusant*. I hear they want to make them have more children— a subject for a caricature in *Amusant* and *Oskolki:* "The State of Affairs in France." A police commissar comes in and orders those present to have children.

Adieu. I am thinking about where and how I can curl up and fall fast asleep.

I have the pleasure of being respectfully yours,

A. Chekhov

To Nikolai A. Leikin

Moscow, 12 October 1885

Dear Nikolai Alexandrovich;

Your letter reached me at my new apartment. It is beyond the Moskva River in a truly provincial spot: clean, quiet, cheap and a bit slow-witted. The pogrom at *Oskolki*[22] has left me stunned. On the one hand, I feel sorry about my pieces, on the other, it is somehow stifling, eerie. Of course you are right that it is better to cut back and plug the same theme than to strike the stone with the pitcher at risk to the journal. I shall have to bid my time and be patient. But I think I will have to cut back endlessly. What is permissible today will compel you to make a trip to the committee tomorrow, and the time is at hand when even merchants will be off limits. Yes, literature is a precarious way of earning a living, and you were smart to enter this world earlier, when it was easier to breathe and write.

I had not intended to send you anything this week. You had three things of mine, and I thought I could legitimately rest, especially since I am worn out by the move.[23] Having received your letter and learned the fate of my three things, I am sending you a story that I wrote not for *Oskolki* but for "in general," wherever it was best suited. The story is a bit long, but it is about actors which, given the season's opening, is highly appropriate and, I think, humorous. I shall sit down tomorrow and write "September and October and November"—if nothing like my practice, et cetera, interferes.

You advise me to go to St. Petersburg to talk to Khudekov,[24] and you say that St. Petersburg is not China. I know that it is not China, and as you are aware I realized a long time ago I need to make the trip, but what can I do? As my family is big I never have a spare ten rubles on hand, and even the most uncomfortable and straightened circumstances would require the expenditure of fifty rubles at least. Where can I obtain that kind of money? I would not know how to squeeze it out of my family, nor do I regard it as a possibility. Were I to cut meals down from two courses to one, I would wither away in remorse. I once hoped I would be able to extract the money for the trip from my pay from *Peterburgskaya Gazeta,* but now that I have started working for *Peterburgskaya Gazeta* I find that I earn no more than I did before, as I give it everything I formerly gave *Razvlecheniye, Budilnik,* et cetera. Allah alone knows how hard it is for me to make ends meet and how easy it is for me to go astray and founder. If I earn twenty or thirty rubles less next month I think the budget will go up in smoke, and I shall become entangled. When it comes to money I am awfully cowed, and it is probably because of this financial, certainly not commercial, timidity that I shy away from loans and advances. I am not adverse to travel. If I had the money I would always be on the road.

I received my fee from *Peterburgskaya Gazeta* two weeks after sending them the bill.

If you come to Moscow in October, I shall somehow arrange to go back with you. I shall find the money for the trip to St. Petersburg and get what I need for the return from Khudekov (earnings).

I cannot write any more than I do now, for medicine is not law: if you do not work you become stiff. Consequently, my literary earnings are a constant. They can be reduced, but not increased.

I shall be looking to receive *Oskolki* at my new address on Tuesday. It has been a long time since I received it regularly.

Congratulations on your new purchase. I am awfully fond of everything that goes by the name "estate" in Russia. That word has not yet lost its poetic overtones. You should enjoy a rest then this summer.

We are having frosty weather, but there is no snow.

Palmin was here and will be back on Tuesday. On Tuesdays I have gatherings that feature girls, music, song, and literature. I want to draw the poet into society, because he is feeling low.

Yours,

A. Chekhov

To Alexei S. Suvorin

Moscow, 21 February 1886

Dear Alexei Sergeyevich;

I have received your letter. Thank you for your flattering comments on my work and for promising to print my story soon. You can well judge what a rejuvenating and inspiring influence on my writing the kind attention of a person as experienced and talented as yourself has.

I share your view on the discarded conclusion of my story and thank you for useful suggestions. I have been writing for six years now, but you are the first person who did not find it troublesome to give instructions or motivate them.

The nom de plume A. Chekhonte probably is odd and recherché. However, it was chosen at the dawn of a vague youth, and I have become accustomed to it. Perhaps that is why I do not notice how odd it is.

My output is relatively low: no more than two or three short stories a week. I will have time to work for *Novoye Vremya* but am nevertheless glad that you have not made meeting strict deadlines a condition of becoming a contributor. Deadlines mean haste and a sense of being weighed down. Both make it harder to work. In my case deadlines are also inconvenient because I am a doctor and have a practice. I cannot give you any assurance that tomorrow I shall not be torn from my desk for the entire day. I run the continual risk of failing to meet the deadline and falling behind.

The fee you indicated is now quite sufficient. If you could have the newspaper sent to me I would be very grateful to you, as I rarely see it.

This time I am sending you a story that is exactly twice as long as the last one, and twice as bad, I am afraid.

I have the pleasure of being respectfully yours,

A. Chekhov

c/o Klimenkova, Yakimanka

To Dmitry V. Grigorovich

Your letter, dear, kind bearer of glad tidings, left me thunderstruck.[25] I could barely keep from crying, lost my composure, and now feel that it has left a deep mark on my soul. May God soothe your old age as you have shown kindness to my youth. I can find no way to thank you. You know how mere mortals look upon such members of the elect as you, so you can well judge what your letter has done for my self-esteem. It is better than any diploma, and for the novice writer it is remuneration for the present and future. I feel as though I were intoxicated. I do not have the power to judge my worthiness for this honor. I can only repeat that it has left me thunderstruck.

If I have a gift that ought to be respected, then I must confess to your pure heart that I have not respected it up to now. I sensed that I had one, but was accustomed to considering it meager. A body can find sufficient reasons of a purely external nature to be unjust towards itself, mistrustful and suspicious in the extreme. And, as I now recall, such reasons were sufficient in my case. Everyone in my family has always been patronizing toward my writing and has continually given me the friendly advice not to trade my current vocation for hack writing. I have hundreds of acquaintances in Moscow, a couple score write, but I cannot think of one who would read my work or regard me as an artist. There is a "literary circle" in Moscow: the talented and mediocre of every age and stripe gather once a week at a restaurant and give their tongues an airing. If I were to go there and read even a small portion of your letter to them, they would laugh in my face. In five years of roaming from newspaper to newspaper that general view of my literary insignificance was impressed upon me; I quickly became accustomed to regarding my work condescendingly and— went off to write! That is the first reason. The second is that I am a doctor and up to my ears in my medicine, so no one has lost more sleep over the saying about the two hares than I.

I say all this only to somewhat justify my grave sin in your eyes. Up to now the attitude I have taken to my literary work has been extremely lighthearted, flippant, feckless. I cannot remember working on a *single* story more than a day, and "The Hunter," which you liked, was written in a river bathhouse! I wrote my stories like reporters write up fires: mechanically, half-aware of what I was doing, concerned neither for the reader nor myself. I wrote and did everything I could to keep from wasting images and characters dear to me that I have perceived and carefully concealed, God knows why.

What first prompted me to take a critical look at my work was a very kind and, if I recall, honest letter from Suvorin. I made up my mind to write something worthwhile, but still I did not have faith in my literary worth.

And then your letter came out of the blue. Forgive the comparison, but it had the same effect on me as an order from the governor to "depart the city within twenty-four hours!" In other words, I suddenly felt the urgent need to get out of the spot I was stuck in as soon as I could.

I agree with you in every instance. I myself noticed the cynical moments you indicate when I saw "Witch" in print. Had I written that story over three or four days rather than in one, they would not have been there.

I shall free myself of work that must be done hastily, but not soon. There is no opportunity to get out of the rut I am in. I am not against starving and have done it before, but others are involved. I devote my free time to writing, two to three hours during the afternoon and a bit of the night, in other words, time that is only suitable for doing inconsequential work. In the summer, when I shall have more time and fewer expenses, I shall get down to serious work.

My real name cannot be put on the book because it is too late: the vignette is ready, and the book has been printed. Many Petersburgers before you advised me not to spoil the book with a pseudonym, but I did not listen, probably out of pride. I am very displeased with the book. It is mix, a hodgepodge of student pieces plucked over by the censors and the editors of humorous publications. I believe many people will be disappointed once they have read it. Had I known that you were reading my work and had your eye on me, I would not have published the book.

The future is my only hope. I am just twenty-six years old. Perhaps I shall manage to do something, although time is passing swiftly.

Kindly excuse the length of this letter and do not judge a man too harshly for having allowed himself the pleasure of writing to Grigorovich for the first time ever.

Please send me your photograph, if you could. You have flattered and excited me so that I feel I could write you not a quire but a whole foot. God grant you health and happiness, and please believe the sincerity of one who esteems you deeply and is gratefully yours,

A. Chekhov

To Nikolai P. Chekhov[26]

My dear little Zabelin,[27]

I was told that you are offended by the gibes Shekhtel and I have made. Only noble souls are capable of taking offense, however, if it is possible to laugh at Ivanenko,[28] at me, at Mishka, and at Nelly,[29] why is it not possible to laugh at you? That is not fair. But if you are not joking and really are hurt, I hasten to apologize.

People only laugh at things that are funny or that they do not understand. Take your pick.

The second is more flattering, of course, but—alas—you are not a cipher to me. It is not hard to understand someone with whom you have shared the delights of Tatar hats, Vuchina,[30] Latin, and finally, Moscow existence. Besides, your life is psychologically so straightforward that it is comprehensible even to someone who has not been to the seminary. I will be frank out of respect for you. You are angry and hurt, but the reason is not the gibes or Dolgov[31] with his amiable chatter. The reason is that, being a decent person, you sense that you are on the wrong track; and whoever thinks himself guilty inevitably tries to find some external justification: the drunk blames grief, Putyata[32] blames the censor, he who departs Yakimanka[33] for the sake of fornication blames the chilly room, gibes, and so forth. Were I to abandon the family to the whims of fate now, I would try to find vindication in Mother's character, blood-spitting, and so forth. That is natural and pardonable. Such is human nature. But it is also true that you sense you are on the wrong track, otherwise I would not call you a decent person. If you lose your decency it will be quite another matter: you will be reconciled to lies and stop knowing them for what they are.

It is also true that you are not a cipher to me, and at times I find you wildly funny. After all, you are a mere mortal, and we mortals are only enigmatic when we are stupid and funny forty-eight weeks of the year. Right?

You have often complained to me that you are "misunderstood"! Not even Goethe and Newton complained of that. Only Christ did, and even then he was speaking of his teachings, not himself. You are understood quite well. If you do not understand yourself, it is not the fault of others.

I assure you as a brother and someone who feels close to you that I understand you and sympathize with you with all my heart. I know all your good qualities like the back of my hand, value them, and have the most profound respect for them. If you like I can even list them to prove I understand you. In my opinion, you are kind to the point of spinelessness, generous, unegoistical, capable of sharing your last kopeck, sincere; envy and jealousy are alien to you, you are ingenuous, pity man and animal, and exhibit no greed, rancor, or mistrust. In addition you have been given something others have not: you are talented. That talent places you above millions, for there is only one artist for every two million people on earth. Your talent has set you apart: even if you were a toad or a tarantula you would still be respected, because a person with talent is forgiven everything.

You only have one failing. Your fallacious ways and your grief and your intestinal troubles can all be traced to it. It is your extreme ill breeding. Please forgive me, but *veritas magis amicitiae*.★ The fact of the matter is that life lays down certain rules. To feel at ease in an intellectual environment, to avoid sticking out and being a burden to it, you must be well bred in a certain way. Talent has brought you into that milieu, you belong to it, but you are being drawn away from it, and you must strike a balance between cultured society and the folks vis-à-vis. Philistine flesh that was raised on birchings, by the Rhein wine cellar and on crumbs, will out. Triumphing over that flesh is hard, terribly hard.

Well-bred people should, to my mind, observe the following rules of conduct:

1) They respect the individual, so they are always indulgent, gentle, courteous, tractable. They do not kick up a fuss over a hammer or lost eraser; when living with someone they do not represent it as a favor and when leaving do not say, "You're impossible to live with!" They forgive noise and cold and overcooked meat and jokes and the presence of visitors in their home.

2) They do not just pity the poor and cats. Their hearts ache, too, over things that are not plain to see. So for example, if Pyotr[34] knows that his father and mother are becoming gray out of anguish and do not sleep at night because they rarely see Pyotr (and if they do he is drunk), he will hurry back to them and give up vodka. They do not sleep at night so that they may help the Polevayevs, pay their brothers' university bills, and clothe their mother.

3) They respect others' property, so they pay their debts.

★ (Lat.) truth before friendship.

4) They are sincere and avoid lies like fire. They do not even lie about little things. Lies offend the person to whom they are told and lower the teller in his eyes. They do not pose or comport themselves in public as they would at home; they do not show off for their younger brothers. They are not gabby and do not force unsolicited candor on anyone. Out of respect for others' ears, they are frequently silent.

5) They do not disparage themselves with the aim of eliciting another's sympathy. They do not play on the strings of another's heart, so that he or she will sigh and join them in moaning. They do not say, "No one understands me!" or "I've squandered my talent!" because that tries for a cheap effect, vulgarly, stalely, hypocritically.

6) They are not vain. They are not interested in such fake diamonds as knowing celebrities, shaking the hand of Plevako[35] when he is drunk, having a thrilling encounter at the Salon, or being a familiar face at the bars. They laugh at the words "I am a representative of the press," which only suit Rodzevichs and Levenbergs.[36] When they have done a pittance they do not run around with their hundred-ruble paper case or brag that they were let into such and such a place while others were not. The truly gifted are always in the shadows, in the crowd, far from exhibitions. Even Krylov[37] said that an empty barrel rings louder than one that is full.

7) If they have talent they respect it. For its sake they sacrifice rest, women, wine, the hustle and bustle. They are proud of their talent. Consequently, they do not get drunk with the supervisors of a petty bourgeois school or Skvortsov's guests, for they realize that they are called to set them an example, not live with them. Moreover, they are fastidious.

8) They develop a sense of personal aesthetics. They cannot sleep in their clothes, see bugs in cracks in the walls, breathe bad air, walk on a floor covered with spittle, or cook on a kerosene stove. They do their best to curb and ennoble the carnal instinct—endure her logic, not take a step from her side—and all that for what! In that sense the well bred are not so parochial. What they need of a woman is not sex or sweat or native wit that expresses itself in the ability to fake pregnancy and lie tirelessly. They, artists in particular, need freshness, grace, humanity, the ability to be a mother, not a . . . . They do not guzzle vodka in passing or sniff cupboards, because they know they are not pigs. They only drink when they do not have any obligations to meet, when the opportunity arises, for they need *mens sana in corpore sano*.

And so on. Such are the well bred. To acquire breeding and avoid being inferior to the society in which you find yourself it is not sufficient to have read *Pickwick* and learned the monologue from *Faust* by heart. It is not sufficient to get in a cab and go to Yakimanka, only to take off a week later.

What is needed is unceasing work day and night, continuous reading, study, willpower. Every hour is precious.

Trips to Yakimanka and back will not help. You have to gather your courage and make a clean break. Come here, smash the vodka decanter, and lie down to read, at least Turgenev, whom you have not read.

You have to relinquish your pride: you are not a little boy anymore. You shall soon be thirty! It is high time!

I am waiting. We are all waiting.

Yours,

A. Chekhov

To Alexander P. Chekhov

Moscow, 10 May 1886

My Dear Mr. Alexander Pavlovich Chekhov,

If you have not changed your mind about writing me, send your letters to this address: Dr. Anton P., Voskresensk (Moscow Gubernia).

I am just back from St. Petersburg, where I spent two weeks and had a wonderful time. I have never come to such a great understanding with Suvorin and Grigorovich. There are too many details to relate in a letter, so I shall wait until I see you. Do you read *Novoye Yremya?*

"The City of the Future" is a splendid subject, both new and interesting. If laziness does not overtake you I think you will do a pretty good job with it, but God knows you are so lazy! "The City of the Future" will be a work of artistic merit only if the following conditions are met: 1) the absence of long passages of a politico-socio-economic nature; 2) objectivity throughout; 3) authenticity in the description of characters and settings; 4) extreme brevity; 5) audacity and originality, avoid clichés at all cost; 6) warmth.

In my opinion, descriptions of nature should be very short and apropos in character. Hackneyed phrases like "the setting sun, dipping into the waves of the now dark sea, spread a carpet of crimson and gold," "The swallows chirped merrily as they skimmed the surface of the water"—hackneyed phrases like that must go. In describing nature you need to latch onto small details, grouping them so that when you read the passage and close your eyes a picture forms. For instance, you can achieve a moonlit night if you write that a piece of glass from a broken bottle twinkled brightly on the mill dam, and the black shadow of a dog or wolf glided past, et cetera. Nature becomes animated if you do not balk at using analogies with human actions, et cetera.

Employ detail, too, when dealing with the human psyche. Lord preserve us from hackneyed phrases. It is best to avoid describing the mental state of your characters: try to let their actions speak. There is no need to strive for a large cast of characters. The focal point should be two people: him and her.

I tell you this as a reader with specific tastes. I also tell you this so you will not feel alone when you write. It is hard to do creative work alone. Better bad criticism than no criticism at all. Don't you agree?

Send me the beginning of your novel. I shall read it the day I get it and return it to you with my comments on the next. Do not be in a hurry to finish it, as not one Petersburger will read your manuscript before the middle of September—X is abroad, Y is at his country home.

I am glad that you have gotten down to business. At thirty years of age a man needs to be useful and display character. I am still a fop and can be excused for fooling around. Incidentally, my five stories in *Novoye Vremya* created a commotion in St. Petersburg that has left me singed.

Mishka has sent you your fee from *Sverchok* and *Budilnik*[38] in two installments.

And so, be healthy and do not forget your

A. Chekhov

The weather is bad: windy.

To Maria V. Kiseleva[39]

Moscow, 29 September 1886

Yesterday Alexei Sergeyevich gave me your "Galoshes," dear Maria Vladimirovna. As soon as he did I grinned maliciously, winked, gleefully rubbed my hands, and began to read.

You shall have my comments on "Galoshes" later. In the meantime I can say that the story is literary, lively, short, relative, and approximate. I think my comments shall be favorable.

The pen name Pince-nez is a good choice.

Of course, there is no need to assure you that I am very glad to be your literary-honorary hof-broker and cicerone. That office coddles my vanity and performing it is as easy as carrying your pail when you return from fishing. If you need to know my terms, then allow me to state them:

1) Write as much as possible! Write, write, write until your fingers break. (The main thing in life is penmanship!) Write in quantity, bearing in mind not so much the intellectual development of the masses as the fact that initially the better half of your vignettes will be rejected since you are new to the "minor press." As far as rejections are concerned, I shall not deceive, dissemble, or prevaricate—you have my word. But do not let rejections upset you. Even if you get back half you will still be better off than you would be working for *Children's Bohemian Leisure.*[40] As for pride, I do not know about you, but I became accustomed long ago.

2) Write on different subjects, amusing and melancholy, good and bad. Let's have stories, vignettes, anecdotes, jokes, puns, and so on and so forth.

3) Reworking foreign material is certainly not against the law, but only in the event that sinning against the eighth commandment does not bother you. (For "Galoshes" you are due in hell after 22 January!)[41] Avoid popular subjects. However obtuse our venerable editors may be, it is not easy to catch them up on the literature from Paris, especially when it comes to Maupassant.

4) Write in a single sitting and have complete faith in your quill. I can honestly say, without dissembling, that in comparison with you, eight out of ten writers in the minor press are cobblers and fodder.★

5) Brevity is regarded as the first virtue in the minor press. The best measure is stationery (the stuff I am using now). As soon as you get to page eight or ten, stop! Besides, stationery is easier to send. There you have all the terms.

Now that you have listened to the instructions of this brain and genius, please be so kind as to accept the assurance of my most sincere devotion. Should they wish, Alexei Sergeyevich, Vasilisa, and Sergei may have the same assurance, provided they sign for it.

I have still not seen widow Khludova. I go to the theater on occa-

---

★ In other words, drunks and failures.—Tr.

sion. Not one sweet. They are all phizedrons, mugetons and snoute-monds. It is quite horrible.

Good-bye and my respects to all.

Yours,

A. Chekhov

Life itself is gradually becoming one big snoutemondery. Things are gray and happy people are nowhere to be seen.

Nikolai is staying with me. He is seriously ill (a bleeding stomach, which has completely worn him down). Yesterday he gave me a bad scare, but today he has improved to the point that I am allowing him a spoonful of milk every half hour. He is lying there sober, meek, pale.

Everyone is wretched. On those occasions when I am serious it seems to me that anyone who is repulsed by death is irrational. As far as I have been able to make out the order of things, life consists solely of horrors, garbage, and vulgarities, converging and alternating. But now I have gotten into the vein of *Novoye Vremya* literature. Pardon me.

Ma-Pa[42] is well. There is no money.

To Maria V. Kiseleva

Moscow, 14 January 1887

Your "Larka" is very sweet, dear Maria Vladimirovna; there are some uneven moments, but the brevity and manly style make up for all that. Not wishing to be the sole judge of your creation, I have sent it to Suvorin, a man of great intelligence. I shall eventually let you know what he thought. But in the meantime permit me to snap at your criticisms. Even your praise of "En Route" has not softened my authorly wrath, and I hasten to avenge "The Mire."[43] Watch out and to keep from fainting take a tighter hold of the back of your chair. Here I go.

Every critical article, even that which is abusive and unjust, is usually greeted on the author's part with a silent bow—such is literary etiquette. Responding is not pleasant, and all who do are justly accused of excessive pride. However, as your criticism is of the nature of "an evening chat on the porch in Babkino or on the terrace of the owner's house, in the company of Ma-Pa, Forger,[44] and Levitan," and as your criticism passes over the literary aspect of the story and puts the matter in a general context, I shall not be committing a breach of etiquette if I allow myself to continue our discussion.

First of all, I, too, do not like the type of literature in question. Speaking as a reader and everyman, I make an effort to steer clear of it, but if you wish to know my honest and sincere opinion, then I must say that the question of its right to exist is still open and has not been resolved by anyone, though Olga Andreyevna[45] thinks she has. Neither you, nor I, nor the critics of the world have any solid facts that give us the right to repudiate that literature. I do not know who is correct: Homer, Shakespeare, Lope de Vega, and the ancients as a whole, who were not afraid to dig around in the "manure pile" but were much more upright than we are, or the modern writers, prim and proper on paper, but cold and cynical at heart and in life? I do not know who is in bad taste: the Greeks, who were not ashamed to praise love as it really is in wondrous nature, or the readers of Gaboriau, Marlit, and Pierre Bobo?[46] Like such questions as nonresistance to evil, freedom of will, et cetera, this can only be resolved by time. We can only bring it up; resolving it is beyond our competence. Citing Turgenev and Tolstoy, who avoided the "manure pile," does not clarify matters. Their squeamishness proves nothing: they were preceded by a generation of writers who thought not only that "scoundrels male and female" were filthy, but that even describing peasants and untitled bureaucrats was. Besides, no single period, however prolific, gives us the right to decide in favor of one or another trend. Citing the growing influence of the trend in question does not resolve the matter, either. Everything in this world is relative and approximate. There are people who are even corrupted by children's literature, who take special pleasure in reading the spicy parts of the Psalter and Solomon's parables, and there are those who become purer as they learn about life's filth. Journalists, lawyers, and physicians, who have been initiated into all the mysteries of human sin, are not known for their immorality; realist writers are often more moral than archimandrites. Besides, when all is said and done, no literature can surpass life for its cynicism; you cannot make a drunk inebriated with a single shot when he has already imbibed a whole barrel.

2) It is true that the world "is swarming with scoundrels, male and female." Human nature is imperfect, so it would be strange if the world were peopled solely by the righteous. Thinking that one of literature's duties is to dig the "kernel" out of the pile of scoundrels means denying literature's very essence. Literature has that name because it shows life as it really is. Literature's objective is the truth, unconditional and honest. Narrowing its functions down to something as specific as

extracting the "kernel" is as deadly for it as if you were to make Levitan draw a tree and ordered him not to touch the dirty bark or the yellow leaves. I agree that the "kernel" is a good thing, but a writer is not a confectioner or a cosmetician, or an entertainer; he is duty bound, obligated by the recognition of what he must do and by his conscience; in for a penny, he must not say that he is not in for a pound; and, no matter how awful he may find it, he is obliged to overcome his squeamishness and sully his imagination with the filth of life. He is like any ordinary reporter. What would you say about the reporter who, out of a feeling of squeamishness or a desire to please his readers, only wrote about honest mayors, exalted ladies, and virtuous railway men?

For the chemists there is no such thing as impurity in the world. A writer should be as objective as a chemist; he should renounce mundane subjectivity and recognize that manure piles in the landscape play a very honorable role, and evil passions are as natural as their virtuous counterparts.

3) Writers are children of their age, so they, like everyone else, should bow to social convention. Thus, they must be irreproachably proper. That is all we have the right to demand of realists. Incidentally, you do not say anything against the manner of execution or form of "The Mire." I must have been proper.

4) I confess that I rarely confer with my conscience when I write. Put it down to habit and the shallowness of my work. Therefore, when I propound one or another opinion on literature, I do not have myself in mind.

5) You write, "Were I an editor, I would have returned that satire to you for your own good." Why not go one step further? Why not take to task the editors who print such stories? Perhaps a stern reprimand should also be issued to the Chief Administration for Press Affairs for failing to ban immoral newspapers?

Literature (great and small) would have a sorry fate if it were to be put at the mercy of personal opinion. That is one. Secondly, there is no police force that would consider itself qualified to regulate literary affairs. I agree that bridles and sticks are necessary to keep cheats from worming their way into literature, but, think what you may, literature could not be better policed than it is by the critics and the writer's own conscience. After all, inventions have been made since the creation of the world, but nothing better has been invented.

You would like to see me suffer a loss of 115 rubles and be raked over the coals by my editor. Others, including your father, were delighted by the story. A fourth group has been sending Suvorin abusive letters that revile the newspaper and me, et cetera. Who is right? Who is the real judge?

6) You continue, "Permit the like to be written by scribblers as poor in spirit and slighted by fate as Okreits,[47] Pince-nez, Aloe." Allah forgive you if you were being sincere when you wrote those lines! Adopting a condescending, disdainful tone towards little people for the mere reason that they are little does not do the human heart honor. The lower ranks are as essential to literature as they are to the army— so says the head, and the heart should say it even more.

Ugh! I have wearied you with my rumination. Had I known that my critique would be so long, I would never have undertaken it. Please forgive me!

Devotedly and Respectfully Yours,

A. Chekhov

TO VLADIMIR G. KOROLENKO

Thank you very much, Vladimir Galaktionovich, for the book[48] which I have received and am now rereading. As you already have my books, I can unfortunately only send you these thanks.

Incidentally, to keep this letter from being altogether brief, I can tell you that I am extremely happy to have made your acquaintance. I say this sincerely and without ulterior motive. First, I deeply value and admire your talent, it is dear to me for many reasons. Second, I think that if you and I are to live another ten to twenty years in this world we will undoubtedly find we have certain things in common. Of all the successful Russian writers today, I am the most frivolous and least serious; I am in bad standing with myself. To use the language of the poets, I loved my pure-hearted muse but did not respect her; I cheated on her and took her more than once to places that were not befitting of her. You, however, are serious, stalwart and true. As you can see, the difference between us is great. Nevertheless, having read your work and, now, having made your acquaintance, I do not think we are alien spirits. Perhaps I am not right, but it pleases me to think I am.

Incidentally, I am sending you a clipping from *Novoye Vremya*. I shall cut out and save the Thoreau[49] it mentions. The first chapter is very promising: thoughtful, fresh, and original, but hard reading. The architecture and construction are impossible. Beautiful and ugly, ponderous and imponderous thoughts pile up, one on top of another, crowd together, squeeze the juices from one another, and seem on the verge of squealing in the crush.

When you come to Moscow I will hand Thoreau over to you, but in the meantime I bid you farewell and wish you health.

My play will probably be staged at the Korsh. If so, I will let you know what day it is to be performed. Perhaps it will coincide with your visit to Moscow. Should that be so, I hope you will do me the honor.

Yours,

A. Chekhov

To Alexander P. Chekhov

I received a letter from Suvorin of which I could barely make head or tail. It is incomprehensible: how do his typesetters read his handwriting? Of his play he writes, "I sweated and sweated over my comedy only to abandon it after taking a look at real Russian life this summer." Well he should sweat! Modern playwrights cram their plays exclusively with nothing but angels, scoundrels, and jesters—just try and find those elements in all of Russia! Find them you may, but not in the extreme incarnations playwrights need. So willy-nilly you start to conjure them up, break into a sweat, and abandon the whole thing. I wanted to be original: I did not depict one villain or one angel (though I was unable to resist jesters); I did not blame anyone or vindicate anyone.[50] I do not know whether or not I succeeded. The play is sure to come off—Korsh and the actors are certain. I am not. The actors do not understand it; they babble and claim the wrong roles while I battle with them in the belief that if the play is not performed with the roles as I assigned them, it will flop. If they do not do as I wish, I shall have to withdraw the play to avoid disgrace. On the whole it is an upsetting and highly unpleasant business. Had I known I would never have gotten into it.

Your Ill-Wisher

To Alexander P. Chekhov

Well, the play went off. I shall describe everything as it occurred. First of all, Korsh promised me ten rehearsals but gave me only four, and only two of them could be called rehearsals, as the other two resembled tournaments at which the esteemed actors practiced their logomachy and epithets. Davydov and Glama[51] alone knew their parts; the others relied on the prompter and inner conviction.

Act One: I am backstage in a small box that looks like a detention cell. The family is in the lower boxes, trembling. All expectations to the contrary, I am calm and collected. The actors are nervous, tense, and cross themselves. Curtain. Enter the actor for whom the benefit is being given. Hesitancy, poor knowledge of the part, and the wreath he is presented combine to make the play unrecognizable to me from the very first lines. Kiselevsky, on whom I had pinned such great hopes, did not deliver a single line right. Literally: *not one.* He delivered something entirely his own invention. Despite this and slips by the director, the first act was a great success. Many curtain calls.

Act Two: A crowd on the stage. Visitors. They do not know their parts, get mixed up, babble. Every word is like a knife in my back. Nevertheless—O muse!—this act was a success, too. Everyone was called to make a bow, including me, twice. Congratulated on a hit.

Act Three: The acting is not too bad. The show is an enormous success. I am called on stage three times. During the curtain calls Davydov shakes my hand continually, while Glama presses my other hand to her heart, as Manilov would. Talent and virtue triumphant.

Act Four, First Tableau: Not too bad. Curtain calls. Then a long and tiring intermission. The audience, unaccustomed to getting up and going to the refreshment room between tableaux, grumbles. The curtain rises. Pretty: a supper table (wedding) is visible in the archway. Flourishes are played. Enter the best men; they are drunk and so must clown and play tricks, don't you know. All the earmarks of low farce and the tavern, leaving me horrified. Next enters Kiselevsky, a lyrical spot that tugs at the heartstrings, but my Kiselevsky does not know his part and is as drunk as a cobbler, so a brief lyrical dialogue becomes interminable and sickening. The audience is bewildered. At the end of the play the hero dies because he cannot take an insult. The now cool and weary audience is confused by this death (on which the actors insisted, though I have another version). Calls are made for the actors

and me to take bows. During one of the curtain calls undisguised hissing is drowned out by the applause and stamping.

Tiring and depressing on the whole. Unpleasant, though the play
was a solid success (Kicheyev[52] and Co. notwithstanding).

Theater people say they have never seen such a foment, such general applause and hissing, and have never heard as many heated discussions as they heard and saw at my play. And never before has an
author had occasion to make a curtain call at Korsh's after the second
act.

The play will have its second performance on the twenty-third, in
a different version and with changes: I am getting rid of the best men.

Details when we meet.

Yours,

A. Chekhov

Tell Burenin that I settled down after the play and got to work on
the Saturday piece.

To Dmitry V. Grigorovich

Moscow, 12 January 1888

12 January, Tatiana Day, University Holiday

There is no need to tell you, Dmitry Vasilyevich, how much I appreciated your last marvelous letter or what it meant to me.[53] I confess it
made such an impression on me that I sent a copy to Korolenko—a
very good man, incidentally. The letter did not make me particularly
ashamed, as it arrived when I was at work on a piece for a fat journal.
There you have the answer to a significant portion of your letter: I
have undertaken a big work; I have already written over two printed
quires and shall probably write three more. For my debut in the fat
journal I have chosen the steppe, which has long gone undescribed. I
depict the plain, the purple horizon, shepherds, Jews, priests, noctur-
nal thunderstorms, coaching inns, caravans, the birds of the steppe, and
so on. Each chapter is a story in itself, and all the chapters are closely
linked, like the five figures of a quadrille. I am attempting to achieve
a single aroma and a single mood, and this may be made easier by the
fact that the same character appears in all the chapters. I sense that I
have brought a good deal off, that there are passages where the smell
of hay comes through, but on the whole the result is strange and

inordinately original. Unaccustomed to writing at length and constantly, habitually afraid of writing something superfluous, I go to the other extreme. All the pages come out compact, condensed as it were; the impressions crowd together, pile up, press in on one another; the pictures, or the flashes as you call them, squeeze tightly together, follow one upon the other in an unbroken chain, and are therefore wearying. The result is not a picture but a dry, detailed list of impressions, somewhat like an outline; instead of an integral artistic portrait of the steppe, I shall present the reader with an "encyclopedia of the steppe." Every beginning is hard. But I am not being timid. And the encyclopedia may do. Perhaps it will open the eyes of my contemporaries and show them what riches, what stores of beauty lie untapped and how little restrained the Russian artist still is. If my novelette reminds my colleagues of the steppe they have forgotten, if just one of the motifs to which I have tersely alluded gives some poet occasion to pause and think, I shall be grateful for that. I know you will understand my steppe and for its sake forgive the sins I have unwittingly committed. I have unwittingly committed them because, as is now clear, I still *do not have the ability* to write big pieces.

I shall return to my unfinished story this summer. It takes up a whole *uyezd* (gentry and zemstvo) and the domestic lives of several families. To some extent the steppe is an exceptional and special subject: if it is described not in passing but for its own sake, the monotony and bucolic hokum weary; in my story I have taken ordinary people and intellectuals, women, love, marriage, children—you do not tire but feel at home.

The suicide of a seventeen-year-old boy is certainly a noble and tempting subject, but so intimidating! This question, which has tormented everyone, requires a tormentingly powerful answer, but does our brother have the inner resources necessary? No. In guaranteeing the success of the subject, you are using yourself as a measure, but people of your generation possess, besides talent, erudition, a school, phosphorus and iron. The talents of today, however, have nothing of the sort, and frankly one must be glad that they leave serious subjects alone. If you were to give them your boy, I am certain that well-intentioned X would lie, slander, and blaspheme without knowing it, Y would take a shallow, pale approach, while Z would put the suicide down to psychosis. Your boy has a nature that is pure, gentle, in search of God, loving, sensitive, and deeply hurt. Anyone who is to comprehend such a character must himself be capable of suffering, but today's bards are only capable of whining and sniveling. As far as I am concerned, I must add to everything said above that I am indolent and lazy.

V. N. Davydov paid a call a few days ago. He acted in my *Ivanov*, which has occasioned our friendship. Upon learning that I was about to write you he mustered his courage, sat down at the desk and wrote the letter I enclose herewith.

Have you read Korolenko and Shcheglov? The latter is the subject of considerable talk. In my opinion, he is talented and original. Korolenko continues to be the favorite of the public and the critics; his book is doing splendidly. Of the poets, Fofanov is beginning to stand out. He really is talented in contrast to the others, who are worth nothing as artists. While the prose writers are so-so, the poets are downright awful. A crowd without education, knowledge, or a view on life. Though Koltsov the cattle dealer could not write grammatically, he was much more rounded, intelligent, and educated than all of today's young poets combined.

My "Steppe" will be published in *Severny vestnik*. I shall write Pleshcheyev and ask him to have an offprint set aside for you.

I am very glad that your pains are gone. They lie at the heart of your disease; the rest is not so important. Your cough is not serious or connected with your illness. It is undoubtedly due to a chill and will pass with the cold weather. Today I shall have to drink again and again to the health of the people who taught me how to cut up corpses and write prescriptions. In all likelihood I shall be drinking to your health, too, as not one anniversary passes here without the drinkers kindly remembering Turgenev, Tolstoy, and you. The writers drink to Chernyshevsky, Saltykov, and Gl. Uspensky, while the public (students, MDs, mathematicians, etc.), to which I belong by virtue of being an Aesculapius, keeps the old ways and does not wish to be unfaithful to names that are like kin. I am deeply convinced that as long as there are forests, ravines, and summer nights in Rus, as long as the stint cries and the lapwings weep, you and Turgenev and Tolstoy shall be remembered just as Gogol is. The people you depicted will die and be forgotten, but you will remain safe and sound. Such is your power and thus, your good fortune.

Forgive me, I have wearied you with a long letter, but what can I do; my hand got away from me and I wanted to have a good long talk with you.

I hope this letter finds you in a warm place, hale and hearty. Come to Russia this summer. They say that the Crimea is just as lovely as Nice.

Thank you once more for the letter. I wish you all the best and remain sincerely and devotedly yours,

Chekhov

TO YAKOV P. POLONSKY[54]

MOSCOW, 18 JANUARY 1888

I spent several days, Yakov Petrovich, trying to think how best to reply to your letter, but failed to come up with anything satisfactory and have concluded that I do not yet know how to reply to letters as good and kind as yours.[55] It was an unexpected New Year's present for me, and if you recall the time when you were starting out, you will understand how much it means to me.

I am ashamed that I did not write you first. Admittedly, I have long wanted to do so, but bashfulness and timidity got the better of me. I reasoned that however friendly our conversation was, it did not give me any right to the honor of corresponding with you. Please pardon my cowardice and pettiness.

I have received your book and photograph.

Your portrait has already been hung above my desk, and the prose is being read by my entire family. Why do you say that your prose has become covered with moss and hoarfrost? If the only reason is that the public today does not read anything but newspapers, that is not sufficient grounds for passing such a truly cold, autumnal sentence. I first came to your prose with a conviction, or rather a bias; the fact of the matter is that even when I was studying the history of literature I was aware of a phenomenon, which I practically elevated to law, namely that all the great Russian poets do a splendid job with prose. That bias cannot be wrested from me, nor did it desert me on those evenings when I read your prose. Perhaps I am wrong, but Lermontov's *Taman* and Pushkin's *The Captain's Daughter,* to say nothing of other poets' prose, give direct proof of the close connection between Russia's lush verse and elegant prose.

I can only acknowledge your desire to dedicate a poem to me with a bow and a request—allow me someday to dedicate to you a story that I write with particular affection.[56] Your kindness has touched me, and I shall never forget it. Beyond its warmth and the innate charm a dedication carries, *At the Door*[57] has special meaning for me: it is worth a whole article of praise by an authoritative critic, since thanks to it I shall grow a whole *sazhen*★ in the eyes of the public and my colleagues.

As regards contributing to the newspapers and illustrateds, I am in complete agreement with you. Is it not all the same whether a nightingale sings in a big tree or a bush? The insistence that all talented people work *solely* for the fat journals is petty, bespeaks the bureaucratic mentality, and is as harmful as all prejudices. This prejudice is silly and amusing. It made sense when those publications were headed by people with distinct personalities, people like Belinsky, Herzen, et cetera, who not only paid fees but took writers under their wings and taught them. Now, when the distinct personalities have been replaced at the head of the publications by nonentities with gray circles for faces and dog collars around their necks, the partiality for the thicker publication does not stand up to criticism, and the difference between the fattest journal and a cheap newspaper is only quantitative, i.e., not worthy of respect or heed on the part of the artist. There is just one undeniable advantage to contributing to a fat journal: long works are printed whole, not chopped up. When I write something big, I will send it to a fat journal, and publish little pieces wherever the wind and my discretion take them.

Speaking of which, I am at work on a big piece of fiction, probably to be published in *Severny vestnik*. In this story I am depicting the steppe and its people, birds, nights, thunderstorms, et cetera. It is fun to write, but I fear that being unaccustomed to writing at length I sometimes let the mood slip, tire, fail to finish thoughts, and lack seriousness. There are many places that neither the critics nor the public will like, to whom they will seem inane, unworthy of serious consideration, but I rejoice in anticipation that these very places will be understood and appreciated by two or three literary connoisseurs, and that is enough for me. On the whole I am not pleased with my tale. To me it seems unwieldy, dull, and of limited appeal. For today's reading public the subject of the steppe, its scenery and people is of limited appeal and little significance.

I will probably go to St. Petersburg in early March to say good-bye to friends and then leave for the Kuban. April and May will be spent in the Kuban and by the Black Sea; then I will go on to Slavyansk or

★ Approximately seven feet.

the Volga for the summer. I cannot stay put in one place in the summer. Permit me to thank you once again for your letter and the dedication. I do not yet merit either of them. Be healthy and happy and believe in the sincere respect and affection of your devoted,

Chekhov

P.S. I returned from the country a few days ago. Winter is also a lovely time to be in the country. If only you could see the blindingly white fields and woods with the sun sparkling on them! It makes the eyes ache. While I was there I had to examine a cow that had suddenly died. Though I am a physician, not a veterinarian, I must occasionally do veterinary work as the proper specialists are lacking.

To Dmitry V. Grigorovich

Moscow, 5 February 1888

Dear Dmitry Vasilyevich,

Three days ago I finished "The Steppe," which I mentioned in an earlier letter to you, and sent it off to *Severny vestnik*. In the end it was about five printed quires, indeed probably more. If it is not rejected it will be in the March issue; I shall send you an offprint and have already written to the editorial office about it.

I know that in the other world Gogol will be angry with me. He is the king of the steppe in our literature. I entered his domain with good intentions but committed quite a few follies. I was unable to bring off three-quarters of the story.

Around 10 January I sent you two letters: one from me, the other from V. N. Davydov. Have you received them? Incidentally, in my letter I commented on your story idea—the suicide of a seventeen-year-old boy. I made a weak attempt to use the idea. All eight chapters of my "Steppe" feature a nine-year-old boy, who will certainly come to a bad end when he eventually gets to St. Petersburg or Moscow. If "The Steppe" is at all successful, I shall continue it. I deliberately tried to give it the feel of an unfinished work. As you will see, it is like the first part of a novel. As far as the lad is concerned, I will tell you why I portrayed him as I did and not otherwise once you have read "The Steppe."

I am not certain I understood you. The suicide of your Russian youth is a unique phenomenon, unknown to Europe. All the artist's energy should be directed toward two forces: man and nature. On the one hand, feebleness, nervousness, early sexual maturity, a passionate thirst for life and truth, dreams of endeavor as vast as the steppe, restless analysis, a dearth of knowledge, hand in hand with a soaring imagination; on the other—the immense plain, the harsh climate, the gray, harsh people with their difficult, cold history, Tatarism, bureaucracy, poverty, ignorance, the dampness of the capitals, Slavic apathy, and so forth. Russian life beats the Russian to a pulp, pounds him like a thousand-pood stone. In Western Europe people die because life is cramped and stifling, here because of the space. There is so much space that the tiny individual does not have the strength to get his bearings.

Those are my thoughts on Russian suicides.

Have I understood you correctly? But it is impossible to discuss this in a letter because there is so little space. It is a good topic for conversation. What a pity you are not in Russia!

It is warm and dry where you are,[58] and I am certain that you no longer have a cough. Go easy on the tobacco and, most importantly, buy better cigarette paper. Often cigarette paper contains much more poison than tobacco does. Good-bye! I wish you health and happiness.

Your sincerely devoted,

Ant. Chekhov

To Alexei S. Suvorin

Sumy, 30 May 1888

The Lintvarev Estate

Dear Alexei Sergeyevich,

This is in reply to your letter, which I received just yesterday; the envelope was torn, crumpled, and stained, which circumstance was given a strong political slant by my hosts and the members of the household.[59]

I live on the bank of the Psel, in one wing of an old manor house. I took the dacha sight unseen, on a chance, and have not yet come to regret it. The river is broad, deep, and replete with islands, fish and crayfish; the banks are lovely, there is a great deal of greenery. But most importantly, it is so expansive that it seems my hundred rubles have given me the right to live in an expanse stretching as far as the eye can see. The scenery and way of life follow the pattern, now so dated, that is rejected by the editors of periodicals: to say nothing of the nightingales that sing day and night, the barking of dogs that can be heard from afar, the old, overgrown gardens, the tightly boarded, very poetic and sad manor houses where the spirits of beautiful women dwell, to say nothing of the old men servant-serfs with one foot in the grave, the girls who thirst for the most hackneyed kind of love; not far from me I have something as clichéd as a water mill (sixteen wheels) with a miller and his daughter, who is always seated at the window, evidently in expectation of something. Everything that I am now seeing and hearing seems long familiar from the stories and tales of yore. The only sense of novelty has been inspired by a mysterious bird, the "water bull," which sits somewhere far off in the rushes and emits a cry day and night that sounds partly like a blow struck on an empty barrel and partly like the bellow of a cow shut in a shed. Every Ukrainian has seen this bird at some time in his life, but each description is different, so evidently no one has seen it. There is a novelty of another sort, but it is borrowed and consequently not so new.

Every day I row to the mill and then in the evenings leave for the islands to fish with the fanatical fishermen from the Kharitonenko factory. We have some interesting conversations. On Whitsun Eve all the fanatics are going to the islands to fish the whole night long; I intend to go, too. There are some marvelous types.

My hosts have proved to be very nice, hospitable people. A family worthy of study. It has six members. The old mother is a kind, podgy woman who has experienced her share of suffering; she reads Schopenhauer and goes to church for acathistus; she conscientiously peruses each issue of *Vestnik Yevropy* and *Severny vestnik* and knows authors I had never dreamed existed; she sets great store by the fact that the artist Makovsky once stayed in her wing and that now a young writer is staying there; when speaking with Pleshcheyev her whole body trembles with awe and rejoices each minute that she has "had the honor" of seeing the great poet.

Her oldest daughter, a female doctor—the pride of the family and, according to the *muzhiks,* a saint—truly does give the appearance of being out of the ordinary. She has a brain tumor; consequently, she is completely blind and suffers from epilepsy and constant headaches. She knows what lies ahead and speaks of death, which is imminent, stoically and with astonishing dispassion. As a practicing physician, I am accustomed to seeing people who will soon die and have always felt somewhat strange when people whose death was imminent talked, smiled, or cried in my presence; but here, when I see this blind woman on the terrace laughing, joking, or listening to my *Twilight*[60] as it is read to her, it begins to seem strange not that the lady doctor shall die, but that we are insensitive to our own deaths and write *Twilight* as though we shall never pass away.

The second daughter—also a female doctor and old maid—is a quiet, shy, and plain creature who is endlessly kind and loves everyone. Patients are pure torture for her, and she is apprehensive to the point of psychosis with them. We never concert in our diagnoses: I am the bearer of good news where she sees death, and I double the doses she gives. But where death is evident and unavoidable, my lady doctor reacts in a quite undoctorly manner. I once saw patients with her at the clinic; one was a young Ukrainian woman with a malignant tumor in the glands of her neck and the back of her head. The lesion had spread so far that there was no sense in treating it. Well, because the woman is not now in pain but will die in six months in horrible suffering, the lady doctor looked at her with an expression of such profound guilt, as if to apologize for her health and declare her shame at medicine's helplessness. She is a diligent housekeeper and understands domestic management in every detail. She even understands horses. When, for instance, the trace horse is not pulling or starts to get restless, she knows how to deal with the problem and instructs the driver. She is very fond of family life, which has been deprived her by fate, and seems to dream of it; in the evenings, when there is music and singing in the big house, she nervously strides up and down the dark avenue of trees, like a caged animal. I do not think she has ever done anyone a bad turn, and if I am right, she has never been happy for a single minute, nor shall she ever be.

The third daughter, who has completed the Bestuzhev higher education courses, is a young unmarried lady of mannish build, strong, bony as a bream, muscular, tanned, loud. Her laugh can be heard a verst away. A fanatic about all things Ukrainian—she has set up a school in the manor house at her own expense and teaches Ukrainian tikes Krylov's fables in Little Russian translation. She makes pilgrimages to Shevchenko's grave[61] like Turks go to Mecca. She does not cut her hair, wears a corset and bustle, keeps the house, loves to sing and laugh heartily, and would not reject the most hackneyed kind of love, though she has read Marx's *Capital*, but marriage is unlikely as she is not good looking.

The oldest son is a quiet, modest, intelligent, unexceptional, and hardworking young man, unpretentious and evidently satisfied with what life has given him. Expelled from his fourth year at the university, something of which he does not brag. Says little. Loves the estate and the land and lives in concord with the Ukrainians.

The second son is a young man who raves that Tchaikovsky is a genius. A pianist. Dreams of living according to Tolstoy's precepts.

There you have a brief description of the folks who now surround me. As for the Ukrainians, the women remind me of Zankovetskaya, all the men of Panas Sadovsky.[62] Guests are numerous at times.

A. N. Pleshcheyev[63] is visiting me. Everyone regards him as a demigod, considers it bliss if he deigns to notice someone's yogurt, presents him with bouquets, invites him everywhere, and so forth. Vata, a young lady student from Poltava, who is visiting my hosts, has been particularly attentive. In the meanwhile he "listens but keeps on eating" and smokes the cigars that give his fair admirers headaches. He is lethargic and lazy in the way of the old, but that does not keep the fair sex from going boating with him, taking him to neighboring estates, and singing romances for him. He has been playing the same part here as he does in St. Petersburg, i.e., that of an icon to which one prays because it is old and once hung alongside miracle-working icons. Beyond the fact that he is a very good, warm, and sincere man, I personally see him as a vessel filled with traditions, interesting reminiscences, and fine truisms.

I have written a story and sent it to *Novoye Vremya*.

What you write about "Lights" is altogether fair. "Nikolai and Masha"[64] run through "Lights" like a red thread, but what can I do? Unaccustomed to writing at length, I become apprehensive; whenever I write I am constantly frightened by the thought that my story is unduly long, and I try to be as brief as possible. The finale of the engineer and Kisochka seemed to me like an insignificant detail that clogged the story line, so I discarded it, inadvertently putting "Nikolai and Masha" in its place.

You write that neither the discussion of pessimism nor the Kisochka story clarified the question of pessimism in the least, let alone resolved it. To my mind, writers of fiction are not the ones to resolve questions of God, pessimism, et cetera. The fiction writer's sole job is to depict how and under what circumstances people spoke or thought about God or pessimism. An artist should not be a judge of his characters and what they say, just a disinterested observer. If I have overheard a muddled, pointless discussion about pessimism between two Russians, I must convey the discussion as I heard it and leave any assessment to the jury, i.e., the readers. My sole task is to be talented, i.e., I must be able to distinguish important evidence from unimportant, depict characters and speak their language. Shcheglov-Leontiev reproached me for ending the story with the phrase, "You cannot make head or tail of anything in this world!" In his opinion, the artist-psychologist *should* be able to do just that if he is a psychologist. But I do not agree. It is time writers, particularly those of fiction, recognized that you cannot make head or tail of anything in this world, as Socrates realized in his day and Voltaire recognized again and again. The crowd thinks it knows and understands everything, and the stupider it is, the broader, seemingly, its vision. If the artist, whom the crowd trusts, makes up his mind to declare that he does not understand anything he sees, that alone is of great significance to thought and represents a big step forward.

As far as your play is concerned, you are wrong to run it down. Its defects have to do with the nature of your creative abilities, not any lack of talent or observation on your part. You are more inclined to a rigorous approach to art, that has been fostered in you by frequent reading of the classics and your love for them. Imagine your *Tatiana* written in verse, and you shall see that its defects take on a different aspect. Had it been written in verse, no one would have noticed that all the characters speak alike, no one would have criticized your protagonists for philosophizing and satirizing instead of talking—in classical poetry form, all that fades into the background like smoke fades into the air—and no one would notice the lack of vulgar language and vulgar, petty actions, which modern drama and comedy should have in abundance but are completely absent in your *Tatiana*. Give your characters Latin names, dress them in togas, and the result will be the same. Your play's defects are insuperable because they are part of its fabric. Be consoled by the fact that they are the product of your virtues, and were your defects to be given to other playwrights, such as Krylov or Tikhonov, their plays would be more interesting and intelligent.

Now about the future. In late June or early July, I shall go to Kiev, from there down the Dnieper to Yekaterinoslav, then to Alexandrovsk and on to the Black Sea. I will stop in Feodosia. If you really are going to Constantinople perhaps I could accompany you? We could pay a call on Fr. Paisi, and he would show us that Tolstoy's teaching is the work of the devil. I shall spend the whole of June writing, so in all likelihood I would have enough money for the trip. From the Crimea I shall go on to Poti, from Poti to Tiflis, from Tiflis to the Don, from the Don to the Psel. In the Crimea I shall begin a lyric play.

What a letter I have dashed off! Time to quit. Please give my regards to Anna Ivanovna, Nastya, and Borya. Alexei Nikolayevich sends greetings. He is a bit under the weather today: his breathing is labored, and his pulse is limping along like Leikin. I shall now see what I can do about doctoring him. Farewell, be healthy, and God grant you all the best. Your sincerely devoted,

Chekhov

To Alexei N. Pleshcheyev

MOSCOW, 15 SEPTEMBER 1888

Dear Alexei Nikolayevich, pray do not order my execution but hear me out! I now see that when I promised you a story for the *October* issue all the arithmetic got muddled in my head. On the journey to Moscow I decided to write a story for *Severny vestnik* in September, finish it on 1–2 October, and send it off no later than 5 October. That knavish *October* got mixed up in my thick head with the *October* issue. Having started writing in early September, I could not possibly make the issue that is printed in September! I urgently entreat you and Anna Mikhailovna to forgive me for being so scatterbrained. My story will be in the November issue without fail (if you do not reject it, that is). I am writing it little by little, and it is turning out angry, because I myself am terribly angry.[65]

As far as the Garshin collection is concerned, I do not know what to tell you. Refusing to contribute is not something I care to do. In the first place, I love people like the late Garshin with all my heart and consider it my duty publicly to acknowledge my affection for them; in the second place, Garshin devoted much of his final days to my personage, which I cannot forget; in the third place, refusing to contribute to the collection would be behaving in an uncomradely manner, that is, swinishly. I sense all this to the marrow of my bones, but imagine the awkward position I find myself in: I have absolutely nothing that is at all suitable for the collection.

Everything I have is either very vulgar, or very gay, or very long.

There was one mediocre little story idea, but I have already put it to use and sent it off in the form of a sketch to *Novoye Vremya,* where I am up to my ears in obligations. Actually, I do have one subject: a young man in the Garshin mold—exceptional, honest, and deeply sensitive—visits a brothel for the first time.[66] Since serious subjects need to be treated seriously I shall be totally frank. Perhaps I shall succeed and write it in such a way that it produces the oppressive effect I want; perhaps it will turn out well and be suitable for the collection, but can you vouch, dear sir, that neither the censor nor the editors themselves will take out what I consider to be important? After all, the collection is to be illustrated, thus subject to censorship. If you vouch that *not one word* will be struck, I shall write the story in two evenings; if you cannot provide any such assurance, then I shall give you my answer in about a week: perchance an idea will come to me!

Yours,

A. Chekhov

To Alexei N. Pleshcheyev

MOSCOW, 4 OCTOBER 1888

My letter to you was barely on its way when I received your communication, Alexei Nikolayevich, containing news which will be very displeasing to Svetlov. I shall immediately let him know your reply and insistently recommend *A Nasty Man.*[67]

Had your letter arrived two hours earlier, I would have sent my story to you, but now it is halfway to Baskov Lane.[68]

I would be happy to read what Merezhkovsky has written. Until we meet. Write me once you have read my story. You will not like it, but I am not afraid of you and Anna Mikhailovna. I am afraid of those who look between the lines for a social stance and are set on finding me to be a liberal or a conservative. I am not a liberal or a conservative, or a gradualist, or a monk, or an indifferentist. I simply want to be a free artist and regret that God has not given me the ability to be one. I hate deception and violence in all its forms, and I am as equally repelled by the secretaries of the consistory as by Notovich and Gradovsky.[69] Pharisaism, stupidity, and despotism reign not in merchants' houses and prisons alone; I see them in science, in literature, among the young. Therefore I feel equally impartial to gendarmes, butchers, scholars, writers, and youths. I regard labels and tags as marks of prejudice. My holy of holies is the human body, health, intelligence, talent, inspiration, love, and absolute freedom, freedom from coercion and deception, whatever form the final two take. There you have the platform I would stand by if I were a great artist.

But I am babbling. I wish you health.

Yours,

A. Chekhov

To Dmitry V. Grigorovich

MOSCOW, 9 OCTOBER 1888

Kudrinskaya-Sadovaya, c/o Korneyev

Winning the prize[70] naturally makes me happy, and I would be lying if I said I was not excited. I feel as though I had just graduated from some third place besides high school and the university. Yesterday and today I have paced from corner to corner like a man in love, not working, just thinking.

Of course—and there can be no doubt about this—I am not obliged to myself for the prize. There are young writers better and needier than I, like Korolenko, quite a decent writer and a noble individual, who would have received the prize had he submitted his book. The idea of trying for the prize was planted by Ya. P. Polonsky, while Suvorin stressed the idea and sent the book to the Academy. You were at the Academy and gave me your solid support.

You must agree that if not for you three I would not have had any chance at the prize. I do not wish to make a show of modesty or persuade you that the three of you were biased, that I am not worthy of the prize, et cetera—that would be old and tiresome; I merely wish to say that I am not obliged to myself for my happiness. I thank you a thousand times and shall thank you all my life.

I have not worked for the minor press since the start of the year. I am publishing my short stories in *Novoye Vremya* and giving the bigger ones to *Severny vestnik,* which pays me 150 rubles per quire. I shall not leave *Novoye Vremya* because I am attached to Suvorin, besides *Novoye Vremya* is not the minor press. I do not have any definite plans for the future. I would like to write a novel, and I have a marvelous idea; at times I am gripped by a passionate desire to set to work on it, but evidently the strength is lacking. I started it and am now afraid to continue. I have decided to write it unhurriedly, only during good hours, correcting and polishing; I shall spend a few years on it; I cannot write it all at once, in a single year, for I do not have the stamina; my impotence is frightening, besides there is no need to hurry. I am inclined to dislike what I wrote the previous year and believe that I will be stronger the next; that is why I am not in any hurry to take a risk and make a decisive step. After all, if the novel turns out badly, it will be all over for me.

The thoughts, women, men, and landscapes that I have accumulated for the novel will be safe and sound. I shall not waste them on work of no consequence, I promise you. The novel will be broad in scope, encompassing several families and a whole *uyezd* with its woods, rivers, ferries, and railway. In the center of the *uyezd* are two main figures, male and female, around whom the other pieces group themselves. I do not yet have a political, religious, and philosophical *Weltanschauung,* it changes every month, so I must restrict myself to merely describing how my characters love, marry, give birth, die, and how they talk.[71]

Until the novel's hour comes I shall continue to write what I love, in other words, short works one and a half quires long and less. Stretching mediocre stories out onto a big canvas is dull, though financially advantageous. It would be a shame to take up big topics and butcher characters and images that are dear to me in day's labor scribbled off to meet a deadline. I shall wait for a better time.

I do not have the right to forbid my brother to sign his own name. He asked my permission first, and I told him I was not opposed.

I had a marvelous summer. I stayed in the Kharkov and Poltava gubernias, traveled to the Crimea, Batum, Baku, and experienced the Georgian Military Road. Numerous impressions. If I lived in the Caucasus, I would write fairy tales. An amazing land!

I will not be in St. Petersburg before November. On the day I arrive I shall present myself at your doorstep, but until then permit me to thank you once again from the bottom of my heart and wish you health and happiness.

Your sincerely devoted,

A. Chekhov

To Alexei S. Suvorin

I have received the beginning of the play.[72] Thank you. Blagosvetlov shall go in entirely as is. You have done a good job on him: he is tiresome from the very first words he speaks, and if the audience listens to him for three to five minutes on end, it will create just the effect needed. The playgoer will think, "Oh shut up, please!" He, i.e., Blagosvetlov, should strike the audience as an intelligent, gouty grumbler and remind them of a dull musical play that has long been running. I think you will see how well you succeeded with him when I finish my draft of the first act and send it to you.

With Anuchin I shall retain the name and "all that," but his dialogue needs a bit of greasing. Anuchin is a podgy, unctuous, affectionate individual, and his speech should likewise be podgy and unctuous, but in your rendition he comes out excessively curt and insufficiently equable. This godfather needs to give off an air of old age and indolence. He is too lazy to listen to Blagosvetlov; instead of arguing he would rather doze and listen to stories of St. Petersburg, the tsar, literature, and science or have a bite to eat in pleasant company.

Allow me to remind you of our playbill:

1) Alexander Platonych Blagosvetlov, a member of the State Council, has a White Eagle and receives a pension of 7,200 rubles; the son of a priest, he attended a seminary. The position he held was attained through personal endeavor. There is not a single blemish on his past. He suffers from gout, rheumatism, insomnia, and buzzing in his ears. The property he owns was part of his wife's dowry. He has a forthright mind. He cannot abide mystics, visionaries, fools of God, lyric poets, or the sanctimonious. He does not believe in God and is accustomed to taking a pragmatic view. Business, business, and business, the rest is nonsense or charlatanism.

2) Boris, his student son, a youth who is very sensitive and very honest, but has not a clue about life. Once imagining himself to be a Populist, he decided to adopt peasant dress and wound up looking like a Turk. He is an excellent pianist, sings with feeling, writes plays in secret, falls in love easily, spends considerable sums of money, and always talks nonsense. He is doing poorly at his studies.

3) Blagosvetlov's daughter, only, please, not Sasha. *Ivanov* was enough to make me sick of the name. Since the son is Boris, why not make the daughter Nastya. (Let us raise a monument to Borya and Nastya[73]

not built by hands.) Nastya is twenty-three or twenty-four. She possesses an excellent education and has the ability to think. St. Petersburg bores her, so does the country. She has never been in love. She is lazy, loves to talk about philosophy, reads books reclining, wants to marry solely for the change it would bring and to avoid becoming an old maid. She says she could only fall in love with an interesting man. She would gladly marry Pushkin or Edison, she would fall in love, but she will only marry a good man out of boredom; she will respect her husband but love her children. Seeing and hearing the Forest Demon, she surrenders to passion, to *nec plus ultra*,★ to convulsions, to silly, indecent laughter. The powder, grown damp in the Petersburg tundra, dries in the sunlight and explodes with a terrible force. I have come up with a phenomenal declaration of love.

4) Anuchin, an old man. He considers himself the happiest man on earth. His sons have moved up in the world, his daughters have been married off, and he is as free as a bird. He has never been ill, never been on trial, never been decorated; he forgets to wind his watch and is everyone's friend. He eats heartily, sleeps well, drinks in quantity and without ill effect. His age angers him and he does not know how to think about death. There was a time when he was dejected and discontent, had a bad appetite, and took an interest in politics, but then a chance occurrence saved him: once, ten years before, he had to ask everyone's forgiveness for some reason at a zemstvo meeting—afterward his spirits suddenly rose, he felt hungry, and, as a man subjective by nature, pragmatic to the marrow of his bones, he concluded that absolute sincerity, such as public repentance, was a remedy for every illness. He recommends this remedy to one and all, including Blagosvetlov, incidentally.

5) Victor Petrovich Korovin, a landowner thirty to thirty-three years old, the Forest Demon. A poet and landscape painter with a tremendous feeling for nature. Once, when he was still in high school, he planted a birch tree in his garden; when it put forth leaves and began to sway in the breeze, rustle and give a patch of shade, his heart filled with pride: he had helped God make a new birch tree; he had seen to it that there was one more tree on earth! This was the start of his unique labor. He realized his idea not on canvas, not on paper, but in the earth, not with dead paint but with living organisms. A tree is lovely, but that is not all; it has a right to life, it is as vital as water, as

★ (Lat.) the utmost point attainable.—Tr.

the sun, as the stars. Life on earth is unthinkable without trees. Forests affect the climate, the climate influences human nature, et cetera. There is no civilization, no happiness if the woods fall under the ax, if the climate is hard and callous, if people are hard and callous, too. A terrible future! Nastya likes him not for his idea, which is alien to her, but for his talent, for his passion, for the sweep of his idea. She likes the fact that he has applied his mind to all of Russia today and a thousand years from now. When he comes running to her father and, with tears and sobs, begs him not to sell his woods for timber, she chortles in delight and happiness that she has finally found a person she did not believe existed when she saw him in dreams and novels.

6) Galakhov is the Forest Demon's contemporary, but he is already a Councilor of State and a very rich man who works with Shalkovsky. He is a bureaucrat to the marrow of his bones and simply cannot get away from that, for it is part of his flesh and blood, handed down from his forefathers. He would like to live by his heart but does not know how. He tries to understand nature and music but does not. An honest, sincere person who understands that the Forest Demon is superior to him and frankly concedes it. He wants to marry for love, thinks he is in love and puts himself in a lyrical mood, but cannot bring off anything. Nastya is a pretty, intelligent girl to him, a good wife and nothing more.

7) Vasily Gavrilovich Volkov, the brother of Blagosvetlov's late wife. He runs his brother-in-law's estate (he had to sell his own some time before). He regrets that he did not steal. He did not expect that his St. Petersburg kin would have so little appreciation of the service he performs. They do not understand him, do not want to understand him, and he regrets that he did not steal. He drinks Vichy water and mutters. His behavior is arrogant. He emphasizes that he is not afraid of generals. Shouts.

8) Lyuba, his daughter. She cares for the things of the earth. Chickens, ducks, knives, forks, the cattle yard, the *Niva* prize that needs to be framed, refreshments for guests, dinners, suppers, tea are her sphere. She regards it as a personal affront if someone else decides to pour the tea: "I guess I'm not needed in this household any more." She does not like those who throw money about and fail to make good use of their time. She respects Galakhov for his rectitude. You do not bring her on right. She needs to emerge from the depths of the garden crying, "How could Maria and Akulina leave the turkey poults to spend the night in the dew?" or something of the sort. She is always

stern, stern with people and with ducks. True mistresses never praise their own handiwork. On the contrary, she tries to show that she lives a life of penal servitude, that there is no time for rest, God knows, with everyone sitting around with their arms crossed while she alone, poor thing, is running herself ragged. She lectures Nastya and Borya on sponging but is frightened of Blagosvetlov.

9) Semyon, a peasant, the Forest Demon's steward.

10) Feodosy the pilgrim, eighty years old, but still not gray. A soldier during Nikolai's reign who served in the Caucasus and speaks Lezghin. Of sanguine disposition. He adores funny stories and gay conversation; he bows to the ground before everyone, kisses everyone on the shoulder, including the ladies, whether they like it or not. A lay brother of the Afon Monastery. He saved up 300,000 in the course of his life, then gave every last kopeck to the monastery and now lives in poverty. He calls people fools or scoundrels regardless of rank or office.

There you have the whole playbill. You shall receive my material for the first act no later than Christmas. I shall not touch Blagosvetlov. He and Galakhov are yours, I renounce all claim to them; the better half of Nastya is yours. I cannot handle her alone. Boris is not important, he is not hard to master. The Forest Demon is mine until the fourth act, and yours in the fourth up to the dialogue with Blagosvetlov. In that dialogue I shall have to maintain the general mood, which you will grasp.

Again, you begin the second act (guests).

Feodosy is an episodic character who will, I think, be needed: I would like the Forest Demon to not be alone on stage, so that Blagosvetlov will feel he is surrounded by fools of God. I left out of the playbill M-lle Emily, the elderly French woman who is also enchanted by the Forest Demon. We need to show what effect these gentlemen forest demons have on women. Emily is a kindly old woman, a governess who has not yet lost her vivacity. When she becomes excited, she mixes up French and Russian. A patient nurse to Blagosvetlov. She is yours. I will leave blanks for her in the first scene.

I see Alexei Alexeyevich every day. He has changed from an architect into an inspector. Bogolepov[74] has become even more like his name.* During a conversation with me today one of the tellers called him "The Sabbath."

If Jesus Christ had been more radical and said, "Love thy enemy as

* (Rus.) in the image of God.—Tr.

thyself," he would not have been saying what he intended. Neighbor is a general concept, enemy is specific. After all, the trouble is not that we hate our enemies, of whom we have few, but that we do not adequately love our neighbors, of whom we have many, more than enough. Had he been a woman, Christ might have said, "Love thy enemy as thyself." Women like to pick bold, striking specifics out of general concepts. Christ, though, who stood above enemies and did not notice them, who was by nature courageous, equable, and broad-minded, scarcely attached any significance to specific aspects of the "neighbor" concept. You and I are subjective. If someone speaks to us of animals, say, we immediately think of wolves and crocodiles, or of nightingales and beautiful roes; to the zoologist there is no difference between the wolf and the roe: it is too insignificant for him. You have mastered the newspaper business on a broad level; the specifics that cause the public worry seem insignificant to you. You have mastered the general concept, so you have succeeded at the newspaper business; those who have only grasped specifics have failed. The same is true of medicine. Those who cannot think medically but judge by specifics reject medicine; Botkin, Zakharyin, Virkhov, and Pirogov, on the other hand, are, without a doubt, intelligent and gifted men; they believe in medicine as in God, because they have reached the concept of "medicine" in their growth. The same is also true of fiction. The term "tendentious" stems from the inability of people to rise above specifics.

However, I am already coming to the end of the third sheet. It is late at night. Please forgive me. Regards to all your family.

I am in fine health.

Yours,

A. Chekhov

Do not tell anyone about the play.

TO ALEXANDER S. LAZAREV-GRUZINSKY[75]

MOSCOW, 20 OCTOBER 1888

Thank you, dear Alexander Semyonovich, for your kind congratulations. As I recall, I have never accused you of flattery or questioned your judgment; I merely told you that great writers, too, sometimes run the risk of writing themselves out, growing tiresome, addling the wits, and suffering a drop in circulation. Personally I run this risk to a great degree, which I hope you, as an intelligent man, shall not attempt to deny. In the first place, I am "a lucky fellow of no family,"[76] in literature I am a Potemkin[77] who has leapt out of the depths of *Razvlecheniye* and *Volna*,[78] I am a petty bourgeois amongst gentry, and such people do not last long, just like an instrument string that has been hurriedly stretched. In the second place, the train in the greatest risk of being derailed is that which runs daily, nonstop, regardless of weather or the quantity of fuel.

Of course, the prize is a big thing and not just for me. I am happy that I showed many the way to the fat journals, and it now makes me no less happy that thanks to me those same many can count on academic laurels. Everything I have written will be forgotten in five or ten years; but the ways I have paved will be intact—that is the sole service I have performed.

Yezhov[79] deserves praise. He has already sent off another "Saturday piece."

I liked your Saturday piece,[80] especially the middle, where the mother instructs the little girl.

There was no need to include stamps.

I have given your Saturday piece to Suvorin *fils*, who is now in Moscow.

Why did you change your mind about publishing as Lazarev?

I like your stories; you write better each year, that is to say with greater talent and intelligence. But you run the risk of missing the boat. Hurry. If you do not start moving double time, you shall be too late: others will take your place.

Your shortcoming is that you are afraid to give your temperament free rein in your stories, you are afraid of being impulsive and making mistakes, the very hallmarks of talent. You do too much polishing and honing. You hurry to put everything that seems daring and outspoken in parentheses and quotation marks (e.g., "In the Manor House"). For heaven's sake, stop using parentheses and quotation marks! There is an excellent punctuation mark for parenthetic clauses, the dash (—whatever—). Quotation marks are employed by two kinds of writers: the timid and the untalented. The former are frightened by their daring and originality, while the latter (the Nefedovs and to some extent the Boborykins) put a word in quotation marks as if to say, "Look, reader, see what an original, daring new word I have thought up!"

Do not imitate Bilibin![31] You need to be brave and strong, but in describing the honeymoon, et cetera, you adopt the sentimental-playful-grannyish tone typical of Bilibin. That is best avoided. Your nature descriptions are not bad and you are right to steer clear of trivialities and conventionalism. But again you do not give rein to your temperament. That is why your devices lack originality. Women should be described in such a way that the reader senses you have unbuttoned your waistcoat and taken off your tie. The same goes for describing nature. Give yourself liberty.

I wish you health. My regards to your wife. I am alive and well. Yours,

A. Chekhov

To Alexei S. Suvorin

Moscow, 27 October 1888

Yezhov is not a flighty sparrow, but rather (to use the noble language of hunters) a puppy that has not yet become a dog. He is still running and sniffing, bounding after bird and frog indiscriminately. It is hard to say as yet what kind of person he is and what his abilities are. His youth, rectitude, and the fact that the Moscow papers have not spoiled him speak strongly in his favor.

I have preached heresy on occasion, but not once have I reached the point of absolutely rejecting a question in art. In discussions with my brothers-in-writing, I have always insisted that it is not up to the artist to resolve very specific questions. An artist should not apply himself to something he does not understand. For specific questions we have specialists; it is up to them to pass judgment on the community, on the fate of capital, on the hazards of drinking, on boots, on female complaints. The artist should only pass judgment on matters he understands; his competence is just as limited as any other specialist's—that I reiterate and invariably maintain. Only the individual who has never written and never dealt with images can say that there are no questions in his sphere, just a solid mass of answers. An artist observes, selects, guesses, arranges—these actions alone must be prompted by a question. If he did not ask himself a question at the very start, there would be nothing to guess and nothing to select. For the sake of brevity I shall finish up with a bit of psychiatry: if the presence of questions and intentions in creative endeavor is denied, then the artist must create inadvertently, unintentionally in moments of insanity; that is why if an author were to boast to me that he had written a story without having thought through his intentions first, on inspiration alone, I would call him mad.

You are right to demand that an artist take a conscious attitude to his work, but you confuse two concepts: *resolving a question* and *posing a question correctly.* Only the second is required of the artist. In *Anna Karenina* and *Onegin* not one question is resolved, but you are quite satisfied solely because all the questions in them are posed correctly. The judge must pose the questions correctly; let them be resolved by the members of the jury, each in accordance with his own taste.

Yezhov has not grown up yet. Another, whom I recommend, is A. Gruzinsky (Lazarev), more talented, intelligent, and stronger.

In parting I admonished Alexei Alexeyevich not to retire on an evening later than midnight. Spending the night at work and in conversation is as harmful as boozing nights. He looked in better spirits in Moscow than he had in Feodosia; we lived amiably and within our means: he treated me to operas while I treated him to bad dinners.

Tomorrow my *Bear* will be performed at Korsh's theater. I have completed another vaudeville: two male roles, one female.

You write that I should have spent more time on the hero of "Name Day." Heavens, I'm not an insensate brute, I know that. I know that I butcher my heroes and spoil them, that I am squandering good material. To be honest, I would gladly have spent half a year on "Name Day." I love taking it easy and can see no charm in hurrying into print. I would have gladly, happily, with feeling and deliberation, described my hero in his *entirety,* described the state of his soul while his wife was in labor and during his trial, his feeling of disgust upon his acquittal, described how the midwife and doctor drank tea late in the night, described the rain. That would have been pure pleasure, as I love to putter. But what can I do? I begin the story on September 10 knowing that I must finish it by October 5—the final deadline. Failing to meet it means breaking faith and remaining without money. I write the beginning in a leisurely fashion, not constraining myself, but toward the middle I become hesitant and fear that my story will be long: I have to remember that *Severny vestnik* does not have much money and that I am one of their expensive contributors. That is why the beginning is always promising, like the start of a novel; the middle is rushed and hesitant, and the end has the fireworks of a short story. When you are working on a story you worry in spite of yourself, about the boundaries most of all; out of a mass of heroes and semi-heroes you choose just one individual—the wife or the husband—place that individual in the foreground and delineate him alone, emphasize him, while scattering the rest in the background like small change; and the result is something like the firmament: one big moon surrounded by a mass of very small stars. The moon does not come out well because it can only be comprehended if the other stars are comprehensible, and they are unfinished. So the result of my endeavors is not literature, but something like Trishka's *caftan*.★ What can I do? I do not know, I do not know. I must put my faith in time, which heals all.

To be honest, I have not yet begun my literary work, the prize notwithstanding. Ideas for five stories and two longer works are languishing in my head. One of the longer works was conceived long ago, so some of the characters have moldered before they had a chance to be put on paper. There is a whole army of people in my head who want to come out and are just waiting for the command. Everything I have written up to now is trifling compared to that which I would like to write and would write with great pleasure. It is all the same to me whether I write "Name Day" or "Lights" or a vaudeville or a letter to a close acquaintance—the result is all dull, automatic, listless. And I feel sad at times for the critic who attaches any significance to, say, "Lights"; I feel as though I were deceiving him with my writings, just as I deceive many with my inordinately serious or happy face. I am not pleased by my success; the story ideas in my head are dispiritedly jealous of what has already been written; it pains me that two-bit stuff has been done while the good material sits in storage like so much discarded printed matter. Of course, my wailing contains a good bit of exaggeration, much is just my *imagination,* but there is a grain of truth, and a big one, at that. What do I call good material? Those images and characters which seem the best to me, which I love and jealously guard to keep from wasting them and sacrificing them on "Name Day," which must be done quickly. If my love is mistaken, then I am wrong, but perhaps she is not mistaken! Either I am a fool and a self-conceited person, or I am a being capable of becoming a good writer; I am displeased and bored with everything now being written, while everything in my head interests, moves, and excites me—whence I draw the conclusion that no one is doing what is needed, and I alone know the secret of how it should be done. In all likelihood everyone who writes

★ A patchwork—Tr.

thinks that. In fact, the devil himself will be brought to his knees by these questions.

My regards to your dear ones.

Yours,

A. Chekhov

A mosquito is flying around in my room. Where did it come from? Thank you for the prominent announcement about my books.

To Alexei S. Suvorin

Greetings Alexei Sergeyevich! I am now donning tails to go to the first meeting of the Society of Arts and Literature, to which I have been invited as a guest. There is to be a formal ball. What the aims and means of this society are, who are its members, and so forth, I do not know. All I do know is that it is headed by Fedotov, the author of many plays. I was not elected a member, for which I am very glad as I certainly have no desire to pay twenty-five rubles in dues for the right to be bored. Should anything interesting or amusing occur, I shall write you about it; Lensky is to read my stories.

Severny vestnik (November) contains an article by the poet Merezhkovsky about yours truly.[82] It is a long article. I call your attention to the conclusion. It is indicative. Merezhkovsky is still very young, a student of science it seems.[83] Whoever has mastered the wisdom of the scientific method and can therefore think scientifically falls victim to quite a few fascinating temptations. Archimedes wanted to upend the earth, while today's hotheads want to scientifically comprehend the incomprehensible, want to find physical laws governing creative endeavor, grasp the general law and formulas that enable the artist, who understands them instinctively, to create musical plays, landscapes, novels, and so forth. These formulas probably do exist in nature. We know that nature contains a, b, c, d, do, re, me, fa, sol, that there are curves, lines, circles, squares, greens, reds, blues; we know that in certain combinations they produce melodies or poetry or pictures, just as chemical bodies in certain combinations produce trees or rocks or seas; but all we know is that such combinations exist; the formulas are hidden from us. Whoever has mastered the scientific method feels in his bones that the musical play and the tree have something in common, that both are created in accordance with the same correct, simple laws. Hence the question: what are those laws? Hence the temptation—to write a physiology of creativity (Boborykin), or, in the case of those who are younger and more timid, to cite science and the laws of nature (Merezhkovsky). A physiology of creativity probably does exist in nature, but dreams of it ought to be quashed at the very start. If critics begin looking to science for explanations, nothing good will come of it: a decade will be lost, a great deal of dead weight will be written, the matter will be further confused, and that is all. Thinking scientifically in every instance is fine, but the trouble is that scientific thought on creativity will inevitably come down to a search for "cells" or "centers" responsible for creativity; and then some obtuse German will discover those cells in the temporal lobe of the brain, a second will disagree with him, a third German will agree, while a Russian will skim an article on cells and fire an abstract off to *Severny vestnik, Vestnik Yevropy* will analyze the abstract, and for the next three years we shall see an epidemic of nonsense that will afford dullards earnings and popularity, while merely causing intelligent people irritation.

For those who long for the scientific method, those whom God has granted the rare talent of scientific thought, there is, in my opinion, just one choice—the philosophy of creativity. They could gather together all the best works of art created down through the ages and then employ the scientific method to discern the *common denominator* that unifies them and determines their value. That common denominator would be the law. Works that are called immortal have a great deal in common; if that common denominator were to be discarded from each of them, the works would lose their value and charm. Accordingly, the common denominator is essential and constitutes a *conditio sine qua non*★ for any work aspiring to immortality.

It is more beneficial for the young to write criticism than poetry. Merezhkovsky writes smoothly and youthfully, but on every page he loses his nerve, hedges and makes concessions—that is a sign that he has not made his own mind up on the matter. He calls me a poet, my stories novellas, my heroes failures; consequently I am in a rut. It is time to be done with failures, superfluous people, et cetera, and come up with something new. Merezhkovsky calls my monk who composes acathisti a failure.[84] What kind of failure is he? God grant everyone a life like that: he believed in God and had enough to eat and had the

★ (Lat.) an indispensable condition.

ability to compose. Dividing people into successes and failures means considering human nature from a narrow, biased point of view. Are you a success or not? Am I? Was Napoleon? Is your Vasily? Where are the criteria? You have to be God to distinguish the successes from the failures without making a mistake. I am off to the ball.

I am back from the ball. The society's aim is "unity." One learned German taught a cat, mouse, marlin, and sparrow to eat out of the same dish. That German had a system, but the society has none. Deadly dull. All present loitered about and pretended not to be bored. A young lady sang. Lensky read my story (On top of which one of the listeners said, "A pretty weak story!" whereupon Levinsky had the stupidity and cruelty to interrupt, "Here is the author himself! Allow me to introduce you," and the listener sank through the floor in embarrassment.); we danced, ate a bad supper, were cheated by the menservants. If actors, artists, and writers do indeed represent the best part of society, more the pity. Society must be splendid if its best part is so barren of colors, desires, intentions, so barren of taste, pretty women, initiative. They put a Japanese puppet in the entrance hall, stuck a Chinese parasol in a corner, hung a rug on the banister, and think it is artistic. They have a Chinese parasol but no newspapers. If an artist goes no further in decorating his apartment than displaying a museum puppet with a halberd and putting shields and fans on the walls, if it is not a product of chance but deeply felt and emphasized, then he is not an artist but a solemn performing monkey.

I received a letter from Leikin today. He writes that he visited you. He is a kindhearted and harmless man, but bourgeois to the marrow of his bones. If he comes here or says something, he invariably has some ulterior motive. Every word he utters has been carefully chosen, and he takes good note of every word you say, no matter how carelessly chosen, in the firm belief that he has great need of it; otherwise, his books will not sell, his enemies will triumph, his friends will desert him, the Credit Association will kick him out. The fox fears for his hide every minute, and so does he. Subtle diplomat! If he speaks of me, it means that he wishes to get in a dig at the "Nihilists," who have spoiled me (Mikhailovsky), and my brother Alexander, whom he hates. In his letters to me he cautions, scares, advises, reveals. Poor unhappy cripple! He could live out his days in peace, but some demon will not let him.

There has been a small *misfortune* in my family, of which I shall inform you when we meet.[85] Trouble is brewing for one of my brothers, and it prevents me from working and living in peace. What kind of commission is it, Creator, to be the head of a family!

Everyone here sends greetings. Please give Anna Ivanovna, Nastya, and Borya my warm regards.

Yours,

A. Chekhov

The vaudevilles may be published in the summer, but the winter is not a good time. I shall produce a vaudeville a month in the summer, but in the winter I shall be compelled to forgo that pleasurable activity.

Please sign me up for the Literature Society. When I come I shall attend.

To Alexei S. Suvorin

Moscow, 23 December 1888

I reread your play.[86] There is much in it that is good and original and has not been seen before in dramatic literature, and much that is not good (for example, the language). Its merits and defects are capital on which a good profit could be made if we had critics. But that capital will lie idle until it molders or is drawn. There are no critics. Cliché-ridden Tatishchev, that ass Mikhnevich, and apathetic Burenin —there you have the extent of Russia's criticism. Writing for them is just as senseless as giving someone with a cold a flower to smell. There are moments when I positively lose heart. For whom and what am I writing? For the public? But I do not see it and believe in it even less than I believe in the house spirit: the public is uneducated and ill bred, while its best elements are unscrupulous and insincere towards us. I cannot tell whether or not that public needs me. Burenin says that they do not and that what I am doing is of small account, while the Academy gave me a prize—the devil himself could not make head or tail of it. Write for the money? But I never have any, and thus unaccustomed, I am all but indifferent to it. I work lethargically for money. Write for the praise? But it merely irritates me. The Literature Society, students, Yevreinova, Pleshcheyev, girls, et cetera, praised my "Nervous Breakdown" to the skies, but Grigorovich alone noticed the description of the first snow. And so forth and so on. Were there criticism, I would know that I am creating material—good or bad, it makes no difference—that for people who have devoted themselves to studying life, I am as vital as stars are for an astronomer. Then I would endeavor to work and would know the reason for my labors. But in the meantime you and I and Muravlin, et cetera, are like maniacs, writing books and plays for personal pleasure. Personal pleasure is a good thing, of course; you feel it when you are writing, but then what? However, I shall close the faucet. In short, I feel hurt for Tatiana Repina and sorry for her, not because she poisoned herself, but because she lived out her life, died in suffering, and was described in a way that was quite futile and did not benefit people. Scores of tribes, religions, languages, and cultures have disappeared without a trace—disappeared because there were no historians or biologists. Likewise, scores of lives and works of art disappear before our eyes due to the complete absence of criticism. They will say that there is nothing for critics to do here, all the works produced today are paltry and bad. But that is a narrow view. The minuses as well as the pluses of life need to be studied. The mere conviction that the eighties have not produced one writer can serve as material for five volumes.

A. Chekhov

To Alexei S. Suvorin

Moscow, 7 January 1889

It would give me great pleasure to present a paper to the Literature Society on how the idea for *Ivanov* came to me. I would publicly repent. I cherished the audacious hope of summing up everything written about discontented, melancholy people and making *Ivanov* my final work on the subject. It seemed to me that all Russian authors of poetry, prose, and plays felt the need to depict the despondent individual and that they were all writing instinctively, without having any definite conceptions or views on the matter. In intention I came close to the mark, but the result was not worth a straw! I should have waited! I am glad that I did not listen to Grigorovich two or three years ago and did not write a novel! I can imagine how much goodwill I would have lost had I listened to him. He says, "Talent and freshness conquer all." Talent and freshness can spoil a great deal—that is closer to the truth. Besides an abundance of material and talent, something else no less important is needed. Maturity is needed, that is one; secondly, a *sense of personal freedom* is needed, and that sense was kindled in me only recently. I did not have it before; my frivolousness, carelessness, and disrespect for my work successfully took its place.

That which gentry writers took free from nature, intellectuals of lower birth are buying at the price of their youth. Write a story on how a young man, the son of a serf, a former shopkeeper, a chorister, a high school and university student, who was raised to respect rank, kiss the priest's hand, worship the thoughts of others, give thanks for every piece of bread, who was thrashed many times, went to school without galoshes, gave and received beatings, tortured animals, loved to eat at the home of rich relations, dissembled before God and man without the least need, solely from a sense of his own insignificance—write how that young man squeezes the slave from himself drop by drop, and how he, awakening one fine morning, senses that what flows through his veins is not a slave's blood, but that of a real human being.

Yours,

A. Chekhov

To Alexei S. Suvorin

Sumy, 7 May 1889

I read your account[87] of Bourget's *Disciple* and the Russian translation *(Severny vestnik)*. Here is how I see the matter. Bourget is a talented, very smart, educated man. He is fully versed in the method of the natural sciences and has a profound feeling for it, which implies that he has studied the natural sciences or medicine. He is no stranger to the field in which he has decided to establish his authority—a virtue unknown among Russian writers new and old. As far as textbook, academic psychology is concerned, he knows it as poorly as the best psychologists. Knowing it is the same as not knowing it, as it is not a science, but a fiction akin to alchemy which should now be consigned to the past. That is why I shall not even attempt to determine whether Bourget is a good or bad psychologist. The novel is interesting. I read it and understand why you found it so engrossing. Intelligent, interesting, witty at times, fantastical in part. As to its defects, chief among them is its pretentious campaign against the materialist trend. Forgive me, but I do not understand such campaigns. They never accomplish anything and only sow unnecessary confusion in the field of thought.

Against whom is the campaign directed and why? Where is the enemy and what are his bad qualities? First of all, the materialist trend is not a school or a trend in the narrow sense in which the term is used by the newspapers; it is not a fluke or a passing phenomenon; it is essential and unavoidable and beyond the power of man. Everything that lives on earth is materialistic of necessity. In animals, in savages, in Moscow merchants, all that is exalted and non–animalistic is a result of unconscious instinct; everything else about them is materialistic and ungoverned by their will, of course. Beings of a higher order, thinking people, are also materialistic of necessity. They look for truth in matter, for there is nowhere else for them to look, as all they see, hear, and experience is matter. Of necessity they can only look for truth where their microscopes, probes, scalpels, et cetera, are of use. Prohibiting the materialist trend is like forbidding man to look for the truth. Beyond material there is no experience or knowledge, thus there is no truth. Perhaps it is deplorable that Mr. Sixte[88] apparently sticks his nose into an area not his own and has the audacity to study man's inner being on a cellular level? How can he be blamed for the fact that psychological phenomena are astoundingly like physical phenomena and you cannot tell where one begins and the other ends? I think that when a corpse is opened up even the most inveterate spiritualist *must* ask himself the question, "Where is the soul?" And if you know how great the similarity is between corporeal and mental illness, and when you know that both illnesses are cured by the same medicines, you simply cannot separate the soul from the body.

As for the "psychological experiments," the implantation of vices in children and the figure of Sixte himself, they are all extremely exaggerated.

Spiritualists are not scientists. It is an honorary title. They are not needed as scientists. In everything they do and try to achieve, they are just as much materialists of necessity as Sixte himself is. If they were to do the impossible, defeat the materialists and wipe them from the face of the earth, by that defeat they would show themselves to be the supreme materialists, as they would have destroyed a whole cult, almost a religion.

At the very least it is premature to speak of the harm and danger of the materialist trend, let alone to wage war on it. We do not have sufficient evidence to form a charge. There are many theories and suppositions, but no facts, and all our antipathy will never amount to anything more than one great hobgoblin. Hobgoblins are anathema to merchants' wives, but no one knows why. Priests speak of lack of faith, debauchery, and so forth. Faith is not lacking. They believe in something, like Sixte, for instance. As far as debauchery is concerned, it is not the Sixtes and the Mendeleyevs[89] who have a reputation for being sybaritic debauchers, lechers, and drunks—it is poets, abbots, and personages who conscientiously attend embassy churches.

In short, I do not understand Bourget's campaign. Had Bourget taken the effort, while he was about it, to point out to the materialists the incorporeal God in heaven and point him out so that they would see him, that would be different, I would understand his excursion.

Forgive the philosophizing. I am off to the post office. My regards to all of yours, and I wish you health.

Yours,

A. Chekhov

To Alexei S. Suvorin

SUMY, 15 MAY 1889

If you have not yet left the country, I am writing in reply to your letter about Bourget. I shall be brief. You write in passing, "Let the science of matter take its course, but permit something to remain that will provide refuge from all that matter." The science of matter is taking its course, and those places where it is possible to take refuge from all that matter are also intact, no one seems to be encroaching on them. If anything is at risk, it is the natural sciences, not the sanctuaries from those sciences. My letter puts the issue more correctly and inoffensively than yours does, and I am closer to "the life of the spirit" than you are. You speak of the right that this or that form of learning has to exist, while I speak not of rights but of accord. I do not want people to see conflict where it is absent. Learning has always been around. Anatomy and belles-lettres have equally aristocratic origins, the same aims, the same enemy—the devil—and there is positively no reason why they should be at war. They are not in a struggle for survival. If an individual knows about blood circulation, he is rich; if he then learns the history of religion and the song *A Wondrous Moment I Remember,* he will be even richer, not poorer—so we must be dealing with pluses alone. That is why geniuses have never warred with one another, and the natural scientist in Goethe got along beautifully with the poet.

It is not forms of learning that clash, not poetry and anatomy, but delusions, i.e., people. When an individual does not understand something, he feels an inner conflict; he looks for the causes of that conflict not within himself, as he should, but beyond, hence the battle with that which he does not understand. In the course of the Middle Ages, chemistry gradually grew out of alchemy by natural, peaceful means; likewise, astronomy grew out of astrology; the monks did not understand, saw a conflict, and waged battle. Our own Pisarev[90] was just such a battling Spanish monk.

Bourget, too, is doing battle. You say that he is not, but I say he is. Imagine what will happen if his novel falls into the hands of someone who has children studying the natural sciences, or into the hands of a priest high in the church hierarchy who is looking for a subject for his Sunday sermon. Will the effect be at all tranquil? No. Imagine what will happen if the novel is spotted by an anatomist or physiologist, et cetera. It will not bring peace to anyone's soul. It will irritate the knowledgeable and reward the ignorant with false notions—and that is all.

Perhaps you will say that he is doing battle not with the quintessence but with deviations from the norm. I agree that every writer should combat deviations from the norm, but why compromise the quintessence? Sixte has the pride, courage, and strength of an eagle, but Bourget has made a caricature out of him. *The Psychological Experiments* slander man and science. Surely if I had written a novel where in the name of science an anatomist dissected his wife and infant children alive, or a learned female doctor traveled to the Nile and fornicated with a crocodile and a rattlesnake for scientific purposes, surely that novel would be slanderous. I could produce something interesting and clever, highbrow, too.

Bourget offers the Russian reader a fascinating change, like a thunderstorm after drought, and that is understandable. The reader found a novel whose heroes and author are smarter than he, and a life that is richer than his; Russian fiction writers are less intelligent than their readers, their heroes are pale and insignificant, the life they fleetingly describe is meager and uninteresting. The Russian writer lives in a drainpipe, eats wood lice, loves fishwives and laundresses; he does not know history or geography or the natural sciences, or the religion of his native land, neither its administrative nor legal procedures—in short, he does not know up from down. In comparison with Bourget, he is nothing more than a ninny. The reasons for Bourget's appeal are clear, but it still does not follow that Sixte is right when he recites the *Our Father,* or that he is being honest then.

Bon voyage.

Yours,

Chekhov

To Alexei S. Suvorin

Moscow, 18–23 December 1889[91]

[E]ssays, satirical articles, bits of fluff, vaudevilles, dull stories, a multitude of mistakes and incongruities, poods of paper covered in writing, the Academy's prize, the life of Potemkin—and not one line that has any real literary significance in my eyes. There has been a great deal of busyness, but not one minute of serious work. When I read Bezhetsky's *A Tragedy in the Family* the other day, I felt something akin to compassion for the author; the exact same feeling comes over me when I see my books. The element of truth in that feeling is the size of a fly, but my suspicion and envy of others' work inflates it to elephantine proportions. How I would like to go into hiding for five years or so and occupy myself with meticulous, serious work. I need to learn, learn everything from the start, for as a writer I am a complete ignoramus; I need to write conscientiously, feelingly, intelligently, not five quires a month but one quire every five months. I need to leave home. I need to start living on seven to nine hundred rubles a year, not three to four thousand as I do now. I need to say to heck with a lot of things, but there is more Ukrainian laziness in me than daring.

I sold *The Forest Demon* to Abramova,[92] more's the pity. My lethargic inner being reasons that I now have enough money for three or four months. There you have my Ukrainian logic. What a deplorable lot today's young people are!

Everyone in the household is enjoying better health. I am not coughing anymore, either. It will be awfully nice to see you. I should arrive in early January.

The days are lengthening. Spring is on the way and we have not yet had winter.

I will be thirty in January. A mean trick. I feel as though I were twenty-two.

Please do not be sick, and tell Anna Ivanovna to give her illness to someone else.

Perhaps I should come to St. Petersburg to see in the New Year?

Yours,

A. Chekhov

To Alexei S. Suvorin

Moscow, 9 March 1890

9 March—Forty martyrs and ten thousand larks

We are both wrong about Sakhalin, but you are probably more so. I embark quite certain that my trip shall not make a valuable contribution to either literature or science: I do not have the knowledge or the time or the pretensions. I do not have the plans of a Humboldt or even a Kennan.[93] I want to write at least one or two hundred pages so that I can compensate my medicine, which, as you know, I have behaved swinishly towards. Perhaps I will not be able to write anything, but even then the trip will still have its appeal: by reading, looking, and listening I shall learn a great deal. I have yet to make the trip, but thanks to the books which I have been obliged to read, I have learned a great deal that everyone should know at pain of forty lashes and that I had the ignorance not to know before. In addition, I presume that the trip will be half a year of unceasing labor, both physical and mental, and that is vital for me since I am a Ukrainian and have begun to show signs of indolence. I need to teach myself discipline. Maybe my trip is frivolity, stubbornness, a caprice, but reflect on the matter a moment and tell me what I shall lose by going? Time? Money? Experience deprivation? My time is worth nothing, I never have any money as it is, and, as for deprivations, I shall spend twenty-five to thirty days in a horse-drawn cart, no more, while the rest of the time I shall be on the deck of a steamship or in my cabin and shall bombard you continuously with letters. Maybe the trip will be of absolutely no benefit to me, but can it really be that the whole trip will not yield two or three days that I shall remember with pleasure or pain for the rest of my life? Et cetera. So there, m'lord. All unconvincing, but you do not do a better job. For example, you write that no one has any need of Sakhalin or interest in it. Can that be true?

Sakhalin can only be of no need or interest to a society that does not exile thousands of people there or spend millions on it. Besides Australia of former times and Cayenne, Sakhalin is the only place where colonization by criminals can be studied; all of Europe is interested in it, but we have no need of it? No more than twenty-five or thirty years ago our own Russian people performed astounding feats in exploring Sakhalin that would make them worthy of idolization; but we do not need that, we do not know who those people were and just sit within our four walls and complain that God did a bad job when he created man. Sakhalin is a place of extreme adversity that a man could hardly endure. Those who worked in and around it have accomplished frightful, important tasks and continue to do so. I regret that I am not sentimental, or I would say that we should make pilgrimages to places like Sakhalin, as the Turks go to Mecca; Sakhalin in particular should be to sailors and penologists what Sebastopol is to the military.[94] From the books I have read it is clear that we have driven *millions* of people into prisons, driven them there to no purpose, thoughtlessly, barbarously; we have driven people in shackles tens of thousands of versts in the cold, infected them with syphilis, corrupted them, and bred criminals, and blamed it all on the jailer and red-nosed guards. Now all of educated Europe knows that it is we, not the guards, who are to blame; but we do not care about that, it is uninteresting. The celebrated sixties did *nothing* for the sick and imprisoned, thereby breaking the chief commandment of Christian civilization. Today something is being done for the sick, but nothing is being done for prisoners; our legal experts are quite uninterested in penology. No, I assure you that Sakhalin is needed and interesting, and it is only to be regretted that I am going, instead of someone who understands more about the matter and would be better capable of awakening society's interest. I am going for trifles.

As for my letter regarding Pleshcheyev, I wrote you that I have caused dissatisfaction among my young friends with my idleness, and in my defense I wrote you that, despite my idleness, I had nevertheless done more than my friends have—they do absolutely nothing. At least I have read the *Maritime Collection* and paid a call on Galkin.[95] That is all, I think.

We are experiencing great student unrest here. It all started at the Petrine Academy, where the administration prohibited girls from visiting state-owned apartments, on the suspicion of not just prostitution but politics, too. From the Academy the unrest spread to the university, where, surrounded by heavily armed, mounted Hectors and Achilles with lances, the students are demanding the following:

1) Complete autonomy for the universities.
2) The lifting of all restrictions on instruction.
3) Free access to the university regardless of creed, nationality, sex, or social position.
4) The lifting of all restrictions on the admittance of Jews to the university and equal rights with other students.
5) Freedom of assembly and recognition of student corporations.
6) The establishment of a university and student court.
7) Elimination of the police function of inspection.
8) Reduction of tuition.

I copied that from the proclamation with some deletions. I think that passions burn most fiercely in a mob, and the sex which wishes to be admitted to the university, though prepared for it five times worse than the men, who are badly prepared as it is and with rare exceptions do atrociously at their studies. . . .

Yours,

A. Chekhov

TO MIKHAIL I. TCHAIKOVSKY

MOSCOW, 16 MARCH 1890

In one and a half to two weeks the book I have dedicated to Peter Ilyich will come out.[96] I am ready to be on honor guard day and night by the wing of the house where Peter Ilyich resides—that is how great a respect I have for him. As to rankings, in Russian art he is second only to Lev Tolstoy, who has long been in first place. (I give third to Repin and take ninety-eighth for myself.) I have long cherished the audacious hope of dedicating something to him. That dedication would, I thought, be a partial, minimal expression of the vast estimation that I, a journeyman writer, have for his magnificent talent but am unable to put down on paper due to my lack of musical talent. Unfortunately, I was compelled to realize my dream with a book that I do not consider one of my best. It is made up of especially dreary, psychopathological sketches and has a dreary title, so my dedication will not at all be to the taste of Peter Ilyich or his admirers.

You are a Chekhovist? Please accept our humble thanks. No, you are not a Chekhovist but simply an indulgent man. I wish you health and all the very best.

Yours,

Chekhov

TO ALEXEI S. SUVORIN

MOSCOW, 1 APRIL 1890

You reprove me for objectivity, calling it indifference towards right and wrong, a lack of ideals and ideas, and so forth.[97] You would like to have me say when I depict horse thieves, "It is wrong to steal horses." But that was clear long before I came along. Let the jury pass judgment, my job is to show what kind of people they are. I write; you deal with horse thieves, so you should know that they are not destitute people, but satiated, that they are part of a cult, and that stealing horses is not just a theft, but a passion. Of course, it would be nice to combine art with a homily, but I personally find that extraordinarily difficult and almost impossible, given the limitations of the genre. In order to depict horse thieves in seven hundred lines, I must constantly speak their language, think their thoughts, and feel their feelings; otherwise, if I add an element of subjectivity, the images will dim and the story will not be as compact as a short story should be. When I write, I place my complete trust in the reader; I presume he will add the missing subjective elements himself. Prosper.

Yours,

A. Chekhov

TO VUKOL M. LAVROV[98]

MOSCOW, 10 APRIL 1890

Vukol Mikhailovich;

In the March issue of *Russkaya mysl,* on page 147 of the bibliography section, I stumbled across the following phrase: "As recently as yesterday even the priests of unprincipled writing, e.g., Messrs Yasinsky and Chekhov, whose names . . . ." Ordinarily no response is made to criticism, but in this instance slander, not criticism, is in question. I might not have responded to slander, either, but within the next few days I shall be leaving Russia for a long journey, perhaps never to return, so I cannot refrain from making a reply.

I have never been an unprincipled writer or, what amounts to the same, a scoundrel.

True, my entire literary career has consisted of an unbroken series of mistakes, at times flagrant, but that is to be explained by the size of my gifts, certainly not by whether I am a good or bad person. I have not committed blackmail, written pasquils or denunciations, toadied, lied, or insulted others; in short, there are many stories and editorials that I would gladly discard as worthless, but there is not one line that now causes me shame. If we presume that by unprincipled you mean the sad fact that I, an educated, frequently published man, have not done anything for those I love, that my work has not contributed in the slightest to, for instance, the zemstvo, the new courts, freedom of the press, freedom in general, et cetera, then in that sense *Russkaya mysl* should in all fairness consider me its fellow, not point an accusing finger, as it has done no more in this direction than I have—and we are not to blame for that.

If I am judged as a writer on outward criteria, I scarcely deserve to be publicly accused of lacking principle in that instance, either. Up to now I have led a cloistered life within the four walls of my home; you and I meet once every couple of years, and I have never laid eyes on Mr. Machtet, for example—so you can judge for yourself how often I go out of the house. I have always persistently refused invitations to literary evenings, parties, meetings, et cetera; I do not turn up at editorial offices without being asked; I have always tried to make my acquaintances see me more as a physician than writer; in short, I have been a modest writer, and this letter is the first immodesty of my decade-long career. I am on excellent terms with my colleagues; I have never presumed to judge them or the journals and newspapers for which they work, as I do not consider myself competent to do so and find that, given the subordinate role in which the press currently finds itself, any word spoken against a journal or writer is not only cruel and tactless but downright criminal. Up to now I have only turned down those journals and newspapers whose inferiority was obvious and proven; and when I have had occasion to chose between them, I have given my preference to those which, due to financial or other circumstances, were most in need of my services; and that is why I did not work for you or for *Vestnik Yevropy* but for *Severny vestnik,* and that is why I received half what I could have received, had I a different view of my responsibilities.

Your accusation is slanderous. I cannot ask you to retract it, as it is already a fact and cannot be hacked out; I cannot explain it away as carelessness, thoughtlessness, or anything of the sort, as I know you have on your editorial staff unquestionably decent and well-bred people, who, I hope, do not read and write articles to no purpose but have an awareness of the responsibility they bear for each of their words. All that remains is for me to point out your mistake to you and ask you to believe in the sincerity of the distress which has prompted me to write you this letter. Obviously, after the accusation you have made, even a nodding acquaintance, much less business dealings, is out of the question.

Yours,

A. Chekhov

To Alexei S. Suvorin

MOSCOW, 9 DECEMBER 1890

Malaya Dmitrovka, c/o Virgang

Greetings, my friend! Hurrah! At last I am seated once again at my desk, praying to my fading penates and writing to you. I have a wonderful feeling that I never left home at all. I am bursting with health and absolutely thriving. There you have the shortest of reports. I spent not two months in Sakhalin, as was printed in your magazine, but three, plus two days. The work I did was intensive; I made a thorough census of the entire population of Sakhalin and saw *everything* except an execution. When we meet I shall show you a whole trunk full of penal odds and ends which are extremely valuable as resource materials. I now know a great deal but have come back low. While I was living in Sakhalin I merely experienced some heartburn, as though from eating rancid butter, but now, looking back, Sakhalin seems like a living hell to me. I worked intensively two months, without sparing myself; then in the third I flagged due to the aforementioned heartburn, boredom, and the thought that cholera was spreading from Vladivostok to Sakhalin and I might have to spend the winter in the penal colony.

But the outbreak of cholera ended, thank heavens, and on 13 October my steamship left Sakhalin. I was in Vladivostok. Regarding the Primorye region and our eastern coast in general, with its fleets, tasks, and Pacific reveries, I have just one thing to say: scandalous poverty—poverty, ignorance, and meanness that can drive a person to despair! One honest man for every ninety-nine thieves sullying the Russian name. We did not call at Japan, as cholera had broken out there; for that reason I did not buy you anything Japanese, and the five hundred rubles you gave me for purchases went to meet my own needs, so you have every legal right to have me exiled to Siberia. The first foreign port on my journey was Hong Kong. The harbor was just lovely, and I had never before seen much sea traffic, not even in pictures. Splendid roads, horse-drawn trams, a railway up the mountain, museums, botanical gardens, and everywhere you look you see evidence of the Britons' tender concern for the welfare of their employees; there is even a seamen's club. I rode *jinrikishas* (i.e., people), bought all kinds of junk from Chinamen, and felt indignant when I heard my fellow Russian travelers censure the British for exploiting other nationalities. I thought, yes, the British are exploiting the Chinese and Indians, but they have given them roads, plumbing, museums, and Christianity, while you exploit people too, but what have you given them?

When we left Hong Kong the ship began to roll. The vessel was empty and made thirty-eight degree swings, so we were afraid it would capsize. I am not prone to seasickness—that discovery came as a pleasant surprise. On the way to Singapore the bodies of two people were thrown into the sea. When you see a dead man wrapped in sailcloth fly twisting into the water, and when you recall that it is several versts to the bottom, a terrifying feeling comes over you and you are suddenly gripped by the thought that you too will die and be thrown into the sea. The cattle on board got sick. On the orders of Dr. Shcherbak and yours truly, they were killed and thrown overboard.

I have a poor recollection of Singapore as I felt unaccountably sad when I toured it; I nearly burst into tears. Then came Ceylon—the place where the Garden of Eden was. I covered over a hundred versts by train in the Garden of Eden and got my fill of palm forests and bronzed women. From Ceylon we sailed for thirteen days without making a port call and went mad from boredom. I take heat well. The Red Sea was dreary; the sight of the Sinai moved me.

The world is a fine place. There is just one deplorable thing about it: us. We have so little fairness and humility, we have such a poor understanding of patriotism! A drunken, haggard, profligate husband loves his wife and children, but what good is that love? The newspapers say that we love our homeland, but how is that love expressed? Impudence and conceit beyond measure instead of knowledge, indolence and swinishness instead of work. There is no justice, and the notion of honor amounts to no more than "the honor of the uniform," the uniform that so often decorates the docks of our courtrooms. We need to work and send everything else to the devil. Justice is the main thing. The rest will come.

God bless.

Yours,

A. Chekhov

To Alexei S. Suvorin

Melikhovo, 25 November 1892

It is not hard to understand what you mean, and you are wrong to rebuke yourself for not being clearer. You are an inveterate drunkard, and I served you a soft drink; while you gave the soft drink its due, you justly noted that it lacked alcohol. Our writings lack the alcohol that would intoxicate and have an effect, and you let me know that. Why do they? Let's leave "Ward No. 6" and myself aside and address the general issue, since it is more interesting. Let's discuss general causes, if you are not bored, and review a whole era. Tell me, honestly, which of my contemporaries, i.e., between thirty and forty-five years of age, has given the world even one drop of alcohol? Have not Korolenko, Nadson, and all of today's playwrights served up soft drinks? Have the paintings of Repin or Shishkin really made your head spin? They are nice and show talent. You praise them, but your desire for a smoke is always at the back of your mind. This is a great time for science and technology, but an amorphous, dull, glum time for our brother. We ourselves are dull and glum. All we are capable of creating are Gutta-Percha boys,[99] and the only person who does not see that is Stasov,[100] who is blessed with the rare ability to become intoxicated even on dishwater. This stems not from our stupidity, not from mediocrity or impudence, as Burenin believes, but from an illness that for an artist is worse than syphilis or sexual debilitation. We lack something, it is true, which means that if you lift the hem of our muse's dress you will find a void. Remember that the writers we call great or simply good, who intoxicate us, share a very important trait: they are bound somewhere and call on you to join them. You sense with not your mind but your whole being that they have an aim, as did the ghost of Hamlet's father, who came and troubled the thoughts with a purpose. Some, depending on their caliber, have the most immediate of aims—serfdom, the liberation of the homeland, politics, beauty, or simply vodka, as in the case of Denis Davydov.[101] Others have more remote aims—God, life beyond the grave, human happiness, et cetera. The best of them are realists and portray life as it is, but since each line is saturated with the consciousness of that aim, as with sap, you sense, beyond life as it is, life as it should be, and that captivates you. And what about us? Us! We portray life as it is, and that is as far as we will go, lash us though you may. We have neither immediate nor remote aims, and our souls are hollow. We have no politics, we do not believe in revolution, there is no God, we are not afraid of apparitions, and personally, I am not even afraid of death or blindness. He who wants nothing, hopes for nothing, and fears nothing cannot be an artist. Be it an illness or not—the name is not the point—we must recognize that we are in a sorry state. I do not know what will become of us in ten or twenty years, perhaps then the situation will change, but in the meantime it would be hasty to expect something really worthwhile of us, whether we are talented or not. We write unthinkingly, submitting solely to the long-established state of affairs whereby some serve, others sell, still others write. You and Grigorovich think me smart. Yes, I am at least smart enough to refrain from denying my illness and lying to myself and concealing my hollowness with such borrowed rags as ideas from the sixties, et cetera. I shall not throw myself down a stairwell, as Garshin did, but neither shall I flatter myself with hopes of a better future. I am not to blame for my illness, nor can I cure myself, as presumably this illness has fine aims that are beyond our ken and has not been inflicted in vain. Not in vain, not in vain did she walk out with the swain!

And now as to intellect, Sir Grigorovich thinks that intellect can overwhelm talent. Byron was as smart as a hundred devils; nevertheless, his talent has survived intact. If we say that X talked nonsense because his intellect overwhelmed his talent or vice versa, then I say X had neither brains nor talent.

Yours,

A. Chekhov

To Alexei S. Suvorin

The fact that the latest generation of writers and artists have no creative aims is a quite natural, logical, and curious phenomenon, but just because some phantom has gone and frightened Sazonova,[102] it does not follow that I was being deceitful or betraying my conscience when I wrote that letter. You yourself saw insincerity in it only after she wrote you; otherwise you would not have sent her my letter. In my letters to you I am often unfair and naive, but I never write something that is not to my liking.

If you would like insincerity, you have a million poods of it in Sazonova's letter: "The greatest miracle is man himself, and we shall never tire of studying him," or "the purpose of life is life itself," or "I believe in life, in its bright moments; for their sake we not only can live but must live. I believe in man, in the fine features of his soul," et cetera. Is that really sincere? Does it really mean anything? Those are not views, they are fruit drops. She emphasizes "can" and "must" because she is afraid of talking about what is and must be reckoned with. First she should state what is, and then I shall listen to what can or should be. She believes "in life," and that means that she does not believe in anything, if she is smart, or simply believes in the peasant God and crosses herself in the dark if she is a country woman.

Under the influence of her letter, you write me about "life for life's sake." Thanks, but no thanks. Her life-loving letter is a thousand times more like the grave than mine. I write that there are no aims, and you take that to mean that I consider such aims vital and would gladly go in search of them, while Sazonova writes that one ought not tempt man with all sorts of blessings he will never receive, "be grateful for what you have," and in her opinion our whole problem is that we are searching for some sort of higher and remote aims. If that is not female logic, it is the philosophy of despair. For those who sincerely believe that higher and remote aims are as much use to man as to a cow, and that those aims are "our whole problem," all that remains is to eat, drink, sleep, or, tiring of that, bashing their heads into the corner of a trunk. . . .

Yours,

A. Chekhov

To Alexei S. Suvorin

I am in good health on the whole but ill in certain particulars, for example, a cough, missed heartbeats, and hemorrhoids. Once my heart skipped beats for six days running, and I felt loathsome the whole time. Since I have completely given up smoking, I never have gloomy or anxious moods. Perhaps because I no longer smoke, Tolstoyan morals have ceased to have a hold on me, and deep in my heart I am hostile to them, which is not fair of course. Peasant blood courses through my veins, so you cannot impress me with peasant virtues. I have believed in progress since childhood and could not do otherwise since the difference between the time when I was thrashed and the time when I stopped being thrashed was enormous. I loved intelligent people, emotion, courtesy, and wit, while I was as indifferent to people picking at their calluses and the asphyxiating smell of their foot bindings as I was to the gentry ladies out and about mornings in their curling papers. But the Tolstoyan philosophy had a profound effect on me and consumed me for six or seven years, though it was not the fundamental principles that attracted me, as I was already aware of them, but the Tolstoyan manner of expression, his good sense, and probably hypnosis of some kind. Now, however, something in me protests; prudence and a sense of justice tell me that there is more neighborly love in electricity and steam than there is in chastity and abstention from meat. War is evil and the judicial system is evil, but that does not mean that I should wear bast shoes and sleep on the stove alongside the workman and his wife, and so on, and so forth. However, the point is not that I am "for or against," but that in one way or another, Tolstoy has sailed away for me; I no longer have him in my heart; he left, having said, "Lo, I leave your house empty." I am exempt from billeting. Debates get on my nerves, while reading frivolous writers like Max Nordau[103] simply repulses me. A patient with a fever does not want to eat, but he wants something, and this is how he expresses his vague desire: "something sour." I, too, want something sour. And it is no fluke, for I notice that the mood is pervasive. It is as though everyone was in love but has now fallen out of it and is looking for a new infatuation. Russians will once more experience an infatuation with the natural sciences, and the materialist trend may well become fashionable again. The natural sciences are now working miracles, and they can overwhelm the public with their vast size. But everything is in God's hands. And philosophizing makes a person dizzy.

Yours,

A. Chekhov

To Anatoly F. Kony

Moscow Gubernia, Lopasnya

Dear Anatoly Fyodorovich, you cannot imagine how happy your letter made me.[104] I saw only the first two acts of my play from the auditorium, then sat in the wings, and felt the whole time that *The Seagull* was flopping. Afterwards, that night and the next day, I was told that I had depicted nothing but idiots, that my play was clumsy in terms of staging, that it was unintelligent, unintelligible, even pointless, et cetera. You can imagine my position—it was a failure far worse than I had dreamed possible! I was ashamed, dejected, and I left St. Petersburg filled with doubts of every sort. I thought that if I had written and staged a play that was evidently bristling with monstrous defects, then I must have lost all sense of proportion, and that meant that my machine was completely broken. When I had returned home, I heard from St. Petersburg that the second and third performances had gone well; several letters arrived, some signed, others anonymous, prizing the play and scolding the critics; I read them with pleasure, but all the same I was ashamed and dejected, and it occurred to me that if kind people found it necessary to console me, then things were bad. But your letter had the most profound effect on me. I have known you for a long time, respect you deeply, and believe in you more than in all the critics put together. You sensed that when you wrote your letter, and that is why it is so splendid and convincing. I have now calmed down and can recall the play and the performance without disgust.

Komissarzhevskaya is a marvelous actress. At one rehearsal many of those present wept when they saw her and said that she was the best actress in Russia today, but during the performance, the general hostility to *The Seagull* evidently unnerved her, and she lost her voice. Our press is cool towards her, but she deserves better, and I feel sorry for her.

Permit me to thank you for your letter, from the bottom of my heart. Be assured that I value more than I can express in words the sentiments that prompted you to write me, and the sympathy, which you term "unnecessary" at the end of your letter, shall never, never be forgotten, whatever happens.

Respectfully and devotedly yours,

A. Chekhov

TO VLADIMIR I. NEMIROVICH-DANCHENKO

MELIKHOVO, 26 NOVEMBER 1896

Lopasnya

Dear friend, I shall address what lies at the heart of your letter—why we so rarely have serious talks. When people are silent they either have nothing to say or are too shy to say it. What is there to talk about? We do not have any politics. We do not share an involvement in community work or study circles, or even street life. Our urban existence is barren, monotonous, slow, and uninteresting. Talking about it is just as boring as corresponding with Lugov.[105] You say that we are men of letters, and that of itself makes our life rich. Is that so? We are up to our ears in our profession; bit by bit it has isolated us from the outside world; and, as a result, we have little spare time, little money, few books which we rarely and reluctantly read, we hear little, travel little. Talk about literature? But we have already. Every year the same thing over and over again, and all our conversations about literature come down to is whose work was better and whose work was worse; conversations on more general, broader subjects never succeed, because when you are surrounded by tundra and Eskimos, general ideas dwindle and fade as fast as thoughts of eternal bliss, since they are inapplicable to the present. Talk about our personal life? Yes, that can be interesting at times, and we might well have a good talk; but we feel too shy, we are reticent, insincere, an instinct for self-preservation constrains us, and we feel afraid. We are afraid that some boorish Eskimo with whom we have a mutual dislike will overhear our conversation; personally, I am afraid that my friend Sergeyenko,[106] whose mind you are so fond of, will raise his finger in every railway car and home and loudly state his opinion on why N and I were drawn together while Z loves me. I am afraid of our morals, afraid of our ladies. In short, do not blame yourself or me for our silence or for the frivolity and dullness of our conversations. Blame "the epoch," as the critics say, blame the climate, the expanse, whatever you like, and allow circumstances to take their fated, inexorable course, while placing your hopes on the future.

Yours,

A. Chekhov

To Fyodor D. Batiushkov[107]

NICE, 23 JANUARY 1898

All anyone can talk about is Zola and Dreyfus. The overwhelming majority of the intelligentsia are on Zola's side and believe Dreyfus to be innocent. Zola has risen a whole three *arshins* in people's eyes; his letters of protest are like a breath of fresh air, and every Frenchman senses that, thank the Lord, there is still justice in this world, and if an innocent man is convicted of a crime, there is someone who will stand up for him. The French newspapers are extremely interesting, in stark contrast to the Russian papers. *Novoye Vremya* is simply abominable. . . .

Respectfully yours,

A. Chekhov

To Alexandra A. Khotyaintseva[108]

NICE, 2 FEBRUARY 1898

Monday

You ask me whether I still think that Zola is right. I must reply by asking you if you really have such a poor opinion of me that you could doubt me to be on Zola's side even for a moment? His finger-nail is worth more to me than all those who now sit in judgment of him in the assizes, all those generals and noble witnesses. I read the court reports and do not find Zola to be wrong, nor do I see what other *preuves*★ are necessary. . . .

Yours,

A. Chekhov

★ (Fr .) evidence.—Tr.

To Alexei S. Suvorin

You write that you are vexed with Zola, while everyone here feels as though a new and better Zola has been born. His trial has had the effect of turpentine, clearing away the soil marks, so that he now stands before the French in all his natural splendor. He has achieved a purity and moral status of which no one suspected him capable. You trace the scandal from the very beginning. Dreyfus's demotion, whether justified or not, cast a pall on everyone (including you, as I recall). It could not escape notice that during the flogging Dreyfus behaved as an honest, well-disciplined officer should, while the journalists who were present, for example, shouted, "Shut up, Judas!" in other words, acted badly, unbecomingly. Everyone returned from the flogging dissatisfied and with an uneasy conscience. Dreyfus's counsel, Démange, was particularly dissatisfied. An honest man, he sensed during the investigation that something was afoot. Then the experts had to convince themselves that they had not made a mistake, so they wandered about Paris talking about nothing but Dreyfus and his guilt. One of the experts proved to be a madman, the author of a monstrously absurd scheme, two were eccentrics. Like it or not, the war ministry's information bureau,* that military consistory which spends its time catching spies and reading other people's mail, was a subject that had to be addressed, since the head of the bureau, Sandherr, proved to be afflicted with progressive paralysis, Paty de Clam showed that he was something like Berlin's Tausch, and Picquart left suddenly, mysteriously, in the midst of a row. As though by design, a whole series of blatant judicial errors were uncovered. Little by little it became clear that Dreyfus had actually been convicted on the basis of a secret document that was not shown to either the defendant or his attorney—and upstanding people saw this as a fundamental violation of the law. If the letter was written by the sun itself, let alone Wilhelm, it should have been shown to Démange. All kinds of speculations were made about the contents of the letter. Wild stories began to circulate. Dreyfus was an officer—the military was on its guard. Dreyfus was a Jew—the Jews were on their guard. There was talk of militarism and Yids. Profoundly contemptible people like Drumont raised their heads; little by little

---

* The intelligence department of the Ministry of War, known as the Second Bureau.—Ed.

trouble was stirred up on anti-Semitic grounds, on grounds that reek of carnage. When something goes wrong, we look beyond ourselves for the cause and soon find it: "It's those damned French, those Yids, that Wilhelm." Capital, hobgoblins, Masons, the Syndicate, Jesuits—they are all apparitions, but how they put our minds at ease! They are a bad sign, of course. If the French are talking about Yids and the Syndicate, they must not feel all right, something must be worming at them, they must need those apparitions to soothe their troubled consciences. Then came that Esterhazy—pugnacious in a Turgenevian way, insolent, long suspect, held in contempt by his comrades, the amazing resemblance of his handwriting to that on the *bordereau*, the uhlan's letters, the threats which he inexplicably failed to carry out, finally the quite mysterious trial where the court came to the strange decision that the handwriting on the *bordereau* was Esterhazy's, but he had not produced it. And the gas built up, the pressure mounted, the atmosphere became depressingly close. The fight in the chamber is something that can be put down to nerves, hysterics resulting from that pressure. Zola's letter and trial are of the same order. What do you expect? The first to raise the alarm should have been the best people, those in the forefront of the nation—and that is what happened. The first to speak up was Scheurer-Kestner. Frenchmen who know him well say (and I quote Kovalevsky) that he is "dagger blades," he is so irreproachable and precise. The second was Zola. Now he is on trial.

You are right, Zola is not Voltaire. None of us is Voltaire, but there are moments in life when it is least appropriate to reproach us for not being Voltaire. Think of Korolenko, who defended the Multan pagans[109] and saved them from penal servitude. Dr. Haas[110] was not Voltaire either, but his splendid life was very well spent.

I am acquainted with the case through the court report. It differs completely from what is in the papers, and I have no doubts about Zola. The main thing is that he is sincere, which is to say he bases his judgments only on what he sees, not on apparitions, as others do. Sincere people can be mistaken, without question, but those sorts of mistakes cause less harm than deliberate insincerity, prejudices, or political considerations. Even if Dreyfus is guilty, Zola is right, since a writer's job is not to accuse, not to prosecute, but to stand up even for the guilty if they have already been condemned and punished. Some may ask, what about politics? The interests of the state? But great writers and artists should get involved in politics only insofar as to defend themselves from it. There are plenty of prosecutors and policemen without them, in the event the role of Paul suits them better than the role of Saul. And whatever the verdict may be, Zola will still experience a lively joy after the trial, he will enjoy a fine old age, and when he dies it will be with a serene or at least lightened conscience. The situation is painful to the French, and they grasp at every word of comfort and every salutary reproach that comes from without. That is why Bjørnstjerne's[111] letter and the article by our Zakrevsky (which was printed here in *The News*) were so well received, and why they are disgusted by the vilification of Zola, in other words, what they are treated to every day by their minor press, which they hold in contempt. No matter how nervous Zola may be, he represents French common sense in court, and the French love him and take pride in him for that, even though they also applaud the generals, who in their artless way scare them first with the honor of the army, then with war.

Yours,

A. Chekhov

To Olga G. Chekhova[112]

Nice, 22 February 1898

You ask my opinion of Zola and his trial. First, I recognize an obvious fact: Europe's intelligentsia to a man is on Zola's side, and all that is vile and dubious is against him. Here is how the matter stands: imagine that the university registrar had mistakenly expelled one student instead of another. You start to protest and are told, "You are insulting science!" though all the registrar and science have in common is the fact that clerks and professors wear their blue tailcoats the same way. You declare, argue, refute, and you are told, "Prove it!" "Let's go to the office and look at the books," you suggest and are told, "No, you may not! It is confidential!" Just see what you can do! The thinking of the French government is obvious. Just as a respectable woman, who was once unfaithful to her husband, then makes a series of stupid mistakes, becomes the victim of impudent blackmail, and eventually takes her own life, all to keep her first mistake from being discovered; so, too, the French government is now barreling along, eyes narrow, lurching left and right—anything to keep from admitting its mistake.

Novoye Vremya is conducting an absurd campaign; however, most of the Russian newspapers are for Zola or at least against his persecution. Nothing will come of the appeal, even if the decision is favorable. The matter will resolve itself, by chance, when the pressure builds up in the heads of the French to the point of an explosion. It will all work out. . . .

Your Papa,

A. Chekhov

TO PAVEL F. IORDANOV[113]

YALTA, 21 SEPTEMBER 1898

My health is good and bad. Bad in the sense that I am out of sorts and have been doing very little work. Having to wander from one health resort to the next is worse than any bug.

Should you happen to be in Moscow, go to the Hermitage Theater where productions by Stanislavsky and Vladimir Nemirovich-Danchenko are given.

The *mise en scènes* are amazing, unlike anything done in Russia before. By the way, my poor, hapless *Seagull*[114] is in production. . . .

Yours,

A. Chekhov

TO VLADIMIR I. NEMIROVICH-DANCHENKO

YALTA, 21 OCTOBER 1898

Dear Vladimir Ivanovich, I am in Yalta for a long stay. The trees and grass are a summer green, and it is warm, clear, quiet, and dry. Today, in fact, it is not just warm but downright hot. It is quite to my liking, and I may well settle down in Yalta for good.

I was deeply touched by your telegram.[115] My great thanks to you and Konstantin Sergeyevich and the actors who thought of me. In general, please do not forget me and write, if only once in a great while. You are now a busy man, a director, but even so, do write an idle fellow once in a while. Write and tell me what is going on, how the actors reacted to the success of the first performances, how *The Seagull* is doing, what changes have been made in the casting, et cetera. Judging by the papers, the beginning was brilliant, and that makes me very, very happy, happier than you can imagine. Your success proves once again that the public and actors need intelligent theater. But why do you not say anything about Irina—Knipper? Did something go wrong? I did not like your Fyodor, but Irina seemed extraordinary; now, though, there is more talk of Fyodor than of Irina. . . .

Yours,

A. Chekhov

My regards to Sumbatov.

To Alexei M. Peshkov (Maxim Gorky)[116]

YALTA, 16 NOVEMBER 1898

Dear Alexei Maximovich, I received your letter and book[117] some time ago and have long intended to write you, but business of various kinds has continuously interfered. Please forgive me. As soon as I have a free hour, I shall sit down and write you a proper letter. Last night I read your *Fair in Goltva*. I liked it very much and felt compelled to write you these lines so that you will not be angry and think badly of me. I am very, very glad to make your acquaintance and very grateful to you and Mirov,[118] who wrote you about me.

And so, until such time as I am more at leisure, I wish you all the best and shake your hand in friendship!

Yours,

A. Chekhov

To Alexei M. Peshkov (Maxim Gorky)

YALTA, 3 DECEMBER 1898

Dear Alexei Maximovich, your last letter gave me great pleasure. I thank you from the bottom of my heart.[119] *Uncle Vanya* was written a long, long time ago; I have never seen it performed. In recent years it has frequently been put on by provincial theaters—perhaps because I published a collection of my plays. I do not think much of my plays on the whole; I ceased having anything to do with the theater a long time ago and no longer wish to write for it.

You ask me what I think of your stories. What do I think? Without a doubt you have talent, and genuine, big talent at that. It came through with unusual force in your story "In the Steppe," for instance, and I even felt envious that I had not written it myself. You are an artist and a man of intelligence. You have an excellent feel for things. You are rounded, which is to say when you depict something you see it and feel it. That is true art. Now you know what I think, and I am very glad that I have had a chance to tell you. I repeat, I am very glad, and if we were to meet and chat for an hour or two, you would see what a high opinion I have of you and what hopes I have for your gift.

Discuss defects now? But that is not as easy. Discussing the defects of a talented individual is like discussing the defects of a big tree that grows in the garden; what is really in question is the taste of the viewer, not the tree itself. Don't you agree?

To begin with, it seems to me you lack restraint. You are like a play-goer who is so unrestrained in expressing his enthusiasm that neither he nor the others can hear what is happening on stage. This lack of restraint is especially evident in the nature descriptions that break up the dialogue; reading them, one wishes they were more compact, shorter, two or three lines long. Frequent references to bliss, whispers, velvetness, and so forth give those descriptions a slightly rhetorical and monotonous effect—and the result is dampening, almost wearying. This lack of restraint also comes through in the portrayals of women ("Malva," "On the Rafts") and in romantic scenes. It is not a matter of sweep or broad brushstrokes, but a lack of restraint. Then there is the frequent repetition of words, quite unsuited to the stories you write. Accompaniment, disc, harmony—these words are out of place. You frequently mention waves. In your descriptions of the intelligentsia, a tension comes through, almost a wariness; that is not because you have rarely observed the intelligentsia—you are familiar with them, but you do not quite know how to approach them.

How old are you? I do not know you. I do not know where you are from or who you are, but it seems to me that while you are still young you would be well advised to leave Nizhny and spend two or three years in a literary milieu, rubbing elbows with literary people; not to get some learning from our cock and become even more clever,[120] but so that you will take the final plunge into literature and come to love it; besides, the provinces age a man quickly. Korolenko, Potapenko, Mamin, and Ertel[121] are splendid people. You may find them a bit dull at first, but in a year or two you will come to know and appreciate them. Moreover, their society will more than recompense the annoyance and inconvenience of life in the capital.

I must hurry off to the post office. I wish you health and success and firmly shake your hand. Thank you once more for your letter.

Yours,

A. Chekhov

To Pavel F. Iordanov

YALTA, 25 JANUARY 1899

My *Seagull* is playing to packed houses in Moscow and the tickets are all sold out. They say the production is extraordinary. Muscovites have sent me congratulations. . . .

Yours,

A. Chekhov

To Alexander I. Urusov[122]

YALTA, 1 FEBRUARY 1899

Frequent inordinate praise eventually deprives us of the ability to acknowledge it properly; your review[23] in *Kurier,* the congratulations, the letters from Moscow, the buzz of acclaim that is carried here once in a great while by the north wind have left me drained. I feel exhausted and cannot collect myself to write you, dear Alexander Ivanovich. Kindly forgive me, absolve me of my sins, and believe me when I say that I am endlessly grateful to you. If I did not live in Yalta, this winter would be the happiest of my life.

So, I am still in Yalta. It is evening now. The wind is blowing as it does in the fourth act of *The Seagull,* but no one has come to see me. On the contrary, I shall have to put on my fur coat and leave soon after ten. On the whole, life is dull. I must make an effort to live here day in and day out and not grumble about my lot. I read the papers, read about the Pushkin Dictionary, and naturally I envy those who are lucky enough to be assisting you.[124]

I have sold Marks my works for time immemorial and have already sent him material for the first volume, a whole pood of my *"lycée period"*[125] stories that were not included in any of the collections. They are as tiny as smelts, and taken together they resemble a Lenten smelt soup. It will probably be a good edition.

Yours,

A. Chekhov

To Lidia A. Avilova[126]

You write that I have an uncommon ability to live. Maybe so, but God does not give horns to a cow that butts. What is the use of knowing how to live if I am away all the time as if in exile? I am the one who walked down Pea Street and could not find a pea.[127] I was free and did not know freedom. I was a writer and could not spend my life in the company of writers. I sold my works for seventy-five thousand and have already received a portion of the money, but what use is it to me if I have spent the past two weeks now cooped up in the house and dare not poke my nose outside. About the sale, I sold Marks everything, past, present, and future. This I did, dear, so as to put my affairs in order. Fifty thousand remain, which (I shall only receive the total sum in two years) will provide me with two thousand annually. Before the deal with Marks, I earned about three and a half thousand annually from my books, and last year, thanks probably to "Peasants,"[128] I received eight thousand! Now you know all my financial secrets. Do with them what you will, only please do not envy my uncommon ability to live.

Still and all, should I suddenly find myself in Monte Carlo, I shall definitely gamble away a couple thousand, for that is a luxury of which I have not even dared to dream before. And what if I won? The writer Ivan Shcheglov calls me Potemkin and also praises me for my ability to live. If I am Potemkin, why am I in Yalta, why is it so terribly boring here. The snow is swirling about, the wind is blowing at the windows, heat is coming from the stove; I have absolutely no desire to write and have not written a thing.

You are very kind. I have said that a thousand times, and now I shall say it again.

Be healthy, wealthy, and happy, and may the heavens watch over you. I warmly press your hand.

Yours,

A. Chekhov

To Alexei S. Suvorin

Yalta, 4 March 1899

Regarding the student disturbances, here as everywhere there is much talk and vociferation, but nothing in the papers. People have received letters from St. Petersburg expressing support for the students. Your letters on the disturbances[129] did not meet with favor, and rightly so, because you cannot pass judgment in print on the disturbances when you cannot go near the facts. The state has forbidden you to write, forbidden you to tell the truth. That is tyranny, but unperturbed you speak of rights and the prerogatives of the state—it is baffling somehow. You speak of the state's right, but you do not take the standpoint of the law. Rights and justice are the same for all, no matter what juridical person is in question, including the state. If the state misappropriates a piece of my land, I can sue, and the court will restore my rights. Should the same not hold true when the state beats me with a whip? Am I not allowed to cry out that my rights have been violated if it uses force against me? The concept of the state should be founded on certain legal norms. Otherwise it is a phantom, a hollow sound meant to inspire fright. . . .

Yours,

A. Chekhov

To Ivan I. Orlov[130]

Yalta, 18 March 1899

Spring has already come to Yalta: everything is budding and blooming, and new faces have appeared on the promenade. Mirolyubov and Gorky are arriving today, the season is beginning, and in two or two and a half weeks I shall probably depart for more northerly climes, nearer to you. My house is under construction, but my muse is quite out of sorts: I have written nothing and have absolutely no desire to work. I need to breathe different air: the south is such a lazy place! For the most part I am in a foul mood thanks to the letters I have been receiving from friends and acquaintances. Now and again in my letters I must either comfort or lecture or snarl like a dog. I have received many letters about the student events, from students and adults alike; I even received three from Suvorin. And students who were expelled have come to see me. In my opinion, the adults, that is the fathers and powers that be, made a big blunder. They behaved as the Turkish pashas did with the Young Turks and softas, and this time public opinion has demonstrated quite eloquently that Russia is not Turkey anymore, thank God. . . .

Yours,

A. Chekhov

To Alexei M. Peshkov (Maxim Gorky)

MOSCOW, 25 APRIL 1899

You have vanished from sight, dear Alexei Maximovich. Where are you? What are you up to? Where are you off to?

I paid a call on Lev Tolstoy three days ago; he praised you highly and called you "a marvelous writer." "The Fair" and "In the Steppe" met with his approval, but "Malva" did not. He said, "You can invent anything you like except human psychology, but Gorky sometimes does that very thing. He describes states he has not experienced." There you are. I said that when you are in Moscow we will pay him a call together.

When will you be in Moscow? On Thursday there is to be a private performance of *The Seagull* for yours truly. If you come, I will give you a seat. My address is Malaya Dmitrovka, c/o Sheshkov, Apt. 14 (entrance on the Degtyarny Ln. side), Moscow. Sometime after 1 May I shall leave for the country (Lopasnya, Moscow Gubernia).

I have been receiving sad, seemingly almost repentant letters from St. Petersburg, and I feel bad because I do not know how to respond or act.[131] Life certainly is a queer thing when it is not a psychological invention.

Scribble off two or three lines. Tolstoy questioned me at length about you. You whet his curiosity. He is evidently touched.

Well, I wish you health and all the best. My regards to your little Maxim.

Yours,

A. Chekhov

To Pavel F. Iordanov

MELIKHOVO, 15 MAY 1899

The Seagull was performed for me at the Arts Theater in Moscow. The production is astounding. If you like, I can insist that the Arts Theater make a stop in Taganrog next spring when it moves southward in toto—with the troupe, decorations, et cetera. The Maly Theater has paled, and as far as *mise en scènes* and productions are concerned, even the Meiningens[132] are far behind the new Arts Theater, which now performs in a wretched location. Incidentally, one of the actors in *The Seagull* is Vishnevsky, our Taganrog Vishnevsky who has irritated me so with his constant references to Kramsakov, Ovsyanikov,[133] et cetera. All those involved in *The Seagull* were photographed with me. It turned out to be an interesting group.

To Alexei M. Peshkov (Maxim Gorky)

YALTA, 3 SEPTEMBER 1899

Dear Alexei Maximovich, greetings once more! I am writing in answer to your letter.

First, I am categorically opposed to dedications to the living. I once made such dedications, but now I feel that I was probably wrong to do so. That is a general answer. In this particular case, dedicating *Foma Gordeyev* to me will only give me pleasure. But how do I come to merit such an honor? However, it is yours to judge, mine simply to acknowledge the honor and thank you. Try to make the dedication as succinct as possible, in other words, just write "dedicated to so-and-so" and let it go at that. Only Volynsky[134] likes long dedications. Here is another practical piece of advice for you, if you wish: have more copies printed, no less than five or six thousand. The book will sell like hot cakes. The second printing can be run off at the same time as the first. Another piece of advice: when you read the proofs, cross out as many nominal and verbal attributes as you can. You have so many attributes that the reader is hard put to sort them out and eventually grows tired. When I write "the man sat on the grass," it is clear what I mean. The sentence is plainly worded and does not arrest the attention. If, on the other hand, I write "a tall man of medium build with a narrow chest and a small red beard sat down on the green grass trampled by passersby, sat down noiselessly, looking timidly and anxiously about," the result is ponderous and hard to understand. It does not go straight in, and the writer must get his point straight across, in a second. Another point: you are a lyrical writer by nature; your heart has a gentle timbre. Were you a composer you would avoid writing marches. Being rude, loud, caustic, and furiously denunciatory is not suited to your talent. So you will understand if I advise you when reading the proofs to be ruthless with the sons of bitches, curs, and pipsqueaks that pop up here and there in *Life*.

Expect you in late September? Why so late? Winter will come early this year, autumn will be short, so you need to hurry.

Well, Sir, I wish you health. Stay in fine fettle.

Yours,

A. Chekhov

The Arts Theater will start giving plays on 30 September. *Uncle Vanya* will be performed on 14 October.

Your best story is "In the Steppe."

TO THE MOSCOW ARTS THEATER

YALTA, 1 OCTOBER 1899

Unendingly grateful / congratulate / send heartfelt best wishes / we will work conscientiously energetically untiringly as one / to ensure that this splendid beginning will serve as a guarantee of future achievements / to ensure that the theater will represent a bright phase in the history of Russian art and each of our lives / your sincere friend / Chekhov.

To Olga L. Knipper

Sweet actress, you exaggerate everything greatly in your gloomy letter; that is clear, for the newspapers received the first performance quite well.[135] Be that as it may, one or two unsuccessful performances is no reason to hang your head and not sleep at night. In art, especially the theater, you are bound to fall flat once in a while. Ahead lie many bad days and even bad seasons; there will be big misunderstandings and vast disappointments—you must be prepared for all that, realize that, and stubbornly, zealously stick to it, no matter what.

And of course you are right: Alexeyev should not have played Ivan the Terrible. It is not his forte. When he directs, he is an artist, but when he acts, he is a rich young merchant dabbling in culture.

As for me, I was under the weather for three or four days and am now staying in the house. I have an unbearably large number of visitors. Idle provincial tongues wag, and I am bored and cross, cross and envious of the rat that lives under the boards of your theater.

You wrote your last letter to me at four in the morning. If it seemed to you that *Uncle Vanya* did not enjoy the success you wished, please go to bed and get a good night's sleep. Success has gone to your head, and you can no longer abide the normal humdrum order of things.

It appears that Davydov will play *Uncle Vanya* in St. Petersburg, and he will be good, but the play will probably flop.[136]

How are you? Please write more. As you can see, I write you almost every day. An author writing an actress so often—my pride may soon begin to suffer. Actresses need to be kept in line, not spoiled with letters. I constantly forget that I am the actress inspector.[137]

I wish you good health, my angel.

Yours,

A. Chekhov

To Vladimir I. Nemirovich-Danchenko

Dear Vladimir Ivanovich, please do not take offense at my silence. My whole correspondence has come to a standstill. That is because I am writing, first; second, I am reading the proofs from Marks; third, I am very busy with out-of-town patients, who come to me for some reason. Reading proofs for Marks is drudgery. I barely finished the second volume, and had I known earlier that it was this hard, I would have gotten Marks to pay me not 75, but 175 thousand. The patients from out of town are mostly poor and ask me for help with arrangements, so I must do a great deal of talking and letter writing.

Of course, I am desperately bored here. I work during the day, and then as evening draws near I start to ask myself what I can do, where I can go. By the time the second act is underway in your theater, I am already in bed. I rise while it is still dark, if you can imagine, with the wind howling and the rain beating down.

You are wrong to suppose that I get "letters from every corner." My friends and acquaintances do not write me whatsoever. In all this time I have received just two letters from Vishnevsky,[138] and one of them does not count, since in it Alexander Leonidovich criticized reviewers whom I have not read. I received a letter from Goslavsky, too, but it does not count either because it was about business, about business in the sense that it is unanswerable.

I am not writing any plays. I have an idea for a play called *The Three Sisters,* but it will have to wait until I finish the stories that have long been preying on my conscience. Next season will not feature a play by me—that is certain.

My Yalta *dacha* turned out very well, cosy, warm, and attractive. The garden will be exceptional. I am planting it myself, with my own two hands. I planted a hundred rose bushes alone—and all the finest, most noble varieties—as well as fifty pyramid acacias, a great many camellias, lilies, tuberoses, et cetera.

There is a barely audible note in your letter, faint and trembling as though made by an old bell; it comes through in those places where you write about the theater, about being wearied by the trivial aspects of life in the theater. Please do not weary, do not lose interest, whatever you do! The Arts Theater represents the best pages of the book that will someday be written about modern Russian theater. That theater is your pride and it is the only theater I love, though I have not once been there. If I lived in Moscow, I would try to obtain a position on the staff, say even as a watchman, to make some contribution and, if possible, keep you from losing interest in that dear enterprise.

It is raining cats and dogs and the room is dark. I wish you health and happiness.

My kind regards to you. Please give my compliments to Yekaterina Nikolayevna and everyone at the theater, especially Olga Leonardovna. Yours,

A. Chekhov

To Olga L. Knipper

Greetings, sweet actress! Are you angry that I have not written in so long? I wrote you often, but you did not receive my letters because they were intercepted at the post office by an acquaintance of ours.

I wish you a happy New Year, a happy New Year and all the very best. I really do wish you a happy year and send you my kindest regards. May you enjoy happiness, wealth, health, and the best of cheer.

We are doing passably well. We eat, talk, and laugh in abundance, and remember you very often. Masha will tell you and let you know how we spent the holidays when she returns to Moscow.

I have not congratulated you on the success of *The Lonely*.[139] I still harbor the illusion that you will come to Yalta, enabling me to see *The Lonely* and genuinely congratulate you in all sincerity. I wrote Meyerhold and tried to persuade him not to be so extreme in his depiction of high-strung people. After all, the vast majority of people are high-strung, most suffer, few experience acute pain, but where— in public or in private—have you seen people rushing about clutching their heads? Suffering has to be expressed as it is expressed in life, in other words, not with arms and legs but with the tone of voice and facial expression, not with gesticulation but with graceful gesture. The delicate emotion characteristic of cultured people needs to be expressed delicately. You say, a theatrical convention. No convention justifies lies.

My sister tells me you were marvelous in the part of Anna. Oh, if only the Arts Theater would come to Yalta!

Your troupe was praised highly in *Novoye Vremya*. They have adopted a new line: evidently they intend to praise all of you during Lent. The February issue of *Zhizn*[140] will contain a story of mine—a very strange one—many characters along with descriptions of nature. It has a half moon. It has a bittern bird that cries somewhere far, far away, Moo! Moo!, like a cow in a shed. It has everything.

Levitan is staying with us. He has depicted a moonlit night during the haying season, [hanging] above my fireplace. A meadow, haystacks, woods in the distance, and the moon reigning over the whole scene.

And so, I wish you health, my sweet, exceptional actress. I miss you. Yours,

A. Chekhov

When will you send me your photograph? What sort of barbarism is this!

To Mikhail O. Menshikov[141]

YALTA, 28 JANUARY 1900

Dear Mikhail Osipovich, I cannot understand what this illness is that Tolstoy has. Cherinov[142] has not sent me a reply, and it is impossible to make anything out of what I have read in the newspapers or what you now write me. Ulcers in the stomach and intestines would have a different effect; either they are not there, or he received some injuries when gallstones passed through and scratched the walls, causing bleeding. He does not have cancer either, because it would first affect his appetite, as well as his general state of health; most importantly, his face would show signs of cancer if he were suffering from it. Most likely, Lev Nikolayevich is in good health (aside from the gallstones) and will live another twenty years. His illness scared me and has kept me in suspense. The thought of Tolstoy's death frightens me. If he were to die, he would leave a large void in my life. First of all, I have never felt such great affection for anyone. I am not a religious man, but of all the faiths I find his the most sympathetic and pertinent to me. Second, when Tolstoy exists, being a writer is easy and pleasant; even the realization that you never have and never will accomplish anything is not so horrible since Tolstoy makes up for everyone. His work serves to justify the hopes and expectations placed on literature. Third, Tolstoy stands firm, his prestige is enormous, and as long as he is alive, bad taste in literature, everything that is trite, brash, and mawkish, all coarse, bad-tempered pride will be far overshadowed. His moral authority alone is capable of keeping the so-called literary moods and trends at a certain level. Without him we would have a shepherdless herd or a difficult muddle to sort out.

To conclude the subject of Tolstoy, I must say a word about *Resurrection,* which I read not by bits and snatches but all at once, without a break. It is a marvelous work of fiction. What is least interesting is everything concerning Nekhlyudov's feelings about Katyusha, while most interesting are the dukes, generals, matrons, peasants, prisoners, and guards. The scene with the general, the commander of the Peter and Paul Fortress, the spiritualist, was so good it took my breath away. And Mme. Korchagina in the chair, and the peasant, Fedosya's husband! That peasant calls his wife "deft." Well, I would say that Tolstoy has a deft pen. The novel does not have an ending, and what it has cannot be called an ending. To write and write and then go and dump it all on a passage from the Gospels is awfully theological. Resolving everything with a passage from the Gospels is just as arbitrary as dividing the prisoners into five categories. Why five and not ten? Why a passage from the Gospels and not from the Koran? First you have to make people believe in the Gospels, make them believe that they are the truth, and then you can resolve everything with a passage from them.

Yours,

A. Chekhov

Write!

TO OLGA L. KNIPPER

YALTA, 9 AUGUST 1900

My dearest Olga, my sweet, greetings! I received a letter from you today, the first since your departure. I read it, then reread it, and now I am writing you, my actress. After I saw you off I went to Kist Hotel and stayed the night there. The next day I went to Balaklava out of boredom and the lack of anything better to do. I spent the whole time hiding from the ladies who recognized me and wished to give me an ovation. I stayed the night there and left the next morning for Yalta on the *Tavel.* Dreadfully rough crossing. Now I am pining away in Yalta, lonesome and cross. Alexeyev came to see me yesterday. We talked about the play,[143] and I gave him my word; in fact I promised to finish the play no later than September. See how smart I am?

I keep thinking that any moment now the door will open and in you will walk. But that is not to be. You are now in rehearsal or on Merzlyakovsky Ln., far from Yalta and me.

Adieu. May the heavenly hosts watch over you and keep you. Adieu my darling girl.

Love,

Antonio

TO IVAN A. BUNIN

YALTA, 15 JANUARY 1902

Dear Ivan Alexeyevich, greetings! I wish you a happy New Year! May you achieve world fame, find yourself the best of women, and win 200,000 on all three bonds.

I was under the weather for about a month and a half but now consider myself well, although I have a cough, do practically nothing, and feel as though I am waiting for something, probably spring.

Have I written you about "The Pines"?[144] First of all, thank you very much for the offprint you sent. Second, "The Pines" is very new, very fresh and very good, but too condensed, like consommé.

So I shall be looking forward to your arrival! Come as soon as you can; I shall be very glad to see you. I give you my very fondest regards and wish you the best of health.

Yours,

A. Chekhov

I told *Yuzhnoye obozreniye* that, though not indisposed to contributing, I am not writing at present, please forgive me, and when I do write something, I shall send it to them. That is the answer I give everyone.

TO ALEXANDER N. VASELOVSKY[145]

YALTA, 25 AUGUST 1902

Dear Alexander Nikolayevich;

Last December I received word that A. M. Peshkov had been elected an honorary member of the Academy. A. M. Peshkov was in the Crimea at that moment, and I lost no time in paying him a call. I was

the first to bring him the news of his election and the first to congratulate him. Then, somewhat later, the newspapers reported that, as
Peshkov was under investigation for violation of Article 1035, the election had been declared invalid. Moreover, it was specifically stated that
the announcement was made by the Academy of Sciences. As I am an
honorary member of the Academy,[146] the announcement was made
in my name, too. My congratulations were heartfelt, and at the same
time I declared the election invalid—I cannot grasp this contradiction,
nor have I been able to come to terms with it. The matter was made
no clearer to me when I acquainted myself with Article 1035. After
giving the matter a great deal of thought, only one course of action
seems open to me, and though I find it extremely difficult and regrettable, I must respectfully ask you to petition to have me divested of
the title of Honorary Academician.

With great respect I have the pleasure to remain your humble
servant.

Anton Chekhov

TO SERGEI P. DIAGHILEV[147]

YALTA, 30 DECEMBER 1902

Dear Sergei Pavlovich;

I have received the issue of *Mir iskusstva* with the article on *The
Seagull* and read it—thank you so much. When I had finished reading
the article, I wanted to write another play, which I shall probably do
after January.

You write that we talked about a serious religious movement in
Russia. The movement we talked about was not in Russia but among
the intelligentsia. I have nothing to say about Russia, while the intelligentsia has so far merely played at religion, chiefly for lack of anything to do. As to the educated segment of our society, it has moved
further and further away from religion, no matter what it says or
which philosophical-religious societies meet. I shall not attempt to
judge whether that is good or bad, except to say that the religious
movement of which you write exists on its own, as does the whole
of modern culture, and the former cannot be made the determinant
of the latter. Today's culture represents the start of work in the name
of a great future, work that may well continue for tens of thousands

of years, so that at least in the distant future mankind will perceive the truth about the real God; in other words, so that instead of guessing or searching for him in Dostoyevsky, it will perceive him as clearly as it has perceived that two times two is equal to four. Today's culture represents the start of work, while the religious movement we spoke of is a holdover, practically the conclusion of something that has outlived its time or is living it out. But this is a long story, too long to fit in a letter. Please pass on my heartfelt thanks to Mr. Filosofov[148] when you see him. I wish you a happy New Year and all the very best.

Sincerely,

A. Chekhov

To Alexander I. Sumbatov-Yuzhin[149]

Yalta, 26 February 1903

Dear Alexander Ivanovich, thank you very much for your letter. I agree with you that Gorky is hard to assess, as one must sort through the volumes that have been said and written about him. I have not seen his play *The Lower Depths* and only have a vague idea of what it is about, but stories like "My Companion" and "Chelkash" permit me to say that he is not a minor writer by any means. *Foma Gordeyev* and *Three* are not worth reading—they are bad—and I find *Petty Bourgeois* an immature work, but what makes Gorky so valuable is not that he is liked but that he was the first person in Russia and the whole world to speak with disdain and disgust of the petty bourgeoisie, and he spoke at a time when society was ready to listen to his protest. From a Christian or economic or whatever point of view you like, the petty bourgeoisie is a great evil; it, like a dam on a river, has always served only to hold things in check, while the down and out, though inelegant, though drunk, are nevertheless a reliable implement, at least they have proved to be; and the dam, if not broken, has sprung a large and dangerous leak. I do not know if I am expressing myself clearly. As I see it, there will come a time when Gorky's writing will be forgotten, but he himself will scarcely be forgotten in a thousand years. That is what I think, or that is how it seems to me, but perhaps I am wrong.

Are you in Moscow now? Or have you left for Nice or Monte Carlo? I often remember the years of our youth when you and I sat side by side and played roulette—with Potapenko. Speaking of whom, I received a letter from Potapenko today. The nut wants to publish a magazine.

I send you my regards and wish you good health and prosperity.
Yours,

A. Chekhov

To Sergei P. Diaghilev

Dear Sergei Pavlovich, I have been somewhat delayed in replying to your letter, as I received it not in Narofominsk, but in Yalta, where I arrived a few days ago and shall probably remain until the fall. I gave your letter considerable thought, but although your proposal, or offer, is tempting I must ultimately give you an answer that will please neither of us.

I am unable to be an editor for *Mir iskusstva* because I cannot live in St. Petersburg, and the journal will not move to Moscow for my benefit. Editing by mail or by telegraph is impossible, and there is no advantage to having me as a nominal editor of the journal. That is the first consideration. Second, just as a picture is painted by one artist and a speech is made by one speaker, a journal is edited by one person. Of course, I am not a critic and would no doubt do a poor job of editing the reviews section, but how could I live under one roof with D. S. Merezhkovsky, who has particular beliefs, didactic beliefs, while I lost my faith long ago and can only look in bewilderment at any intelligent believer? I respect D. S. and have an appreciation for him as a human being and man of letters, but hitch us up to the wagon, and we will start pulling in opposite directions. Whether or not I am mistaken, I have always thought and am now convinced that there should be one editor, just one; and in the case of *Mir iskusstva,* you alone should be that editor. That is my opinion, and I do not think I shall go back on it.

Please do not be angry with me, dear Sergei Pavlovich. I think that if you had edited the journal another five years you would agree with me. In a journal, as in a painting or poem, the force of one personality, one will, should be felt. That has been true up to now with *Mir iskusstva,* and it worked well. You should stick to that.

I wish you all the best. It is cool in Yalta, or at least not hot, and I am jubilant.

Please accept my deep regards.

Yours,

A. Chekhov

TO VLADIMIR G. KOROLENKO

YALTA, 15 JULY 1903

Dearly beloved associate, magnificent man, my thoughts are with you today in particular. I am deeply in your debt. Thank you very much.

Chekhov

TO VLADIMIR L. KIGN–DEDLOV[150]

YALTA, 10 NOVEMBER 1903

Dear Vladimir Ludvigovich, your two books and letter unexpectedly arrived, and I do not know what words to use to express my very sincere, heartfelt thanks. I started with *Simply Stones* and read almost all the stories in one sitting; they contain much that is old and outdated, but there is also something new, a fresh spirit of some kind that is very good. I shall read *Lyrical Stones* today.

My health is constantly poor, old age is catching up with me, Yalta is boring, and I sense that life is passing me by, that I am not seeing much which, as a writer, I should be seeing. All I see and, fortunately, realize is that life and people are becoming better and better, more intelligent and honest—that is the main thing—while more trivial matters have merged in my eyes into a monotonous, gray field, for my vision is no longer what it once was.[151]

Nakrokhin was indeed talented. I read his *Idylls in Prose*. However, he merely described the flower bed by the house, the front garden; he could never make up his mind to enter the house itself. By contrast, Bezhetsky, whom you mention, is already forgotten, and that is as it should be. I. Shcheglov (the author of war stories) is also forgotten.

I wish you health and happiness. Are you not married? Why? Excuse me for asking. I married two or three years ago and am very happy. I think it has changed my life for the better. The things that are usually written about married life are utter nonsense.

My regards to you.

Yours,

A. Chekhov

Thank you once again!

To Alexander V. Amfiteatrov[152]

YALTA, 13 APRIL 1904

Dear Alexander Valentinovich, my humble thanks to you for your kind letter and both reviews,[153] which I read (I shall not conceal the fact) twice, with great pleasure. Your reviews conjured up a sense of the distant but forgotten past, as though you were a relative or neighbor; and I vividly recalled the anniversary picture in *Budilnik*,[154] where you and I and Passek, with a telephone receiver to his ear, stand next to Kurepin and Kicheyev;[155] it seems as though that anniversary was a hundred or two hundred years ago. Incidentally, I have the anniversary issue, and when you come to Yalta I shall find it and show it to you.

As soon as you arrive in Yalta please ring me up on the telephone that very evening to let me know, do give me that pleasure. Again, I very much wish to see you, so keep that in mind. If you leave St. Petersburg after 1 May and stop in Moscow for a day or two, we will arrange a meeting in Moscow, in some restaurant.

I now write little and read a great deal. I read *Rus*, to which I subscribe. Today I read the *Collection* published by Znaniya: Gorky's "Man" reminded me strongly of a sermon by a young priest who does not yet have a beard and speaks with a deep bass, enunciating his *o's*, and there is a splendid story by Bunin, "Black Earth." It is a superb story indeed—some passages are simply breathtaking—and I recommend it to you.

If I am in good health, I shall travel to the Far East in July or August, in my capacity as a physician, rather than as a correspondent. I think a physician can see more than a correspondent would.

Yesterday I received a letter from Vladivostok from a cheerful young man—a writer.[156] He went to Vladivostok in the best of spirits but has now suddenly become despondent.

Fondest regards.

Yours,

A. Chekhov

NOTES

1. Alexander P. Chekhov (1855–1913)—Chekhov's eldest brother. A talented writer in his own right, he was the first to have his work published but did not enjoy his brother's success and scraped together a living as an ordinary reporter. At the start of Anton's literary career, Alexander was one of his first readers and critics, but soon the roles changed.

2. Alexander and Anton's brother Nikolai.

3. Actor and director.

4. Chekhov has in mind employees of sensationalist newspapers and magazines.

5. Moscow publishing house.

6. In an 1882 letter from Taganrog, Alexander gave a detailed description of "a service marking the end of navigation" held "on the piles" at the wharf. Hatteras is a reference to Captain Hatteras of the novel by Jules Verne.

7. The story was never published.

8. N. A. Chmyrev wrote for the sensationalist newspaper *Moskovsky Lisrok*.

9. An unpublished story by Alexander Chekhov.

10. Pimenovna was a Taganrog cook; Nikolai Stamatich was a broker who patronized the shop run by their father, Pavel Ye. Chekhov, when the family lived in Taganrog.

11. According to Saltykov-Shchedrin, with the rise of political reactionism policemen were given the authority to "read hearts."

12. This may be a reference to Maria Pavlovna Chekhova's unsuccessful attempt to enter the College of Painting, Sculpture, and Architecture.

13. G. N. Fedotova, an actress at the Maly Theater in Moscow.

14. University friends of Alexander Chekhov.

15. The youngest of the Chekhov brothers, Mikhail.

16. P. I. Kicheyev worked for the sensationalist press.

17. The Tretyakov brothers' uncle.

18. Anton Pavlovich's friend and classmate at the Taganrog high school and Moscow University.

19. Maria, Alexander's newborn daughter.

20. Nikolai A. Leikin (1841–1906)—writer, humorist, editor and publisher of *Oskolki,* to which Anton Chekhov contributed from 1882 to 1887. Leikin bragged to acquaintances that he had "discovered a new Shchedrin."

21. A novel by Nikolai Leskov, one of Chekhov's favorite writers.

22. Leikin had informed Chekhov of "a whole pogrom" carried out by the Moscow censorship committee against an issue of *Oskolki.* The material banned included stories and sketches by Chekhov.

23. The Chekhov family had just moved to a new apartment.

24. The editor and publisher of *Peterburgskaya Gazeta.*

25. Chekhov is replying to a letter from Dmitry Grigorovich of 25 March 1886 in which the latter hailed Chekhov as "a real talent" and set him "far above the new generation of writers."

26. Nikolai P. Chekhov (1858–1889)—the elder brother of Anton Pavlovich Chekhov. A talented artist, he attended, but did not complete, the College of Painting, Sculpture, and Architecture, and worked for humor magazines, occasionally illustrating his brother's stories. Nikolai led a bohemian life and caused Anton much distress.

27. The name of a landowner who suffered from alcoholism.

28. A musician and close acquaintance of the Chekhovs.

29. An acquaintance of the Chekhovs.

30. A Taganrog teacher.

31. A pianist and acquaintance of the Chekhovs.

32. Nikolai Putyatin—a journalist and editor.

33. The street in Moscow on which the Chekhovs then lived.

34. Pyotr Polevayev—a friend of Nikolai and Alexander Chekhov.

35. Celebrated lawyer.

36. Second-rate journalists.

37. A writer famous for his fables.

38. Humor magazines.

39. Maria V. Kiseleva—children's writer and wife of the owner of the Babkino Estate outside Moscow where the Chekhov family spent three summers.

40. Chekhov's youngest brother, Mikhail, contributed to *Detsky otdykh* [Children's Leisure] under the nom de plume Bogemsky [Bohemian]—thus Anton's humorous rendition.

41. This refers to a letter from Maria Kiseleva of 9 September 1886 in which she complained of the cold, rainy weather and said, "If this continues much longer I shall succumb in the flower of my middle years before 22 January."

42. The family nickname of Maria Chekhova.

43. Stories by Chekhov.

44. The Kiselevs' dog.

45. Olga A. Golokhvastova—writer and acquaintance of Maria Kiseleva.

46. The writer Pyotr D. Boborykin.

47. Stanislav Okreits—writer and publisher of arch conservative, anti-Semitic magazines.

48. *Essays and Stories* (1887).

49. At the advice of Lev Tolstoy, on 15 November 1887 *Novoye Vremya* published the first chapter of *Walden or Life in the Woods* by the American writer Henry David Thoreau.

50. Chekhov is referring to his play *Ivanov.*

51. The actress who played Sarah in *Ivanov.*

52. A contributor to *Novoye Vremya* whose impertinent attacks on writers made Chekhov increasingly indignant as years went by.

53. Grigorovich had made another attempt to persuade Chekhov to "stop writing those hastily executed, trifling stories, particularly for the newspapers."

54. Yakov P. Polonsky (1819–1898)—writer of poetry and prose.

55. Polonsky wrote of his impressions of Chekhov's stories "Kashtanka" and "A Fairy Tale" ("Untitled").

56. Chekhov dedicated the story "Happiness" to Polonsky.

57. The poem Polonsky dedicated to Chekhov.

58. Grigorovich was wintering in Nice.

59. The liberal Lintvarev family was the object of police suspicions.

60. A collection of Chekhov's stories.

61. Renowned Ukrainian poet.

62. Ukrainian actors.

63. In his youth Alexei N. Pleshcheyev was exiled for belonging to Petrashevsky's revolutionary circle. He subsequently worked for two journals headed by Nikolai Nekrasov: *Sovremennik* and *Otechestvenniye zapiski*. Revolutionary democrats Chernyshevsky and Dobrolyubov were closely involved with the former, satirist Saltykov-Shchedrin with the latter.

64. This is probably a reference to characters from another story, as they do not appear in "Lights."

65. Chekhov is referring to "Name Day."

66. This was to become "Nervous Breakdown."

67. Pleshcheyev advised N.V. Svetlov, a member of Korsh's company, to give a benefit performance for himself of Rosen's *A Nasty Man,* translated from the German by Pleshcheyev

68. The address of the *Severny vestnik* editorial offices.

69. Journalists: Notovich was the publisher and editor of *Novosti i Birzhevaya Gazeta* which published a weekly supplement; Gradovsky—a publicist.

70. On 7 October 1888, the Academy of Sciences awarded half the Pushkin Prize (500 rubles) to Chekhov for *Twilight.*

71. The novel was never written.

72. Chekhov and Suvorin planned to collaborate on a play to be called *The Forest Demon*. The project was abandoned, and the material later served as the basis for Chekhov's *Uncle Vanya*.

73. Suvorin's children.

74. Employee of Suvorin's Moscow bookshop.

75. Writer.

76. Chekhov is quoting Pushkin's poem *Poltava*.

77. A favorite of Catherine the Great who made a dizzying rise to the heights of power and influence.

78. Minor Moscow magazines.

79. Writer and humorist.

80. The story "The First Lesson."

81. Writer and humorist.

82. It was entitled "An Old Question About a New Talent."

83. A mistake on Chekhov's part: Merezhkavsky was in the History and Philology Department of St. Petersburg University.

84. A character from Chekhov's story "On Holy Night."

85. It had come to the attention of the authorities that Nikolai Chekhov did not have the proper papers to reside in Moscow.

86. Chekhov is referring to Suvorin's play *Tatiana Repina*.

87. An article by Suvorin entitled "A New Novel" had been published in *Novoye Vremya*.

88. The hero of Bourget's novel.

89. Russian chemist, creator of the Table of Elements.

90. Russian literary critic of the 1860s who often took extreme positions in the heat of a debate (e.g., questioning Pushkin's significance).

91. The beginning of the letter is lost.

92. An actress and impressario who staged a production of *The Forest Demon*.

93. In 1829 the German scientist Alexander Humboldt made a journey through Siberia to study its geology and geography. The purpose of the trip made by American journalist George Kennan is indicated by the very title of his book, published in London in 1890: *Siberia and Exile*.

94. For Russians of the late nineteenth century, Sebastopol exemplified glory and tragedy: the site of a heroic defense effort, it came to symbolize the ignominious collapse of the regime of Nicholas I (1796–1855), who had gotten the country involved in the unwinnable Crimean War (1853–1856).

95. M. N. Galkin-Vrasky, the head of the Chief Prison Directorate.

96. Chekhov dedicated *Dreary People* to Peter Tchaikovsky.

97. Suvorin had commented on "Horse Thieves."

98. The editor and publisher of *Russkaya mysl*.

99. Chekhov is referring to Dmitry Grigoravich's story "The Gutta-Percha Boy."

100. Well-known arts critic.

101. Russian poet of the early nineteenth century.

102. Writer and contributor to *Novcye Vremya*.

103. German writer and philosopher whose books bear such indicative titles as *The Illness of the Century* and *Denigration*.

104. Kony wrote that the play had given him "profound pleasure": "Life itself has been depicted on stage, with its tragic unions, eloquent madness and silent suffering; ordinary life, comprehensible to all, though its cruel inner irony is understood by almost no one. . . ."

105. Contemporary writer.

106. Writer whom Chekhov had known since his Taganrog days.

107. Literary historian and critic, in 1902 he became the editor of the journal *Mir Bozhi*.

108. A talented artist and caricaturist who was a friend of the Chekhovs.

109. Korolenko was actively involved in the defense of a group of Udmurts, from the village of Stary Multan in Vyatka Gubernia, who were accused of having made human sacrifices to their pagan gods.

110. A Moscow prison doctor of the last century who selflessly defended the rights of prisoners.

111. Chekhov is referring to the Norwegian writer Martinius Bjørnstjerne.

112. The wife of Chekhov's younger brother Mikhail.

113. Sanitary inspector who later became the mayor of Taganrog.

114. In September 1898 Chekhov attended several rehearsals of *The Seagull* at the new Moscow Arts Theater.

115. The telegram from the troupe of the Moscow Arts Theater expressed condolences on the death of Chekhov's father, Pavel Yegorovich.

116. Chekhov's first letter to Gorky.

117. The two volume *Essays and Stories* published that year in St. Petersburg.

118. V. S. Mirolyubov (Mirov), the editor of *Zhurnal dlya vsekh*, introduced the writers.

119. Gorky had given an enthusiastic account of his impressions of a production of *Uncle Vanya* at the Nizhny Novgorod Drama Theater.

120. Chekhov is paraphrasing a quotation from Krylov's fable *The Donkey and the Nightingale*.

121. Writers Vladimir Korolenko, Ignati Potapenko, Dmitry Mamin-Sibiryak, and Alexander Ertel.

122. Legal expert and writer.

123. A review of *The Seagull*.

124. Urusov tried to compile a dictionary of words used by Pushkin, to coincide with the centenary of the poet's birth.

125. In other words, early.

126. A writer who was later to publish reminiscences of her relationship with Chekhov, which she said was depicted in the story "About Love" and *The Seagull*.

127. A line from P. I. Grigoryev's operetta, *A Comedy with Dear Uncle*.

128. Chekhov is referring to his story "Peasants."

129. Suvorin's "Little Letters" were a regular feature in *Novoye Vremya*. Those he devoted to the student disturbances caused a great public outcry.

130. Zemstvo physician.

131. The letters were from Suvorin.

132. A German theater troupe under the patronage of Herzog Meiningen.

133. Taganrog teachers.

134. Literary critic.

135. Chekhov is speaking of a production of Alexei K. Tolstoy's *The Death of Ivan the Terrible* with Konstantin Stanislavsky (Alexeyev) in the lead.

136. The production did not take place.

137. An affectionate nickname given to Chekhov at the Arts Theater.

138. Writer and playwright.

139. By Gerhardt Hauptmann.

140. "In the Gully" actually appeared in the January issue.

141. Journalist and critic.

142. Professor of internal medicine.

143. *The Three Sisters*.

144. A story by Bunin.

145. The chairman of the Society for the Appreciation of Russian Literature.

146. Chekhov had been elected an honorary member in 1900.

147. The guiding light behind the *Ballet Russe* and the editor of *Mir iskusstva*, a groundbreaking journal of the arts. Diaghilev tried to persuade Chekhov to join the journal staff.

148. Critic and journalist.

149. For biographical information see Nemirovich-Danchenko's reminiscences in this collection.

150. Writer, journalist, and critic who published under the name Dedlov.

151. Kign-Dedlov replied, "You just think that you are not seeing something, that everything is monotonous and gray in your eyes. Everything is as before—your splendid command of Russian and your technique—sure, concise, and straight to the mark . . . and as to the most important quality a major talent must have—the courage to be truthful—it is growing all the time in you. You look life straight in the eye, never blinking or averting your gaze. You look with your own eyes, never surrendering to the temptation to see what you would like to see. That is the most difficult of arts, and the rarest among authors."